DVOŘÁK

AND HIS WORLD

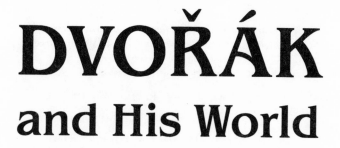

DVOŘÁK
and His World

EDITED BY

Michael Beckerman

PRINCETON UNIVERSITY PRESS

PRINCETON · NEW JERSEY

Copyright © 1993 by Princeton University Press
Published by Princeton University Press, 41 William Street,
Princeton, New Jersey 08540
In the United Kingdom: Princeton University Press, Chichester, West Sussex

Library of Congress Cataloging-in-Publication Data
Dvořák and his world / edited by Michael Beckerman.
p.   cm.
Includes bibliographical references and index.
ISBN 0-691-03386-2 — ISBN 0-691-00097-2 (pbk.)
1. Dvořák, Antonín, 1841–1904. I. Beckerman, Michael Brim, 1951– .
ML410.D99D88   1993
780'.92—dc20   93-4037

This book has been composed in Baskerville
by the Composing Room of Michigan
Music typeset by Don Giller

Princeton University Press books are printed on acid-free paper and meet the
guidelines for permanence and durability of the Committee on Production
Guidelines for Book Longevity of the Council on Library Resources

Printed in the United States of America

10 9 8 7 6 5 4 3 2 1

10 9 8 7 6 5 4 3 2 1
(Pbk.)

Designed by Laury A. Egan

To Brooke and all the Ellisons

with love and admiration

Contents

Contents

Acknowledgments

I would like to thank the following people for their assistance with this project: John Tibbetts, for his enthusiasm for Dvořák and for getting me involved in this project in the first place; and Leon Botstein, for telling me that he would devote one of his festivals to Dvořák only if I agreed to do this volume—and giving me about five minutes to decide. Thanks to Elizabeth Powers and Lauren Oppenheim for being the best in the business. Special thanks to David Beveridge, Jan Smaczny, Joseph Horowitz, Susan Gillespie, and Tatiana Firkušný for their contributions to the volume, and to Mark Loftin for keeping everything together.

I would also like to thank the following people in the Czech Republic whose help made this volume possible: Marketa Hallová, a wonderful friend and the director of the Dvořák Museum in Prague; Nina Všetecková of the Music Information Center in Prague; Milan Kuna, editor of the Dvořák correspondence; and Alena Němcová, for her constant support.

I would like to thank Paul Bertagnolli, Sarah Stoycos, Nga Hean Ong, Eric Entwistle, Garry Ziegler, Stephanie Campbell, Judith Mabary, and James Doering, members of my graduate seminar on Dvořák, for their help and inspiration and for putting up with the commuting schedule of their somewhat peculiar professor. I would especially like to thank Judith Mabary for her help. I would also like to thank Wanda Harry, Peggy Bischoff, Betty Rich, and Laura Savoldi of the Washington University Music Department for their assistance.

I owe a debt of gratitude to Donna Saar, Nancy Lynch, and Martina Darnell of the University of California, Santa Barbara, for their assistance and moral support.

I would especially like to acknowledge the help of two eminent Dvořák scholars, Alan Houtchens and Maurice Peress, and thank them for their advice and knowledge; and a special mention is owed to John Tyrrell for his many helpful comments.

I would also like to thank the brilliant, marvelous, and always memorable Jarmil Burghauser for all the assistance and stimulation he has given me, both for this project and over the years.

ACKNOWLEDGMENTS

Finally, I could not have completed this project without the love and forbearance of my beloved Bernie, Charlie, and Karen.

Michael Beckerman

DVOŘÁK

AND HIS WORLD

Introduction: Looking for Dvořák in December 1992

MICHAEL BECKERMAN

The road to Vysoká leads upward from the town of Přibram, around winding roads and through fields and forests. It is the beginning of December. In the valley below it is raining, and we can see deep green winter wheat, which imparts a false sense of spring to the scene. Up on higher ground (Vysoká itself means "high place") it is snowing. Dvořák's summer villa, now called "Rusalka," has been turned into a wonderland; clean white snow clings to all the branches, and a trackless plain stretches before us along the outbuildings to the main house. We are three: Marketa Hallová, the director of the Antonín Dvořák Museum in Prague; Paní Johnová, the granddaughter of the composer; and myself.

Inside the villa it is icy. A thick metal key unlocks the downstairs bedroom, where Dvořák and his wife slept. Photographs, scrapbooks, and memorabilia are everywhere. The two women begin to argue some fine point of identification in a faded photograph. The guest book lists visitors from France, Japan, the United States, and Germany. They expect seventy million tourists in Prague this year—no doubt some of them will overflow to this peaceful country retreat. Upstairs, dirt and plaster are everywhere, and scores and books are covered with dust. The composer's copy of *Siegfried* stands wrinkling in the corner, and his many decorations lie faded on walls and tables. The upright piano, with gold candelabra on either side, is too cold to touch.

We are looking for several things: a scrapbook of Dvořák's time in the United States, which is supposed to be there, and a "Hiawatha" libretto, which is less likely to be found. Neither turns up. It seems that the legacy of Dvořák is divided equally among the five surviving relatives who use the facility somewhat like a lending library. We retreat in frozen torpor from the scene.

Outdoors once again, Marketa Hallová leads me to a wooden gazebo. Inside is a table covered with several inches of snow. "Josef Suk, the composer's son-in-law, carved his initials into this table." We scrape the snow off, trying to find the magic letters from the past. No matter how much snow we brush away we can see nothing. Finally Paní Johnová appears. "Well, you see," she laughs, "they wanted to preserve the table, so they put another tabletop over the original." She lifts off the false top, and a worn wooden surface appears, surprisingly clear; the subject of our quest stands out in sharp relief.

How do we assemble a coherent image of a composer from sketches, scores, documents, memorabilia, photographs, and recollections? The legacy of the last decades in literary studies has suggested that even though there is nothing *but* the text—no biography, no special pleading, no context—the text does not even really *exist*. One can be sympathetic to this thought among the winter orchards in Southern Bohemia, where Dvořák seems almost to be an elaborate fictional character, created by and for our own needs. But that is our conceit: the past *was*; the composer *did* exist; he did have a presence, intentions, a context.

Antonín Dvořák visited the United States one hundred years ago, and despite an enormous amount of attention from scholars and critics since that time, he remains an elusive figure. Fundamental questions about him remain unanswered. Was he a nationalist or a cosmopolitan artist? One could argue both, or even maintain that such designations, seemingly of critical importance to the nineteenth century, no longer matter. As I shall try to show later, Dvořák staked his claim as a national composer with great care, and throughout his life he identified himself as a Czech composer and his music as Czech music. Yet there was no composer more at home in different worlds than Dvořák. He spoke Czech, German, and English quite well, was a hero in many countries outside of the Czech lands, and for at least part of his career seems to have self-conciously cultivated an "American" compositional style. Though he had satisfying artistic and intellectual friendships among his Czech colleagues, his connections with the leading German musicians and critics of the day were noteworthy : Richter, Von Bülow, Brahms, Seidl, and Hanslick were friends who revered him, and his works were programmed by the finest conductors throughout his life.

Where was his position in the central aesthetic battles of his time: was he a Brahmsian or Wagnerian? Although his reputation as a Brahmsian formalist was virtually codified in the Czech lands, at least in comparison to Smetana, Dvořák was a passionate Wagnerian for his entire life. He once said, "You know, you can talk a great deal about Wagner, and you can criticize a great deal, too—but he is undefeatable. What Wagner did nobody did before him and nobody can take it from him. Music will go its way, will pass Wagner by, but Wagner will remain, just like the statute of that poet from whom they still learn at school today—Homer. And such a Homer is Wagner." Though Dvořák revered Brahms, as David Beveridge makes clear in his study in this volume, he was a kind of "Wagner freak" in his youth: "I had just heard *Die Meistersinger*, and not long before Richard Wagner himself had been in Prague. I was perfectly crazy about him, and recollect following him as he walked along the streets to get a chance now and again of seeing the great little man's face."

It is also difficult for us to determine what Dvořák was really like. There has been a consistent attempt in the literature to portray the composer as a kind of innocent saint, a naive figure who loved pigeons, sat in pubs chatting with his pals and playing Darda (a card game popular at the time that has vanished so quickly that virtually no one now remembers how to play), and was content to remain in the bosom of his family. But there is evidence that throughout his life he knew exactly what he was doing, as far as his career was concerned. He certainly understood the value of speaking (or not speaking) to the press, and there is some evidence that his seemingly artless persona was carefully crafted. Furthermore, to contradict the image of the benign country boy, it appears that the composer was afflicted with a kind of agoraphobia, a fear of open spaces, which haunted him throughout his mature life; and several descriptions, by Kovařík, Otakar Dvořák, and others, reveal a deeply tormented figure.

One hagiographic image of Dvořák is that of the simple rural musician who has gone out into the world and come back unchanged. He is depicted as a village lad grown up, at peace with his family and his world, the perfect Victorian paterfamilias. But many scholars think that he was passionately in love with his wife's sister, Josefina, almost his entire adult life. The most compelling evidence for this is the Cello Concerto, in which Dvořák included a fragment of a song he had written for Josefina years earlier. How do we reconcile these oppositions?

These questions, unanswered and perhaps unanswerable, reveal how little we really know about Dvořák, and this shadow extends to his music as well. We still cling to an image of Dvořák as a composer of instrumental music when it is clear that, at least toward the end of his life, he was passionately involved with the composition of opera. We invest Dvořák with nationalist laurels even though there is arguably

more pure nationalism in one act of *Die Meistersinger* than in all of
Dvořák.

·

This series of books attempts to approach questions about composers
and history in a distinctive manner. It originated, in fact, in conjunction with the annual Bard Music Festival in Annandale-on-Hudson,
New York, which took as its mandate the need to present significant
composers in a wider context not only by presenting their lesser-known
works but also by featuring works of these composers' contemporaries—
and this in the context of detailed and imaginative commentary. The
previous volumes on Brahms, Mendelssohn, and Strauss compiled in
association with the festival have combined broadly inquisitive essays
with newly translated or freshly presented documents, which in turn
offer another perspective on the lives, times, and thoughts of the
composers.

A generation after Dvořák's death Bohuslav Martinů wrote about
staging in regard to his opera *The Plays of Mary*: "By combining various
scenes and texts, often strange and which do not completely fit into the
play, I want the viewer to orient himself and to straighten out the
components—through imagination. In the course of the story and
during the first hearing there is of course a certain disorientation, but
during the play the viewer is compelled to return and to supplement, to
arrange the components—to cooperate."

Though it is probably too late in the century for us to subscribe to a
broad theory of national aesthetics, Martinů believed that his ideas
were particularly Czech, a local alternative to Wagnerian music drama.
Reacting against dogmatic and excessively authoritative art, he sought
to juxtapose images in ways that would allow the audience to cooperate
in the process of making the story, drawing morals, and coming to
conclusions.

In the spirit of Martinů, this collection of interconnected essays,
letters, memoirs, and commentary is meant to illuminate some aspects
of the composer that have remained in shadow. Five essays attempt to
address broad questions about Dvořák and his world. Leon Botstein
seeks to place the composer in the broadest context, focusing on the
fundamental issue of musical personality and the manner in which it
reveals a great deal about the ideals and expectations of nineteenth-
century society. David Beveridge undertakes an exhaustive exploration of the Brahms-Dvořák relationship and seeks, finally, to interpret
the key documents frequently alluded to in the Dvořák literature, in
order to reveal not only the extent of Brahms's admiration for the

younger composer but also a certain almost intangible ambivalence toward him. Joseph Horowitz uses a single event—the premiere of the Symphony "From the New World"—to illuminate musical life in the United States, and he reveals our most glittering moment as a musical nation. Figures such as Dvořák, Henry Krehbiel, Jeanette Thurber, James Huneker, and Anton Seidl reflect an age of passion, ambition, and extraordinary achievement, while the premiere acts as a prism, refracting many different impulses and projecting them as a powerful collective force.

Jan Smaczny writes about Dvořák as a dramatist and in doing so contributes to a view of the composer that flies in the face of the way he is presented in most historical writings. Here we find not a composer whose primary commitments are to some notion of "absolute" music but instead someone who wrote nothing *but* program music and opera for the last years of his life. In the concluding essay to Part I, I address the question of "nationality" and try to determine how and why Dvořák employed national themes and what they meant to him, and how, after playing the role of a Czech composer, he suddenly took on the task of becoming an actor on the stage of American music.

These essays are followed by a series of documents—letters, memoirs, and criticism—that are complementary to our discussions. Although they constitute a rather eclectic collection, we have taken special care, considering that this year marks the hundredth anniversary of the premiere of the Symphony "From the New World," to offer many documents from the New World. This allows us, first, to reflect on our own musical world and answer, if we can, some of the questions that critics of the late nineteenth century posed about the future of "American music"; and second, to publish a substantial number of documents in their original language—for no matter how polished and beautiful a translation may be, it remains a translation. We have also included material newly translated from the Czech, to offer an account of Dvořák in the words of his Czech contemporaries. Translated here from the original German for the first time, Hermann Krigar's biographical sketch of the composer, with critical commentary by Jarmil Burghauser, provides the earliest full-blown contemporary portrait of Dvořák. Finally, a special place is devoted to the idiosyncratic but pungent analyses of Dvořák's symphonic poems by one of his closest friends, the volatile Leoš Janáček.

Though we have tried to probe Dvořák's life and works, we admit that no ultimate understanding of any creative figure exists—anywhere. If Dvořák were to return today, he could sit at the feet of any high-school student and hear astonishing tales about *scientific* progress, from atomic theory to black holes. If, though, he wanted to hear similarly probing insights into music and its relationship to human nature from the same student, he might indeed be puzzled and disappointed. Our questions remain the same as they have always been: what motivates human beings? How do great ideas take shape? What is the relationship between theater, music, art, and society?

Our questioning takes us around and around in a mighty sequence of circles, and we pose the same riddles again and again. The search for Dvořák is like the search for Suk's signature on the wooden table: one peels away the accumulated layers of time only to find a false front. Most of those who, like Paní Johnová, could reveal more of the truth are gone. And if, finally, the truth were to appear as if by magic, it would simply become the basis for another question. All this rootless exploration might seem ultimately futile, suggesting a cynicism about historical inquiry. But the truth is quite different: listening to music with passionate curiosity leads to the most powerful experience. It is to this experience that our book is dedicated.

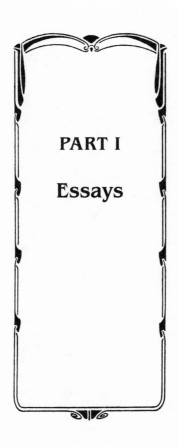

PART I

Essays

Reversing the Critical Tradition: Innovation, Modernity, and Ideology in the Work and Career of Antonín Dvořák

LEON BOTSTEIN

Today when we open a published history of music, we encounter in every second sentence the word *evolution* . . . This is the conventional mode of presentation, in which the simple always functions as precursor of the more complicated, and the more complex is regarded as a more advanced elaboration of the primitive. This mode of conceptualizing is the result of the fact that contemporary musical scholarship is a consequence of the nineteenth century. The nineteenth century was, however, in all its perspectives dominated by Darwinian theories of evolution. The way in which this theory of evolution has been interpreted has doubtlessly led to a dangerous misunderstanding.
—Paul Bekker (1926)[1]

The de-romanticizing of the world, which we now face, was set in motion already before the war, but it was completed by it . . . The machine, which conquers distances in shorter and ever shorter times, is self-evidently opposed to the romantic. The romantic thrives on distances, and even creates them artificially. With the discovery of the railroad, the romantic certainly was not killed, but the commerce and worldwide traffic that the railroad set in motion gave it its first and painful wound. A glorious isolation of the artist became a rarity. . . . by necessity, a leveling process will spread throughout the world. To the extent the machine shines in all corners of the world, then the romantic must die.
—Adolf Weissmann (1928)[2]

Modernism and Dvořák's Reputation

These reflections by two of Germany's most respected critics were written during a pivotal period in twentieth-century musical life. By the mid-1920s, the modern, in terms of music, had taken its essential shape. The post–World War I alternatives to the common, late-romantic language of expression had appeared before the public. A spirit of change pervaded musical life. "Progressive" composers such as Schoenberg and Busoni had undertaken "a radical dismantling of the established syntax of Western music."[3] And a neoclassic and neo-romantic reaction to these new developments was audible.

In the years between the two World Wars the audience for music in the home and in public had enlarged well beyond the social and economic range deemed possible during the later nineteenth century. Radio broadcasts and the gramophone were perhaps the most significant factors. Interest in music theory, history, and criticism had become widespread. In German-speaking Europe, and in England and America, the popularity of a handful of works by Antonín Dvořák, who utilized the "established syntax" of music in a wide-ranging and eclectic manner, represented the apex of the rapid democratization of a high art musical culture which began at the fin de siècle. Not surprisingly, the first serious, full-length, English-language biography of Dvořák appeared in the 1920s. It was written by the Czech piano pedagogue Karel Hoffmeister and translated by that tireless advocate of Czech music, Rosa Newmarch.

Hoffmeister concluded his biography with an extended plea on behalf of Dvořák. His audience was twofold: his fellow Czech readers and the greater European audience. To his Czech compatriots, Hoffmeister called for a reconciliation between the followers of the two warring camps in Czech musical life, one that claimed Smetana as the true exemplar of Czech music and another that traced its lineage proudly to Dvořák.[4] For his European audience, Hoffmeister sought to raise the standing of Dvořák to that of "Brahms, Bruckner, Tchaikovsky, Borodin and César Franck."[5]

From the mid-1870s to the present, Dvořák's accessibility and popularity have remained linked to the critical estimation of his music. His music seemed *merely* beautiful. Dvořák's success, his appeal to the audiences of the fin de siècle, stemmed, in the view of critics both pro- and anti-Dvořák, from the fact that his work was essentially "naive," simple and spontaneous. These epithets mirrored, for both progressive and conservative critics, a pervasive cultural nostalgia. Dvořák's popularity appeared symptomatic of either failed expectations or the basic mistrust of the widening audience for music that surfaced during the last quarter of the nineteenth century.[6] Hoffmeister's argument was understandably defensive. He struggled to reverse a standard interpretive line. At the 1901 libel trial brought against the *Musical Courier* by Victor Herbert, a friend and colleague of Dvořák's, an expert witness— John Goodrich—testified that Dvořák was an "unoriginal" composer who developed "other people's ideas."[7]

The near–hit tune popularity of the Ninth Symphony (and to a lesser extent the Slavonic Dances, the Eighth Symphony, and the Cello Concerto) did not help the cause. Viewed by cognoscenti as a weaker but more accessible work (in comparison to Dvořák's mature Sixth and Seventh Symphonies), the "New World" Symphony was one of the very few works from the nineteenth-century concert-hall tradition to have won the hearts of a mass audience by the mid-1920s.[8]

In making his argument, Hoffmeister conceded, albeit inadvertently, much ground to Dvořák's critics. He accepted a portrait of Dvořák as a "quiet cautious conservative peasant." Dvořák was "intuitive" as opposed to "intellectual"; a "simple soul" (clearly in the best sense) and not possessed of a wide and profound "spirit." His musical achievement was "lyrical" rather than "dramatic."[9]

Typical of the critical conception of Dvořák's place in musical history and culture that Hoffmeister sought to overcome were the arguments leading European and American critics put forward in 1904 following Dvořák's death. The obituary feuilletons by Richard Aldrich in the *New York Times* and Robert Hirschfeld in the *Wiener Abendpost* articulated a conventional but curious mix of affection and condescension.

Aldrich granted Dvořák the quality of genius but raised doubt as to whether he would be "numbered among the immortals." Despite Dvořák's "provincialism" and "a certain primitiveness," Aldrich saw Dvořák's passing as marking the end of an era of symphonic music. Dvořák left no "successor" who could successfully resist "the prevailing tendencies" of the day. Aldrich concluded:

> He seemed, indeed, the last of the naive musicians, the direct descendant of Haydn, Mozart and Schubert, rejoicing in the self-sufficient beauty of his music and untroubled by the philosophic tendencies and the searching for new things to be said in a new way which animate the younger men of today . . . Dvořák's Schubert-like fecundity was not without its penalties . . . his admirers . . . would have preferred to hear less of the obvious, less of the first impulse, and more of the reflection that shapes and finishes to perfection.[10]

The very same week, in Vienna, Hirschfeld wrote:

> Dvořák's music has no profundity. He does not, as Bruckner, dig into the depths of his soul to bring forth an Adagio. Everything came too easily to him. One can see it in his last quartets . . . : he tossed them off as he did with the first quartets. Though he equips them more richly here and there, no more challenging problematic of counterpoint or ideas commands his attention. He does not strive to go beyond the beautiful, harmonious sound and a healthy reality . . . Dvořák did not stand in the great line of historical evolution. He was a follower and stood to the side, a strong and shining personality who in his works gave voice to a national sensibility. In the music history of his people his work will resound gloriously. In the world history of the arts, a single line, albeit one of honor, will suffice. Outside the borders of his homeland, one will reach for this or that selection from his most beautiful chamber music works with optimism (a quality of Dvořák's artistry), with delight in the sounds and filled with pleasure; but without being drawn to it by inner necessity, or the hope of stirring the soul or being drawn toward a glimpse of a secret, mysterious other world.[11]

By the 1920s the residue left by these attitudes was the relative neglect of much of Dvořák's music in the concert hall. The famous works were hallmarks of "popular," high art music—examples of Weissmann's contemporary "leveling" of taste. They were dismissed as easy to listen to and superficial. Heinrich Schenker, an admirer of Smetana's who had reviewed Dvořák's music unfavorably in the 1890s, reacted to two broadcasts of Dvořák's music—the Eighth Symphony in particular—in the late 1920s with withering contempt.[12] Schenker's dismissal of Dvořák was reminiscent of Hugo Wolf's anti-Dvořák reviews from the 1880s. A line of anti-Dvořák criticism in the German and Austrian world remained strong. The claims of later Czech writers notwithstanding, even Bülow and Joachim were never free of doubt.[13] Dvořák, despite his talent and pleasing surface, was no match for Brahms or Beethoven. Bruckner was reported to have commented, when a student praised Dvořák's orchestration, that "when you paint a pair of sausages green or blue, they still remain a pair of sausages."[14] Max Bruch, no doubt spurred by envy, had limited respect for Dvořák.[15]

In textbooks on theory and analysis from German-speaking Europe, including those by Paul Hindemith, Arnold Schoenberg, and Felix Salzer, examples from Dvořák are notably absent. For the authors of those texts, Dvořák was explicitly not a composer from whom one might learn the craft of composition. German critics, sensitive to the accusation that it might be Dvořák's Czech identity that accounted for his not being taken seriously, used Smetana as a foil, as did a comparable group of Czech critics, celebrating the latter's invention and command of form invidiously against Dvořák.[16]

As Bekker correctly diagnosed, a teleological logic within the narrative of the history of music held sway. His reference to Darwin was not arbitrary, for the consequences of the spread of a progressive evolutionary conception of music history were twofold. First, composers who did not appear to contribute to an avant-garde, a cutting edge in technique, style, and form, were set to the side. Second, the criteria of dominance, influence, and originality (analogues to the idea of successful mutation and to the victors in the struggle for survival and natural selection) were used to validate aesthetically a normative sequence of style and periodization. The primitive was superseded by the complex. In this context the marginal place assigned to Dvořák by Aldrich and Hirschfeld in comparison to Brahms and Bruckner seemed justified. A lack of pivotal historical significance, particularly in the evolution toward innovation and complexity, meant qualitative inferiority.

Schenker's disregard for Dvořák may have been immune from a pseudo-Darwinian logic, but Theodor W. Adorno's was not. For Adorno, the ascendant innovative forms in history contained their dialectical opposites. The power of regressive tendencies and tastes threatened cultural and political progress. Dvořák's work and popularity were evidence of corrupt imitation and decline, of the dismembering of the unity of the symphonic form propelled by political reaction and nationalism.

As Weissmann's lament implied, Dvořák's music and its popularity signaled a late nineteenth-century shift away from the ideals of high musical art inherent in the premodern and capitalist tradition. For Adorno, the symptoms of that shift were the orchestral medley masquerading as a symphony, and the commercial hit tune. Both these evils were present in Dvořák's work.[17] Adorno understood, albeit implicitly, that part of Dvořák's explicit project as a composer was to bridge the gulf between the public of the concert hall and the emergent world of modern popular music—a project later embraced by Victor Herbert and George Gershwin in America and Kurt Weill and Hanns Eisler in Germany.

The early twentieth-century devaluation of Dvořák was a consequence of the idea that genuine musical modernism needed to be part of an aesthetic critique of modernity. Progressive composers and reactionary critics in the early twentieth century sustained the late nineteenth-century faith in music's inherent immunity to ordinary representation and therefore to appropriation by extramusical factors. Even when music was integrated with the poetic and the visual, it had the power to resist, for example, Weissmann's dreaded machine.

The modernist rejection of the "syntax" inherited from the nineteenth century reflected the effort to restore the unique autonomy of musical communication. The redemptive power of the aesthetic through music seemed to demand a rejection of an affirmative relationship to the audience and therefore a sacrifice to the conventions of surface comprehensibility on which Dvořák's music thrived. Dvořák's reputation suffered as a result of contemporary critics' expectations of some sort of disturbing profundity in his work. Without this significance, music was mere entertainment, without access, as the virulently antimodern critic Hirschfeld put it, to "a secret, mysterious other world."

This belief in music's special role, particularly as a means of resistance and rejection of a corrupt and harsh external world, was a legacy of Richard Wagner's polemics. Aesthetic formalism (e.g., as championed in the writings of Eduard Hanslick) was regarded as supportive of the idea that music was merely decorative, a private pleasure—affirming, in a complacent sense, a dubious present. Hanslick's aesthetics robbed music of its critical edge. Formalism separated aesthetics from ethics and politics. It was an insufficient theoretical description of the power and essence of music. In Wagnerian terms, music needed to function on behalf of a community. Music was a spiritual agency acting to transform the economic and political future.

The utopian (and in Weissmann's terms, the romantic) content of Wagner's ideas and the special power of Wagner's music had not been lost on the Nietzsche of *The Birth of Tragedy* (1872). Even after his break with Wagner, Nietzsche's use of music as metaphor and his references to music sustained the myth of its special character and power as a medium of resistance and authenticity. His cunning sarcasm notwithstanding, Nietzsche used music, to the end, as a foil by which to pierce the pretentions, horrors, and corruptions of modern life.[18]

These issues were addressed explicitly in the writings of Hoffmeister's teacher, the most significant and influential Czech aesthetic theorist of the late nineteenth century, Otakar Hostinský. For Hostinský, Dvořák's contemporary, the criteria of aesthetic judgment vis-à-vis music had to be part of a larger philosophical and political project. Within the Czech context, Hostinský (whose sentiments were rather pro-Smetana) saw in music the power to reach beyond mere formal beauty, without sacrifice to the unique autonomy of music. A reconciliation of Hanslick and Wagner could ensure the possibility that music's impact on the public would remain at a level of Schopenhauerian intensity peculiar to music. For Hostinský, formalist aesthetics "set to the side" the "content, the cultural moment of art" in favor of the purely "aesthetic," which ultimately was only "one of the many possible tasks of art, but not the exclusive one."[19]

In his theoretical amalgam of Hanslick and Wagner, Hostinský accepted the need for music in the "cultural moment" designed to further a social and cultural movement. Czech national identity needed to be advanced through music based on the most rigorous formal aesthetic expectations as well as on the poetic and the visual. Music's aesthetic integrity, Hostinský argued, could be preserved in mixed forms. Music, in the work of Smetana and later Zdeněk Fibich (the third man in the trio of leading nineteenth-century Czech composers), advanced a cultural project explicitly critical of the status quo. By transforming, for example, speech in the melodrama "into music as much as possible," music as an aesthetic force could be linked directly to content and act as a leading force in cultural change.[20]

The "progressive" critique of Dvořák in the twentieth century stemmed from variants on Hostinský's argument. Despite the ravages of industry, technology, and commerce, music (defined as derivative of instrumental music from the classical era and early romanticism—the age before modern industrial capitalism) retained its unique potential as a means of liberation. By the 1920s, however, the "progressive" extramusical project was no longer the idea of national regeneration of the 1870s and 1880s. Music needed to become either a force of liberation against the evils of reaction, nationalism, and capitalism or serve as an antidote to the debasement of taste.

What linked the aspirations of Hostinský to the critique of Adorno was a suspicion of the nexus of easy musical communication. Offering the audience what it was comfortable with, given that the audience was largely middle-class (and therefore philistine and presumably smug), became for Hostinský and Adorno a concession. Dvořák's immediacy and seemingly trouble-free accessibility deprived music of its redemptive historical and spiritual power. For Adorno, Dvořák's music conceded to fin-de-siècle regressive listening habits whose dominance was being accelerated by the commercialization of the gramophone, the mannerisms of star performers, and the emergence of a standard repertoire.[21] Music needed to rouse and inspire the audience (as in the generation of Wagner, Hostinský, and Smetana) or make them critical and uncomfortable (as in the generation of Adorno and Schoenberg).

The critical estimate of the work of Antonín Dvořák has remained fixed within the framework set up by Louis Ehlert's path-breaking critical article of 1878, which followed on the heels of Brahms's 1877 advocacy of Dvořák. Ehlert wrote that he was delighted to find in the Slavonic Dances and the Moravian Duets compelling alternatives to academic formalism, romantic excess, and the desire to achieve profundity. Although he identified Dvořák's work as possessing "freshness" and "humor," and evoking "spring" as opposed to the "serious" and "quarrelsome" present, Ehlert did not challenge the criteria of ultimate musical greatness. He never argued that Dvořák successfully integrated an instinct for natural melodic beauty with the formal depth and spiritual profundity characteristic of Beethoven, Brahms, and Wagner.[22]

Ehlert's praise was rather an expression of relief, an articulation of a frustration with modern taste and fashion. The critical embrace of Dvořák outside of Prague became located in a species of reminiscence for a lost and more simple world. Dvořák provided an escape from the dense, intense, crushing realities of modern life, including (in the sense of the late Nietzsche) Wagnerian decadence. A pre-urban, pre-industrial landscape was evoked by Dvořák's music.

This view pervaded Sir Henry Hadow's perceptive and appreciative 1895 essay on Dvořák, the first important critical assessment of Dvořák's work in England. Hadow underscored Dvořák's classical as opposed to romantic instincts. But for all his virtues, Dvořák, unlike Beethoven and Brahms, lacked "economy," "fine reticence and control." He was "spontaneous" and "eloquent"; "warm and sympathetic in temper of mind."[23]

Smetana, following Wagner, sought to critique the present by an open progressive and revolutionary stance. In musical terms this meant arguing, through dramatic music, a national agenda on behalf of a Czech cultural transformation and revival.[24] In contrast, Dvořák appeared to his non-Czech defenders, Hadow and Ehlert, as a benign exponent of an endangered but more humane strategy. Music became, again, a source of apolitical pleasure and nonideological happiness. Therefore, Hadow argued, Dvořák represented an advance beyond the more primitive Smetana. Dvořák rendered the national element in music less crude and confrontational. In Dvořák's hands it became aestheticized in the specific sense of Hanslick's formalism; it became "richer, and the designs more complex and beautiful."

Within this critical tradition, the affirmative aspect of Dvořák's music brought the listener the private pleasure of nostalgic daydreaming (much like the vision of "lovely girls pelting each other with sweet scented flowers on which the dew was still sparkling" that Ehlert described having while reading through the Moravian Duets). It also provided, as Hirschfeld noted, a soothing and untroubling "healthy" assertion of reality. In an era in which social critics feared the power of high culture to inspire "degeneracy," fin-de-siècle critics such as Arthur Elson delighted in the idea that Dvořák's music "was eminently sane, robust, healthy."

Furthermore, when Dvořák became the object of newspaper publicity, he was seen as the family man, the antithesis of the image of the artist as an antibourgeois, deviant madman or Wagnerian-style decadent narcissist. "His was a genius that can ill be spared in a period when our great symphonists are leading us astray on the path of morbid programmes pictured by arbitrary tonal devices," continued Elson.[25]

Among the aspects of Dvořák's personality that rendered him popular in Germany and England, and particularly among the growing numbers of urban middle-class concertgoers seeking social improvement through musical culture, was the rags-to-riches story of his life— the explicit parable of the power of talent to engender social advancement.[26] Dvořák was the composer whose journey, as one Victorian critic put it, "from the log cabin to the White House" was most remarkable.[27]

To sympathetic English and German critics, Dvořák was an Eliza Doolittle character.[28] Despite social advancement, the simple peasant nature never entirely left Dvořák. The "childlike simplicity and naturalness" of his personality and music were a welcome relief from the heady, dangerous, pretentious artist and art to which modern audiences were subjected.[29] No doubt the "exotic" aspect of Dvořák's music—its Czech origins and, in a few cases, its roots in American folk music—enhanced its status as natural and refreshingly premodern in its sentiment.

And yet the music could not be dismissed, as Hugo Wolf might have liked, as trivial.[30] As Gerald Abraham noted half a century ago, even the choral music was embraced in England as a breath of fresh air. It was "pleasant" but also "interesting" music that could overcome the divisions between progressives and conservatives and lighten the moribund lethargy that had settled over the Victorian choral tradition.[31]

Furthermore, by the mid-1920s, as Adolf Weissmann's tirade against technological progress revealed, the cultural politics of aesthetic nostalgia in music had turned into an audience reaction against modernism. Like Aldrich, Weissmann lamented the dangers inherent in a glib critical aesthetic endorsement of modern trends simply because they seemed the inevitable consequences of a progressive historical process.

The changes in the musical culture in the decades following his death in 1904 helped add two new twists to the assessment of Dvořák. Modernity, in its pejorative sense, had brought with it avant-garde music that seemed to mirror the worst qualities of the machine. Modernism seemed explicitly destructive to a nineteenth-century aesthetic of the beautiful in music that Dvořák helped to popularize. At the same time, the basis of the reaction against modernism was a broad-based but sentimental and superficial aesthetic. It represented, in Weissmann's view, a "leveling." It signaled a species of cultural decline predicated on a severely debased level of aesthetic education characteristic of a materialistic age.

Weissmann sought to restore the romantic essence of music, which demanded more than Dvořák's music seemed to offer. Against the modern desacralization of music and art, Dvořák's naive and healthy music, given its apparent lack of profundity, provided no antidote. Unlike Ehlert and Hadow, Weissmann was no longer content with daydreaming and the suggestion of innocence, even though, like Hirschfeld, he maintained that the "healthy" ultimately meant the anti-modern.

For Weissmann, like Schenker and Adorno, the popularity of Dvořák's music in the two decades following the composer's death (and therefore the manner in which it was being listened to) was emblematic of the corruption of taste, the involuntary and uniform embrace of cheap sentimentality. The love of Dvořák's music was a symptom not of autonomy of the individually motivated act of judgment but of false consciousness and manipulation by a mass culture dominated by the worst aspects of modernity.

Darwinism and Dvořák:
The Culture of Fin-de-Siècle Criticism

Although the consequence of Dvořák's reception has been to place him on the sidelines of the history of music (so to speak), with regard especially to twentieth-century modernism, Dvořák's skill has been acknowledged, particularly with respect to the way he appropriated folk materials. Yet as late as Gerald Abraham's important article from the 1940s and Donald Francis Tovey's fine essays on the major symphonies, the late nineteenth-century parallelism between Dvořák's use of folk elements and the pejorative notion of the naive remained.[32] In this sense, the continued use of the epithet *naive* (for example by Carl Dahlhaus) and the acceptance of Dvořák's central role in the late nineteenth- and early twentieth-century obsession with the relation of folk music to the art music tradition seem odd and contradictory.[33]

The ambivalence and condescension regarding Dvořák's craft and his role in the evolution of musical nationalism and the integration of folk origins have their roots in the later nineteenth-century shift away from an early nineteenth-century romantic fascination with folk and national elements.[34] Beginning with J.-J. Rousseau and J. G. von Herder, European interest in the differentiation of cultures according to race and nation (which, in part, was spurred on by the interaction with the New World) had its roots in politics. The issues at stake were progress and reason in civilization.

During the first decades of the nineteenth century, in the wake of the French Revolution and Napoleon, a challenge to an eighteenth-century construct of reason and history helped shift the focus from reason as the determining common characteristic of humanity to an emphasis on the historical roots of human differentiation. What Hegel described as the "cunning" of reason in history, the disjointed pattern of change over time and the persistence of violence and irrationality, demanded explanation.

The influence of new theories of history that sought to explain the historical differentiation of culture by looking to pre-Christian roots did not challenge the idea of an objective, normative aesthetic in the realm of civilized high art. The use of simple material evocative of distinct nations and races by Liszt and Chopin, and later by Brahms, did not seem to require an aesthetic yardstick distinct from the one used to judge Beethoven, Haydn, and Mozart. Schubert, to whom Dvořák was consistently compared, was perhaps the best example.[35] In Schubert's work, the folk element offered merely a memorable and distinct inspiration, either in rhythm or in melodic structure. Except for explicitly lighter works, in compositions inspired by folk elements, through techniques of musical elaboration the significance of the folk origins of the music was diminished.

During the second half of the nineteenth century, the direction of political, social, and aesthetic theory shifted dramatically. By the 1890s, owing in part to Darwinism and European imperialist expansion into the non-European world, the interest in race and its expression through culture characteristic of early romanticism changed following the lines of contemporary scientific explanations of historical and bio-logical development. Natural and social science sought to illuminate a progressive transformation from the primitive and savage to the com-plex and civilized.

Dvořák's entrance onto the larger European scene in the late 1870s coincided with the popularization of theories that sought to explain the origin and development of music in terms of the evolution of advanced Western European high culture from the barbaric and primitive. The critical interest in Dvořák as a composer fit into the framework of a discussion of the evolutionary development of culture and civilization that sought scientific justifications for hierarchical comparative judgments. Dvořák's origins in a markedly lower social class and a marginal national culture deemed more primitive—as well as his use of folk elements—shaped the aesthetic evaluation of his work outside of the Czech lands.

Before the advent of romanticism, an ideology of political equality articulated by social contract theory (that mix of myth, metaphor, and presumed history concerning the development of human society) helped deflect a facile endorsement of the civilized over the primitive. Locke underscored the possibilities of rational social progress on account of the essential equality and malleability of all humans. Rousseau inverted the conventional hierarchy of values between the primitive and the advanced by celebrating the ethics and culture of man before the influence of reason and the civilizing process. Even Herder's seminal fascination with cultural differentiation remained within an eighteenth-century universalist framework.

Succeeding Herder and Rousseau, in the mid- and late nineteenth century, came theories that rejected political ideas that argued the possibility of timely political realization of social justice based on natural equality. Cultural, economic, and social hierarchies—superiority and inferiority—appeared to be symptoms of stages of development governed by an inexorable process susceptible to scientific description and explanation. Inequalities—qualitative differences in the development of societies and their cultures—were consequences of objective historical transformations immune to radical intervention.

The extensive late nineteenth-century inquiry into the origins of music was part of the search for the scientific underpinnings that could legitimate differentiation between higher and lower cultures and societies. In the *Descent of Man* (1871), Charles Darwin argued that the production of repeated tones, the consequence of the universal sexual dynamic and its mating rituals, was the decisive impetus of all human musical development. Darwin argued that speech descended from song, thereby challenging Herbert Spencer's notion that music descended from language use. By implication, music was tied not to the faculty of reason but to emotion.

Darwin underscored the need to distinguish between common origins and subsequent differentiation. It was wrong to infer easy musical communication among diverse peoples and cultures from the assumption that music, in all races and cultures, originated out of the mating process; "so different is the taste of the different races, that our music gives not the least pleasure to savages, and their music is to us hideous and unmeaning." Darwin, however, granted the anomaly that among savages "the capacity for high musical development" existed. At the root of music's universal place in social life was its capacity to "excite in us, in a vague and indefinite manner, the strong emotions of a long-past age," particularly those "gentler feelings of tenderness and love," those of "triumph and ardour for war," and ultimately "the sense of sublimity," albeit only within discrete racial and cultural groups.

Darwin doubted whether, in musical communication "amongst the nations," even in Western Europe "the music of one is interpreted in the same sense by others." In other words, difference was far more powerful in reality than any residual shared human capacity. Music presented a variant on the problem of linguistic communication. In ordinary language some system of translation seemed plausible, despite the gap between meaning and significance in the use of literal equivalents in different languages. Music was not susceptible to such translation.

Darwin's scientific intervention exploded the illusion of a single universal musical aesthetic. It also questioned a uniform historical process of evolution by granting the primitive the capacity for "prompt and high development" in music. More than twenty years before Dvořák's praise of African-American and Native American folk music, Darwin singled out specifically "Hottentots and Negroes," although he demurred by acknowledging that "they do not practise in their native countries anything we should esteem as music."[36] Inherent in Darwin's scheme were both the concession to radical cultural differences in types of musical communication, all socially effective, and the judgment that the advanced European form was aesthetically superior.

This mix of admiration for the musical ability of primitive races and the assertion of superiority of European music characterized post-Darwinian theorizing. Two examples are directly relevant to Dvořák. One of the most influential contributions to the study of the origins of music was made by Richard Wallaschek. Wallaschek, who was born in Moravia, began his career in Germany, spent the years from 1890 to 1895 in London, and ended his career in Vienna. He bridged German-speaking Europe and England, two of the three worlds outside of the Czech lands that were crucial to Dvořák. In his two major works, the 1883 *Ästhetik der Tonkunst* and the 1893 *Primitive Music*, Wallaschek sought to prove that all music derived from rhythm. Physical motion, including dance (as opposed to mating calls), was the basis of musical development.

In 1883, Wallaschek distinguished between the uses of the dance among the "cultivated circles within civilized peoples" and the more primitive nationalist dance forms of less developed nations, specifically the Czech, Polish, and Hungarian. Truly civilized nations had no need of the musical residues of folk culture and therefore possessed "no national dances." Their place on the continuum of historical development was higher. They had successfully "ennobled" the primitive uses of the dance and transformed the dance into a true "art form." Schubert's, Chopin's, and Liszt's uses of folk elements were cited as evidence.[37]

Ten years later, Wallashek undertook to reconcile the scientific insights of Darwin in evolution and Francis Galton in heredity to explain not only the origins of music but also the rapid progress of musical culture in Europe during the nineteenth century. That progress was visible in two dimensions, both germane to Dvořák: the spread of musical culture both to a wider range of social classes through education within "cultivated nations" and to more "primitive" races whose progress in music outstripped their development in other arenas.[38]

Although "the sense of beauty" is an "abstract" sensation that neither animals nor savage man possessed naturally, it could be acquired through "tradition and imitation." Wallasheck argued that "it is in no way unlikely that we civilized nations, and for example, the negroes, receive the same degree of musical ability by birth but yet accomplish such different ends . . . they lack examples and the social necessity of coming up to their level. Neither of these can be artificially grafted upon their social status, and therefore they are pretty well lost to musical, and probably any other form of, culture."[39]

The capacity to invent and retain melody and then to employ it in long, discursive forms was the hallmark of advanced musical culture. Wallashek allowed that social institutions of education could accelerate progress within each generation. Using its basic hereditary endowment, a social group could make remarkable strides in musical culture. Progress was measured in terms of the development away from the primitive focus on rhythm, to the utilitarian dance, to the tuneful dance, and finally to an abstraction of the national dance as extended artistic form. Wallaschek's theory of musical development legitimated a social project. In contrast to Spencer and Darwin, whose views he challenged, a civilizing process (which provided "examples" worthy of imitation and "social necessity") could, in principle, help accelerate the entrance of less advanced races, as social entities, into the higher reaches of art. Implicit in the late nineteenth-century assessment of Dvořák was the idea that Dvořák vindicated the attitude Wallaschek articulated.

Crucial to Wallaschek's confidence in the civilizing project was the absence of an "absolute standard of beauty." Science demonstrated that taste was historically contingent. Opinions and tastes would change, permitting music to continue to exert its social function in diverse and unexpected ways.[40] In America, Edward MacDowell, who did not take kindly to Dvořák's appearance on the American scene, sought to fashion a different synthesis of Darwinism and musical aesthetics. Rhythm was the "intellectual side of music" and melody its "sensuous" side. MacDowell skirted the Darwin-Wallaschek debate over priority in the natural or the historical origins of music. In his lectures given at Columbia University in the late 1890s, MacDowell argued, however, that rhythm was the key to the human achievement in music. He wrote, "rhythm denotes a thought; it is the expression of a purpose. There is will behind it . . . melody, on the other hand, is an almost unconscious expression of the senses; it translates feeling into sound."[41] MacDowell sought to restore the rational dimension to musical achievement. Music was more than a response to emotion.

For MacDowell, so-called folk music was like "a twig which has fallen into a salt mine." Over time it gathered attributes of complexity. Its relation to any authentic primitive origins was "general" at best. What passed in the 1890s as folk and national music was a far cry from one-note, primitive musical impulses. The peculiarly American twist that MacDowell put on the late nineteenth-century debate was his effort to underplay cultural differences in music. The "true" folk song "has but few marked national traits, it is something which comes from the heart; whereas nationalism in music is an outward garment which is the result of certain habits of thought, a mannerism of language so to speak."[42]

MacDowell sought to diminish the conceits of aesthetic uniqueness based on race and nation. The "figure"—the essential musical element— of all national folk music was the same "the world over" and related to the same "universal language of savage music." Just as the drum was universally the first instrument, so too was the pentatonic scale employed widely. The evolution of the human race argued for the essential artificiality and interchangeability of national characteristics. Like Wallaschek, MacDowell regarded the artistic transformation of the folk element as the mark of the highest form of musical culture.

Indeed, outside Bohemia and Moravia, Dvořák's music came to be viewed as an example of how and to what extent the folk element had become "civilized." The comparison of Dvořák to Brahms and Liszt in particular rested on how he had transformed national and primitive folk elements. Dvořák, the "peasant" who leapfrogged the historical sequence of economic and social progress, demonstrated Wallaschek's theory that music was unique as a human attribute. The constant reference to Dvořák as "naive" was an aspect of this mode of thought. Naiveté, combined with Dvořák's imitative skill at using many different sophisticated high art forms—the quartet, symphony, and oratorio—explained, as Darwin and Wallaschek suggested, radical incongruities peculiar to how music functioned in human development and evolution.

To exaggerate the context somewhat: Dvořák was a benign example of deviance. He was exotic, not merely for his Czech nature and lower-class origins but for his demonstration of how, through music, the "other" might be civilized rapidly. The fact that rhythm in Dvořák's work (the use of Czech dances from furiant to polka) and the use of harmony (in conjunction with folk melodic patterns) were tied to a folk and national culture that the English and Germans deemed less advanced only heightened the wonderment at Dvořák's mix of the primitive and the complex. Dvořák was a kind of talking monkey.[43] What eluded his German and English audiences was, of course, how aware Dvořák was of the context. Dvořák sought to exploit this dynamic for his own purposes.

In America, the context was different. MacDowell was part of a generation that fought for the rightful place of music in the university and in culture. Music's link to reason was therefore crucial. By cutting through the surface of so-called national and folk distinctions, Mac-Dowell revealed a second aim—to show the futility of finding a distinct American art music. The task was, rather, to enable Americans to gain a foothold in what Wallaschek described as the world of "cultivated people in civilized nations." Dvořák's call in the early 1890s to establish a distinct folk basis for American art music seemed regressive. Like his European counterparts, MacDowell believed that the extent to which the specificity and political significance of a national or folk element was transfigured demonstrated the composer's craft.

MacDowell, however, failed to recognize that Dvořák knew how different America was. Dvořák's enthusiasm for music in America reflected his sense that America could take the best from Europe and leave its worst habits (e.g., national conflict) behind. Furthermore, in his encounter with the folk element in America, Dvořák was forced to reconsider his own use of Czech material. The late symphonic poems are essays in formal experimentation using Erben's poems, icons of Czech national culture. They were a departure from Dvořák's earlier pattern of integrating the folk in traditional classical forms. But unlike

Smetana's *Ma Vlast*, the late symphonic works are not overtly polemical or political.

Before America, Dvořák realized that the achievement of high critical praise demanded concessions to the camouflage of universalism. In a world where hierarchical evolutionary distinctions among cultures were legitimated by science, Dvořák exploited a mixture of assertion and denial. On the one hand, as Wallaschek argued, the use of folk musical elements, unvarnished, was the sign of cultural inferiority. On the other hand, Dvořák wrote music that demonstrated, through its use of classical models—in a microcosm—the successful civilizing process.[44]

Smetana pursued a different route by using the Wagnerian model to create a Czech analogue. Dvořák, anticipating the work of Janáček, Ives, and Bartók, challenged the logic of the dominant English and German critical perspective with his skillful and magical mix of overt concession and covert rebellion. By achieving wide popularity through his compositional strategy, Dvořák helped undermine the ideological bases of late nineteenth-century music criticism.[45]

Between the Czech and the German: Cultural Nationalism in the Habsburg Monarchy

Without doubt, the most important personality among Czech composers is Anton Dvořák. At the same time, his music often enough calls for the application of a different standard from the one applied usually to works of art of the highest level; rhythmic and melodic monomania is given free reign without a sense of limits in a way that sorely tests the patience of the educated listener. One must also accept vulgar violations of primary rules of form. But in this only partially civilized being there lies an impressive creative energy, a real mastery of the grandiose . . . clearly this all works only at climaxes, and even the Russians are barely as skilled at the explosive gesture as this Czech.[46]

No more pithy distillation of the mix of condescension and dismissive judgment toward Dvořák as a "national" composer who used folk material exists than this excerpt from Hugo Riemann's 1901 history of music. As Riemann's analysis suggests, the obvious comparison (for Germans) to be made was to Dvořák's Russian contemporaries, whose music was both exotic and popular. But here the facts of late nineteenth-century politics intervene. The rubric of "nationalism" in

German and English criticism, when it was applied to nineteenth-century Russian composers more frequently than in the case of Dvořák, absolved Russian musical texts of the highest critical expectations (the sort applied regularly to the work of apparently non-nationalist composers, such as Brahms, Bruckner, Mahler, and Schoenberg).

Nationalism, as an evaluative criterion, was applied differentially in the nineteenth century. Indeed, the matter of "nationalism" in Bohemia, Moravia, and the Habsburg Empire in the century between 1815 and 1914 was quite different from what it was in Russia. From the perspective of Western Europe, the geopolitical significance of Russia since the late eighteenth century merged with its oriental strangeness. The Russian was devastatingly attractive. The prominence of Russian literary figures—particularly Tolstoy, Turgenev, and later Dostoyevsky—and the visibility of the Russian émigré intellectual community in the nineteenth century helped add to the special magic. Even though Balakirev and Tchaikovsky (with whom Dvořák maintained a good relationship), like their Russian literary counterparts, Pushkin and Tolstoy, used Western European models to mediate the Slavic and Russian, the national element was expected and embraced.[47] This positive sensibility, both in Germany and in France, lasted into the era of the *Ballets Russes*.

In contrast, Czech culture and therefore "Czechness" were significantly less exotic to the German public. As the 1894 official Habsburg survey of the monarchy pointed out, Bohemia could legitimately be considered the "heart" of Europe, both geographically and in terms of history and culture.[48] There was no decisive religious difference with the rest of Europe, whether in Catholicism or Protestantism. The fact that the Czech nationality seemed more nearly Western than Slavic might appear at first blush to have been an advantage against cultural snobbery and prejudice. But familiarity worked against the recognition of the achievements of the nineteenth-century Czech cultural revival in Western Europe, despite periodic efforts within the Habsburg monarchy to give Bohemia and Moravia a cultural and political status more akin to that which Hungary achieved after 1867.

Germans and their language were integral parts of Czech history. In contrast to the language of Poland, German was, in the Czech lands, at once the language of the foreigner and that of the oppressor, as well as a native tongue.[49] The historic intertwining of the German and the Slavic in Bohemia and Moravia was sufficiently complex as to give credence to the Old Czech political line (led by F. L. Rieger, and to which Dvořák was sympathetic) that called for Czech autonomy in a federal Habsburg empire.[50]

The assertions of cultural autonomy developed by the young Czech movement appeared, as a result, far more labored and awkward than parallels in Russia and Hungary.[51] Leoš Janáček did embrace pan-Slavism, but as indicated by Dvořák's lukewarm reception in Russia, the Russians mistrusted the Czechs, owing to their close relationship, as Slavs, to German culture. The fiasco surrounding Balakirev's 1867 visit to Prague and Smetana's reaction indicated how much more ambivalent the Czechs were toward pan-Slavism than were the Poles and southern Slavic peoples in the Habsburg Empire.[52]

The history of Bohemia and Moravia (the birthplace of many a cosmopolitan figure with little or no conventional nationalist identity, whose career, like Wallaschek's, was made directly through the German language within the Habsburg Empire) was sufficiently tied to Western Europe to permit Smetana and Dvořák, who used both languages, to write music for German texts with little difficulty. The extent of migration by Czechs within the Habsburg Empire during the nineteenth century, particularly to Vienna where Czech was the city's second language, only helped to blur the boundaries of ethnic self-definition already clouded by the multinationalist and dynastic traditions of the Habsburg realm.[53] The Czechs were a distinct element in fin-de-siècle Vienna, for example, but viewed more as lower-class subjects from within the Empire than as a foreign element. The Russian was sufficiently exotic as to elude that special kind of critical contempt reserved for the familiar, the second-class citizen within a given political framework.[54]

No wonder Dvořák was in conflict for most of his life with the radical nationalist politics of his time. He was at one and the same time a patriot in terms of the Empire and a passionate member of the Czech nation in ethnic and cultural terms. He sought a reconciliation of his political and cultural loyalties.[55]

The fate and behavior of the Bohemian and Moravian aristocracy created a further contrast with Russia, Poland (which was regarded in the nineteenth century as a recently dismembered nation), and Hungary. The demise of Czech independence in the seventeenth century in the context of the religious wars resulted in the orphaning of the nineteenth-century Czech national movement from aristocratic patronage.[56] The Czech cultural tradition enjoyed nothing like the advocacy by either church or aristocratic oligarchies characteristic of Russia, Hungary, or Poland. Given the absence of a significant aristocratic role in modern Czech nationalism, it comes as little surprise that modern Czech democracy (in contrast to that of Poland and Hungary, not to mention Russia) uniquely succeeded within a framework of explicit nationalism after 1918. In Hungary, for example, the symbiosis between modern nationalism and an antidemocratic aristocratic sentiment helped doom interwar national democratic movements.

The repeated tone of astonishment, mixed, of course, with admiration for Dvořák's achievement even by supposed friends such as Bülow, Richter, Simrock, and Brahms, was a reflection of social snobbery not only against Dvořák's peasant origins but against the Czech.[57] In the case of Eduard Hanslick, who came from the long tradition of Prague-based and Bohemian German (and later German-speaking Jewish) cultural activity during the nineteenth century, this disregard of the Czech as an autonomous cultural source seemed entirely natural.[58] In contrast, the Russian was, if a bit barbaric, awesome in its raw political might and size. It was, ultimately, a contender for respect and equality as a world culture.[59]

Dvořák's response to and affection for America is quite understandable in this context. The issues of nationality and ethnicity in the America of the 1890s paralleled circumstances in the Habsburg context. The striking and appealing example of a mix of cultural autonomy and political patriotism to America in Spillville and at the 1893 World Exposition in Chicago was not lost on him.[60] The absence of internal political strife among his countrymen in America and their ability to sustain their culture and feel equal and free in political terms not only permitted Dvořák to feel welcome and at home but forced him to reconsider how ethnic and national identity might be expressed through music.

The Roots of Dvořák's Aesthetic

Dvořák, unlike Smetana or Tchaikovsky, developed as musician and composer isolated from the influence of early nineteenth-century musical romanticism. As is well known, Dvořák displayed shifts and apparent inconsistencies in the compositional styles and strategies of his maturity. This has made difficult many a writer's methodological desire to make a coherent developmental whole out of his life's work.[61]

Dvořák struggled to achieve a synthesis between eighteenth-century classicist models (the last of whom—and for Dvořák, the most important—was Schubert) and Wagnerian romantic modernism in a manner quite unlike Smetana despite their similar motivations and impetus. Dvořák was a late adolescent before he confronted the music of the generation of 1809—Schumann, Mendelssohn, and Liszt. He had been steeped in the conservative aesthetics of early nineteenth-century provincial Bohemian musical culture. The models he chose to imitate and adapt reflected the special character of his musical autobiography.[62]

The Horatio Alger–like portrait of Dvořák that so captivated his newspaper-reading contemporaries—that of the butcher's son who became a world-class composer—camouflages a constructive clue to Dvořák's accomplishment. Instead of the condescending surprise characteristic of *haute bourgeois* criticism or the tone of moralistic triumph that runs through the Dvořák literature (particularly commentaries dating from the communist era), one needs to examine the constructive consequences of a kind of Rip van Winkle phenomenon.[63] Dvořák was able to make his own creative breakthrough and synthesis precisely because he jumped, so to speak, an entire era of musical ideas.

The cultural deprivation associated with Dvořák's "humble" origins needs to be regarded as similar to the nonsequential, nonlinear, abrupt breakthrough that eludes the step-by-step paradigm of scientific progress. Dvořák's synthesis of the late eighteenth century with the late romanticism of Wagner, in light of Dvořák's influence on Leoš Janáček and Charles Ives, was crucial to the antiromantic strain in twentieth-century modernism and the modernist interest in the appropriation of folk and popular materials.

Since Dvořák did not work through the models of Schumann and Mendelssohn early in his career, his mature work possessed little of the self-conscious conservatism that came to dominate Brahms's later music. One of the keys to understanding the increasing formal complexity and expressive austerity of Brahms's late oeuvre is not only the self-criticism of maturity but also the keen awareness of his historical responsibility as protagonist of an aesthetic line that descended through Mendelssohn and Schumann to him. Brahms's aesthetic choices after 1875 were mediated by the Wagnerian opposition, by the polemical and ideological aesthetic debates of his time.

Brahms (as opposed to Dvořák) was an avid autodidact in literary, political, and philosophic matters. He was interested in aesthetics and theory. He studied and admired Wagner's achievement, but unlike Verdi or Dvořák, he resisted its influence. Brahms's immunity to the Wagnerian aesthetic was a function of the historical mantle he took on. Dvořák stepped to the side of the kind of aesthetic controversy that engulfed Joachim and Brahms in the late 1850s. As Karel Sazavsky recalled, Dvořák once lamented, "I always envied Wagner that he could write. Where would I be if I could write!"[64] Unlike Smetana, who defined the true national direction for Czech music in prose as well as in music (following no doubt the model of Liszt), Dvořák felt free to be eclectic, change directions, and borrow ideas.

The absence of a rigid aesthetic ideology was, therefore, described by conservatives as a "healthy" instinct, a sign of Dvořák's spontaneous and purely "musical" nature. A strain of Liszt-like orchestral gesture and Wagnerian emulation was never wholly absent from Dvořák's music from the start. As Dvořák's late orchestral writing reveals, his musical ambition led him to develop a unique version of how narrative (i.e., a program) can form the basis of a musical structure or be integrated in the traditional symphony (e.g., the Ninth). Despite his respect for Brahms, Dvořák charted his own course.

Dvořák resisted a Smetana-like monothematic impulse until his very late work, more than a decade after Smetana's death. Likewise (and this defines the contrast with Richard Strauss), Dvořák was not interested in the power of music to wax philosophical. In Dvořák's late symphonic poems, he sought to parallel the experience of hearing and seeing a story told. In the mature symphonies he used form, harmonic contrasts, and thematic differentiation to highlight a leading line, eschewing the multilayered, nearly contrapuntal character of late Brahms.[65] This reconciliation of complexity and surface comprehensibility was similar to techniques of oral narration. The close connection of actual speech patterns to the music of the late poems can therefore be seen as extensions of Dvořák's effort to create the elegant line in symphonic structure, as in the Fifth, Sixth, and Seventh Symphonies. The last symphonic poems mirror the odd mixture of classicism and late romanticism characteristic of Dvořák before 1895.

Gustav Mahler sought to use symphonic structure to integrate the epic narrative. He achieved the scale and weight associated with the extensive Wagnerian music drama. Strauss (after the mid-1880s) abandoned the classic symphonic model and sought to extend the Lisztian paradigm of a parallel between poetic and musical illustration. What is startling, by comparison to Mahler and Strauss, are the substance and subtlety of Dvořák's innovations. In comparison to Bruckner, they appear early.

A close inspection of Dvořák's 1865 symphony, no. 1 in C minor, his only early symphonic work to survive untouched by his revisions from later years, reveals the roots of his aesthetic ambitions. The work shows an extraordinary originality. It indicates that Dvořák might have followed a direction more like the ones Bruckner and Mahler took. A conscious, self-critical process of development, not a lack of originality, led Dvořák to his mature works. This symphony was unknown to

Dvořák's contemporaries. Since *The Bells of Zlonice* is exactly contemporaneous with Bruckner's first efforts in symphonic form (the so-called Zero Symphony and specifically the First, also in C minor), a comparison is apt, particularly since the critical estimation of Bruckner as innovative and profound has been more secure than Dvořák's. Even the use of the term *naive*, common in the critical literature on both composers, has been used differentially. In Bruckner's case, it refers almost exclusively to his character, not to his music. A Bruckner-Dvořák comparison is even more appropriate when one considers that both composers deeply admired the work of Schubert.

In the First Symphony, Dvořák sought to use large episodic frames within the contrasting developmental structure of the symphonic form for dramatic purposes, thereby extending the scale of the symphonic form. Despite resemblances in the finale to Mendelssohn and Schumann, the scope has a late nineteenth-century grandeur. What has struck some commentators as youthful ineptitude was perhaps more a case of daring experimentation.[66] In the first movement, the use of three thematic groups and the juxtapositions of quick modulations give the work an arresting character and imposing sweep. The mastery of instrumentation, particularly the use of obbligato figurations in the strings is uncannily Brucknerian (mm. 283–87).

Like Bruckner, Dvořák's most signaturelike innovations seem located in the scherzo movements. Although the last movement has been criticized as repetitious, Dvořák's use of repetition is comparable to Wagner's and Bruckner's. He retains the dramatic sense by layering sequences and harmonic juxtapositions. The buildup to the climax is successfully paced. The rhythmic transformations in the last 120 bars are unusual and bold. Despite the debt to Schubert, Dvořák's C-minor Symphony shows a fresh dramatic seriousness devoid of pleasing superficialities. If one ever doubted the magnitude of Dvořák's talent and originality, this work, written at age twenty-three, should put such doubts to rest.

The idea that Dvořák was innovative has been a proposition that even writers sympathetic to Dvořák from his own time to the very recent past have failed to argue convincingly. However, the relationship between Dvořák and Janáček and Dvořák's influence on Ives point to his role in inspiring indigenous modernisms at the fin de siècle.[67] Bohuslav Martinů and Aaron Copland may have derived significant impetus from the mature Dvořák.

What renders Dvořák crucial to twentieth-century modernism is his mode of appropriation of validated historical models. The image of Beethoven loomed large for Dvořák but in a manner quite opposite from the way Beethoven figured in the career of Gustav Mahler. Mahler accepted a view of Beethoven entirely mediated by Wagner. Dvořák's Beethoven remained a classical master. Mahler avoided writing for the stage in part because of the shadow cast by Wagner. Dvořák was determined to succeed as an opera composer, because of his desire to emulate Wagner's ambition to gain a wide new audience.[68] But after early attempts at opera, Dvořák turned away; the shadow cast by Smetana was too great. Dvořák veered from both Smetana and the Wagnerian models *before* his discovery by Brahms in 1877. From the time of Brahms's intervention until his return from America, Dvořák experimented in his instrumental work within the classical framework defined by the models of Beethoven and Schubert. A baroque and classical model held sway in the choral music of the 1880s. In these endeavors the Wagnerian call to reach a broader public was not lost on Dvořák.

Dvořák's use of so-called indigenous or "folk" elements after 1875 provides a useful basis for a comparison to Mahler. Mahler and Dvořák were both impelled by an ambivalent psychological nostalgia for childhood in which the distorted memories and expectations of the past became associated with musical images; with the confrontation between a lost world, the fantasy of innocence, and the modern. Mahler's construct of nature was that of an ideal and a refuge, located in an invidious contrast between the urban, the modern, and a vision of the early nineteenth century. The struggle of modernity suggested musical metaphors for the disruptive, the harsh, the fragmented, and the dialectical conflict between the possible and the actual. It is therefore no accident that the popularity of Mahler is closely associated with a view of the modernist movement as a critique of a late nineteenth-century sentimentality. A negative critical dialectic—the fragmentation of false totalities and the disruption of artificial surface syntheses—are associated with Mahler's music. The use of the folk or "banal" elements works as a critique of illusionistic sentiment and unauthentic hopes located in the musical expectations of a philistine bourgeois culture.

Mahler used nature and childhood memories as foils within an innovative, antitraditional aesthetic directed against a late nineteenth-century urban and historicist cultural conceit, as challenges to the facile claims of progress. Dvořák did not celebrate nature as imperiled. He sought a way to integrate the city and the countryside. The age of the machine fascinated him, as did the sheer size of London and New York, with their possibilities for communication with a wide public. Bourgeois philistinism did not concern him. A veteran of a dance band orchestra, Dvořák, like Wagner, never scorned the idea of popularity. Profoundly religious in the traditional sense, he sought to communicate the divine glories of nature as a way of reconciling the present with the past all without trivialization.

Central to Dvořák's project was the task of retaining traditional norms of musical aesthetics, thereby resisting the lure of radical subjectivity in musical style. This adherence to norms justified Dvořák's borrowing from others. Evident eclecticism facilitated the power of new music to communicate with the modern mass audience. The task, as Hirschfeld noted in his review of *St. Ludmila*, was to bridge cultural and national barriers.

One key to understanding Dvořák lies in his awareness of the opportunity for social advancement through cultural achievement. Some of the shifts in Dvořák's style can be ascribed to a double-edged, two-sided process of calculated imitation. He lacked the kind bourgeois conceit and psychological and social confidence to delight in rebellion, to assume the mannerisms of an artist in search of a style marked primarily by surface originality. To gain acceptance and success, Dvořák consistently took the route of caution: the emulation of validated models. He waited a long time to issue his first compositions. He observed and followed a safe route, as in the case of his first big Prague success, the 1872 choral nationalist hymn *The Heirs of the White Mountain*.

Dvořák, as the First Symphony demonstrates, possessed the gift of musical originality. But in his maturity he chose to integrate his own melodic invention, rhythmic ideas, and sense of narrative form within existing models rather than innovate in external structures. Dvořák's achievement, particularly with respect to the twentieth century, rests in his creation of a covert framework, a camouflage through which could be asserted a Czech sensibility, his own voice, and an implicit critique of the German conceit of cultural superiority.

Photography and the Locomotive: Dvořák, America, and Populism

The decisive clue to Dvořák rests not in how Dvořák dealt with aesthetic ideologies but in how he responded to modernity, particularly technological change. Dvořák's journalistic silence on musical matters, apart from his years in America, only forces a closer look at the relationship of his craft as a composer to the extramusical—in Hostinský's terms, the "content, the cultural moment."

Of all the things outside of music that Antonín Dvořák loved, the railroad and the locomotive stand out. Only his pigeons could compete. Few details have been repeated so often and their significance so consistently ignored as Dvořák's railroad obsession, his joy in watching locomotives in Prague (and in New York, inspecting the modern steamships in the harbor) and remembering their identification numbers. Dvořák viewed the progress of the machine, particularly in transportation, and Weissman's much-lamented "shortening" of geographical distance through the railroad and steamship, as a miracle of progress.

Unlike Gustav Mahler, who was nearly twenty years younger and also born in a Czech village, albeit in Moravia, Dvořák possessed no cultural snobbery vis-à-vis America. For all Europeans America was, for better or worse, the harbinger of the future, the material emblem of modernity. Both men went to America to live and work as musicians. Whereas Mahler's departure in 1907 was driven by his weakening political position in Vienna and his exasperation with the intrigue and politics surrounding the musical life there (as well as by the irresistible lure of money), Dvořák went to America not merely for the money but with anticipation regarding the political culture there. Like Beethoven and Haydn, Dvořák had been impressed with England, the continental European's often-inadvertent link to America. Mahler never went to England.

Dvořák's embrace of America is significant when it is compared to the attitude of most of his fellow German-speaking Europeans, including those who also worked and concertized in America, such as Wilhelm Gericke and Hans von Bülow.[69] The fear of America as a heartless place, driven by material greed and a disregard for culture, was a European norm. The vision of America as soulless, as a warning to Europe of its own future in terms of the triumph of calculation and cold rationality over spirit—the idea of America as a futurist nightmare—was commonplace.[70] It led, before 1914, to, among other things, attitudes of cynicism and snobbery regarding the reasons German-speaking musicians traveled to America. Dvořák did not share either sentiment.

Like many immigrants to America, Dvořák associated the industrial and technological progress immediately visible in New York with a constructive future: the breakdown of the remaining vestiges of caste structure and feudal privilege. His delight in his reception in New York particularly by his countrymen has no parallel in the Mahler case.[71] We have become so inured by several generations of historical revisionism that we easily forget simple facts. Among them is the fact that the idealistic attitude to America widespread in Eastern Europe (understandably shared by a Czech artist in the early 1890s) cannot be written off as merely sentimental and naive.

For Dvořák, along with the developments of modernity associated with the American example came the bridging of class and the narrowing of the social and political consequences of economic inequality. Dvořák's amazement at the practice in Boston (which he witnessed before the performance of his *Requiem*) of offering a special performance at cheap prices; his astonishment at the absence, in the halls of New York, of deference to inherited privilege; his respect for the civic philanthropy of Mrs. Thurber; and his experience in Worcester, Massachusetts—all evident in his correspondence—betray a set of political views at once implicitly critical of practices back home and affirmative regarding the kind of rational modernity America seemed to display.[72]

When Dvořák, according to Suk, remarked with regret in 1896 that his mentor, Brahms (who, like Dvořák, loved modern gadgets), seemed to believe in nothing, he was not only referring to Brahms's lack of devout faith. Rather, he reacted in a depressed manner to Brahms's capacity to display a "soul" in his music and yet stick to a pessimistic cosmopolitanism shaped by nearly Burkhardtian dismay at the direction politics and culture were taking.[73] Brahms's dim view of what the future seemed to promise at the fin de siècle was shared by his friends Theodor Billroth and Eduard Hanslick. Their advocacy on behalf of an explicitly anti-Wagnerian aesthetic had much to do with the so-called decadent cultural consequences of Wagnerism, particularly as it was expressed by Hugo Wolf's generation.

In turn, the more sophisticated and less passive pessimism of the younger generation—the generation of Mahler, Franz Kafka, and Thomas Mann, with its embrace of the radical implications in Nietzsche's critique—was, in part, an extension of the cultural pessimism already evident among Brahms's contemporaries. Dvořák did not fear the culture or the politics of the present. The new politics, mass culture, and the explosion of popular forms and expression were associated constructively with the Czech cultural revival and American democracy.

In terms of the consequences of this view of America as prophetic of the modern on the development of aesthetic modernism, Dvořák's reaction to America can be compared with the glowing embrace of America by another citizen of the Habsburg Empire, the young Viennese architect Adolf Loos (1870–1933). Loos, coincidentally, visited America first in part to attend the 1893 Chicago World Exposition at which Dvořák conducted.

By the time Loos returned to Vienna in 1896 he was convinced that in politics and design, Europe had much to learn from America. The future of the modern had everything to do with Europe's discarding a sentimental attachment to the aesthetics of a preindustrial artisanal European past. The cloying historicism of reigning bourgeois aesthetics in Europe needed to be challenged.[74] Loos returned to America celebrating American architecture and design. Dvořák returned with a new conception of the relationship between the public and high art music.

Just as Loos found himself at odds with the Vienna Secession and *Jung Wien* crowd, Dvořák kept his distance during the mid-1890s from the self-proclaimed followers of both Brahms and Wagner. America helped strengthen and direct Dvořák's lifelong distrust of the terms of aesthetic debate that were dominant in Europe. What he returned from America with was an aesthetic of accessible narrative linear and structural simplicity audible in the last symphonic poems. That aesthetic was not dissimilar to the inspiration that Loos took from the architecture of Louis Sullivan, Frank Lloyd Wright, and novel American industrial design. This influence is visible in Loos's great 1910 Viennese building on the Michaelerplatz. The American experience helped Dvořák respond, in the last operas, to Hostinský's challenge to fashion a populist merger between Hanslick's aesthetics and Wagner's *Gesamtkunstwerk*.

Dvořák's stubborn but original eclecticism vis-à-vis contemporary fashions, his failure to be the bearer of a surface cultural critique of either modern progress or America, and his refusal to define the essence of music in either a neo-Wagnerian manner or in imitation of strict Brahmsian withdrawal into surface formalism (with all its innovations in compositional technique) were not necessarily, as commentators have suggested, the function of his simplicity, his peasant origin, his lack of formal education, or his good nature. Dvořák's ability to formulate a populist variant on late romanticism derived, ironically, from the roots of his craft in the eighteenth century.

As in the case of Loos, the direction the innovations with which Dvořák came back from America harked back to an era of classical restraint. For example, the Biblical Songs, *Rusalka* (although it is comparable to the post-Wagnerian, fairy-tale opera movement evident in Humperdinck), and the nearly pre-romantic *Armida* all show a lyrical, populist, and economical strategy. Dvořák's eloquent defense of Schubert, written during his sojourn in America, can therefore be reevaluated as part of Dvořák's formulation of a credo for modernism distinct from the extant conservative and "New German" legacies of the end of the nineteenth century. Central to that credo was the creation of a refined and simplified narrative musical line—stripped of unnecessary decorative complexities—designed to assure wide accessibility.

It was Dvořák's intent to write music for an ever-widening public in Prague and New York. The image of the social and political network generated by the modern railroad was a metaphor for the role of art in contemporary life. As the demographic and economic development of the city of Prague in the years 1860–1904 confirms, Dvořák's personal observation, in Prague, was of a seemingly successful mix of new and old. Unlike in Paris and Vienna, modernity did not bring with it a decisive redesign of the city. The possibilities for integration, as opposed to confrontation, of tradition with progress were strengthened by the late nineteenth-century modernization of Prague. In contrast to Vienna, the central railroad station, for Dvořák, became emblematic of Prague. In Vienna, as Loos had argued, the new had been camouflaged with the distorted and dishonest aesthetics of the old. Likewise, within Vienna, a nostalgia for the "old," premodern city emerged from a cultural resistance to rapid demographic expansion and industrial change.[75]

In Prague, Dvořák observed a more positive symbiosis of a pre–nineteenth-century cultural tradition with the explicitly modern. The answer lay in part with the fact that Czech national revival was not nostalgically antimodern. Dvořák's polemical statements shortly after his arrival in America expressed explicitly his belief that native traditions, traditional aesthetic values, and normative aesthetics could be reconciled with the demands of modern progress.

Dvořák's message to America was that it possessed potentially the cultural equivalents of the locomotive and steamship. America had the means and context to transmit through musical culture the miracles of progress to a mass audience. Dvořák's advice to America, in terms of its musical life, was not to neglect the cultural side of its impressive material and political modernity.[76] Dvořák's advocacy of "Negro" melodies mirrored this mix of aesthetic and political optimism.[77]

Dvořák's fame in music history, as commentators from Ehlert on never tired on pointing out, derived from his identity as a Czech. For Dvořák the attachment to modernity was linked to the national cultural revival. For Dvořák the hope of restoring the Czech nation to its rightful place of equality in the European world rested in part on the making of art. What has helped obscure Dvořák's originality in his compositional craft and his ideas about music, particularly vis-à-vis Smetana, has been the failure of music historians to utilize the interpretive possibilities inherent in the sociology of knowledge in order to understand Dvořák's career and ambitions.[78]

The shift from a feudal rural to a modern urban industrial society altered the dynamics of how social habits and cultural values were transmitted and adapted within the class structure and political life of nineteenth-century Bohemia. Dvořák grew up under the spell of eighteenth-century aristocratic traditions. For Dvořák—unlike Smetana, whose parents and family were more advanced in terms of education, economic standing, and cosmopolitan culture—the Czech national cause was more than a cultural movement.[79] It signaled advancement in social class and economic status.

Dvořák's personal ambition included the achievement of stable middle-class status. Smetana's nationalism was more like Wagner's and other artists from the generation that lived through 1848. Nationalism was essentially a romantic ideology, an intraclass dialogue designed to direct the allegiances of an extant urban middle class. Smetana's and Wagner's conception of the "people" was detached from any direct understanding of the peasant or worker.

Dvořák, who was clearly aware not only of his family's poverty and his rural origins but also of his lack of a middle-class style and cosmopolitanism, used his musical talent as an instrument of social advancement, a means to gain acceptance within the power structure of politics, culture, and society in Prague. Despite his years in Sweden, Smetana was already a part of that world as a young man and engaged, as a legitimate contender, his many rivals. Dvořák was an outsider from the start.

Dvořák's failure to advocate his own work in terms of a worked-out, polemical ideology, as did Wagner and Smetana, only underscored the fact that he knew he could not utilize the weapons of a different class. In Dvořák's mode of cultural advocacy, the overt, aesthetic polemical and literary habits characteristic of Schumann, Berlioz, Wagner, and Smetana, all middle-class composers, were replaced with his own equally original but covert populist strategy of communicating ideas through music.

Dvořák learned in the 1860s that to succeed in Prague he needed to appear to emulate, to follow his elders without exact imitation. He learned how to communicate immediately with his audience by using easily recognized formal surfaces and compositional habits. But he found novel ways to infuse his work with signs of his own stylistic autonomy that could be and were grasped by his hearers. Radical originality in Dvořák is sufficiently submerged by accessibility so as to elude easy discovery.

Take, for example, the central issue of what constituted true "Czech" music and how the aspirations of the Czech nation should be expressed.[80] Unlike Smetana's, Dvořák's command of the Czech language was excellent, his Catholic faith deeper, and his distance from German Bohemian culture greater. He shied away from direct musical illustrations of Czech nationalism in the sense of *Ma Vlast*. In contrast, Smetana's Czechness demanded, psychologically, a direct surface assertion in music. In exceptional cases—for example, in the "Hussite" Overture—Dvořák utilized-evident signs of national identity, but in conservative structural patterns. Smetana, in contrast, in all the movements of *Ma Vlast*, designed the musical structure to parallel the explicitly patriotic dramatic narrative. Dvořák's Czechness (as opposed to his specific politics) demanded no confirmation through music. But his skills as a composer needed to be demonstrated to the urban intelligentsia of the city under the spell of German aesthetic standards.

Dvořák therefore employed two different means of asserting the Czech element. First, as in the Slavonic Dances and the Moravian Duets, he "civilized" the folklike material without robbing it of its evident significance as national. The elevation of the presumably "primitive" folk material into the conventional vocabulary of cosmopolitan lyric, dramatic, and dance music came easily to Dvořák. In musical terms, it represented an exact civilizing analogue to his life and his personal aspirations.

But the more fascinating and innovative strategy evident in the greatest of the symphonic and chamber music of Dvořák is how the national element functioned when it appeared only elusively and was fully integrated. An infiltrating assertion of national identity, particularly to the non-Czech audience, occurred. This was the essence of Dvořák's achievement in the use of nationalism in music.[81]

Dvořák played on the audience's immediate grasp of classical structure and musical flow. By using the national element as a discrete surrogate for "neutral," explicitly international thematic and rhythmic roles in a musical language, Dvořák created a powerful, even subversive declaration whose impact was all the more impressive for its benign formal context. In contrast, Smetana, under the spell of Wagner and Liszt, sought to generate, through the epic tone poem, overt direct narrative forms of national Czech musical expression.

To contemporaries Smetana's strategy was seemingly more modern and radical. But in the long run, it might be Dvořák's more covert strategy, his self-conscious adherence to classical traditions, formal economy, and surface accessibility, that resulted in the far more powerful and far-reaching formulation of Czech identity, particularly outside of Bohemia and Moravia. Dvořák infiltrated, so to speak, the German household and concert hall. The political reaction against his music in Vienna and in Germany in response to Hans von Bülow's advocacy of the *Hussite* Overture reflected not only the German middle-class audience's anti-Czech hostility and snobbery but also their recognition that by clothing the Czech element in their own aesthetic vocabulary, Dvořák's capacity to elicit their approbation made this pattern of aesthetic assimilation more dangerous to their sense of cultural and national superiority than the overtly exotic and nationalistic work of Smetana.[82] Smetana's outspoken musical patriotism made listening safe. The content was evidently politically and emotionally distant.

Four musical examples suffice. In the F-minor Trio, the theme of the Scherzo, the second movement, is subtly related in its opening rhythmic stresses and intervallic patterns to the Hussite chorale "Ye Who Are God's Warriors," which Dvořák used in the *Hussite* Overture. A comparison in communicative effect can be made with Smetana's *Tabor* and *Blanik* from *Ma Vlast*.[83] No listener can mistake the significance of Smetana's material or the import of the story line. The explicit musical leitmotifs and the majesty and eloquence of the rhetoric and instrumentation give both movements an evocative musical nationalism. But the F-minor Trio masquerades, appropriately, as a neoclassical essay in "absolute" formal music.[84] The element of Czechness sneaks in in a manner that makes the player and listener, at the end, acknowledge tacitly the equality and power of the Czech element within the discourse of high art.

In the Fourth Symphony (1874), Dvořák inserts Czech elements within a Wagnerian musical envelope. As in the First Symphony, the work's pace and character achieve a quality suggestive of Bruckner. The explicit references to Wagner, always cited as criticisms, may have been intended to be recognized.[85] Direct allusions and quotations not only elevated the status of the Czech element but turned attention away from their "folk" status.

In the Sixth and Seventh Symphonies, Dvořák's most admired efforts in the symphonic form, this technique reached its perfection. In these three cases, the "civilizing" framework for Dvořák's covert integration of Czech elements is a Brahmsian model, particularly in the Sixth. As Donald Tovey and Robert Layton have pointed out, the furiant of the Sixth and the second movement of the Seventh show contact with Czech sources, but that relationship seems overpowered by the formal mastery of Dvořák's development of the ideas. Tovey even refers to a theme as a "rustic" Tristan, and both Layton and Tovey compare Dvořák's writing in both symphonies favorably to Beethoven, Schubert, Bruckner, and Brahms.[86]

To explicate this confrontation of the Czech with the classical and romantic heritage of symphonic composition, Layton quotes Alfred Einstein's repetition of the notion of Dvořák's "naiveté" and of his "elemental" character.[87] Once again these modifiers are used uncritically with respect to Dvořák's Czech identity and sources. Tovey came closest to the mystery: "With a loud instructive voice the world informed Dvořák that his genius was naive; a certain rustic craftiness, harmless in some earlier civilization, perverted his naiveté thenceforth. He tried to do as he thought the world bid him. . . . Dvořák is not the only artist who injured his own originality and power by strenuously obeying the insistent clamour of the world that he should 'let himself go and be himself.'"[88]

Although Tovey realized how self-aware Dvořák was about his compositional craft, he accepted the commonplace idea that Dvořák somehow failed. Yet Tovey identified the dynamic between the judgment of the external world and Dvořák's "craftiness." The difference lay in the possibility that despite Tovey's claims, Dvořák knew precisely what he was about. What disappointed the critical community were qualities that allowed him to reach a wide public with the covert message of the significance, equality, and centrality of Czech culture. Instead of adapting techniques of musical overt realism to illustrate the national, the "crafty" Dvořák integrated Czechness into classicism without sacrifice to the symbolic power of the Czech element. The "sublimity" that Tovey missed in his comparison of Dvořák to Haydn was there, but not designed for him, as a critic, to embrace. Tovey, along with other critics, displayed resistance to Dvořák's project: the modernization of the musical surface (in the sense of a subsequent twentieth-century anti-romantic neoclassicism) in an effort to render the Czech dimensions international and popular.

Anti-Dvořák criticism outside of the Czech lands was testimony to Dvořák's success in proselytizing the Czech as world-cultural element. Tovey dismissed the choral music written for the English audience as an "unhappy" result. In fact, however, the contemporary English success of *The Specter's Bride* vindicated Dvořák's intent to render the Czech element internationally successful not merely as explicitly exotic (e.g., in contrast to *The Bartered Bride*'s popularity). The contemporary and posthumous reputation of the *Requiem* underscores the power of Dvořák's integration of the Czech element within conservative, canonic, and international aesthetic traditions. In this regard, the comparison (intended as an insult) Nejedlý made to Mendelssohn was apt. Both sought wide acceptance through the accessible adaptation of classical and baroque choral models.

The radical possibilities inherent in Dvořák's approach to the issue of national identity and musical tradition, as opposed to Smetana's, were clearly understood by Leoš Janáček. In Elias's terms, Dvořák's process of civilizing himself resulted in an innovative breakthrough. The result was the transmission of new cultural expressions within traditional rubrics. The result was transformative. Janáček's success vindicated Dvořák's strategy. The link between the two can be found despite Janáček's more explicit pan-Slavism and distrust of all matters German.[89] Janáček understood Dvořák's version of the Czech project.

Dvořák, much more than Smetana, utilized parallels between Czech speech and melodic structure.[90] Janáček's success in translating the patterns of the Czech language into a basis for melodic construction derived from Dvořák's last efforts to integrate the national into a framework whose outward patterns were borrowed from a normative, international model: the tone poem.[91] Janáček premiered *The Wood Dove*. His own orchestral ballads, particularly *The Fiddler's Child* (1912), and his leap into a distinct musical style owe much to the example of Dvořák's late work.[92]

Dvořák's late Erben tone poems were, as scholars have noted, structured as narratives on two levels. The melodic material was directly patterned on Erben's text. The structure was closely linked with the oral patterns of story telling, which included descriptive exposition and repetition. Dvořák's engagement with American folk materials and Longfellow's narrative poem *Hiawatha*, as well as his friendship with Anton Seidl, convinced him that henceforth the way to reach the audience was through illustrative parallelism and narrative structure.[93]

Far from imitating Richard Strauss, Dvořák rejected the dense late-romantic approach. He invented a simpler narrative orchestral form closely tied to linguistic story telling. In contrast to Strauss's *Don Juan* and the earlier *Macbeth*, Dvořák's music is not primarily a symbolic translation of the poetic using thematic identities and rhetorical periods or even metaphoric parallels to a dramatic sequence. Dvořák eschewed Strauss's complex virtuosity in favor of a melodic line, a foreground, with a suggestive background to tell the story and illustrate directly. The musical structure is designed to frame an explicitly simple and direct narrative.

The late symphonic poems are perhaps the closest late nineteenth-century musical equivalent to the photograph. In this sense Dvořák utilized modernity as expressed through technology as a model. He sought to change the significance and meaning of a traditional social and cultural ritual: listening to music. His goal was to borrow from popular techniques to reach a wider public and help an excluded sector of society (the Czech people) in terms of aesthetic internationalism. In this manner Dvořák could challenge the dominance of the German musical world.

Although Dvořák paid homage to his conservative German-

Bohemian teachers, particularly Antonín Liehmann, the image of the railroad and the wonders of modern industry and technology, and the social change that accompanied them (which, as Siegfried Giedion has pointed out, was emblematic of the wider availability of comfort for larger numbers of people—of a democratization of ease), set the pattern and impetus for his aesthetic strategy.[94] The photograph was a modern democratic medium that, like the railroad, increased communication. Without the self-conscious painterly surface, the photograph could be read easily. It represented the pinnacle of realist art in both its methods and its distribution. Like the late symphonic poems, its artistry was submerged beneath its accessibility as an illustration.

The link between the music of Dvořák from the mid-1890s and photography is not arbitrary. During Dvořák's years in America he could not have avoided an encounter with the remarkable craze for photographic travel shows and stereoptical entertainments. The 1893 World Exposition in Chicago, at which Dvořák conducted, was a landmark in the extensive use of photography. As a musician Dvořák must have been aware of the rage in New York for presentations of "illustrated songs." This was a theatrical form that combined music, narration, and the sequential projection of photographic images (a kind of technologically primitive anticipation of MTV).

In 1892 Steele MacKaye, the creator of the monstrous spectacle concept entitled "The Spectatorium," visited Dvořák and Anton Seidl in New York. He tried to enlist their participation in an extravaganza designed to illustrate the voyage of Columbus. Seidl agreed, but Dvořák did not. MacKaye's theatrical scheme involved photographic images, stage machinery, modern lighting gimmicks, symphonic music, and song. He wanted to achieve the pinnacle of realist illusionism by presenting a sequence of *tableaux vivants* to an audience, using the most up-to-date technology. In short, Dvořák during his years in America encountered the powerful presence of photography as part of a novel and rapidly developing popular form of public entertainment. In its theatrical uses, the photography of the 1890s could easily have been suggestive to Dvořák, who struggled with the issues of illustration and narrative in instrumental music.[95]

Dvořák also copied from others the way a photograph reproduces. His explicit referencing of his indebtedness (for example, the resemblances in the Sixth Symphony to Brahms's Second Symphony) was itself a secondary dimension of the photographic illusion of documentary representation that the photographer communicates to the observer. The fact that, in Dvořák, explicit resemblances directly followed, as in the case of the Sixth Symphony, clear Czech elements (e.g., the furiant) was Dvořák's way of replicating the familiar conventions of musical tradition and realism in which the Czech national element appeared.

Critics have undervalued the significance of Dvořák's use of imitation and quotation. The more Dvořák could remind the international musical listener of Handel, Beethoven, Brahms, and Wagner, the more powerful the Czech contribution became. As in photography, the appropriation of the commonplace and recognizable image (the classical model and the Czech element—thereby realizing Hostinský's duality of form and content in music) was only the first step. Dvořák, like the photographer (or the many late nineteenth-century painters who worked off photographic images), altered the images unmistakably with a distinct point of view. Dvořák, in combining the elaborate classical musical procedures with musical materials evoking the native Czech spirit in the model of a modern form of aesthetic communication, achieved an inversion of cultural meaning. At the same time he earned the social approbation and rewards of conventional cultural achievement.

The success that Dvořák had with his American pupils (which in turn, through his pupils' influence, left a powerful mark on American music, the echoes of which are audible in the music of Copland, Gershwin, and Ellington) emboldened Dvořák to take the final step in his career when he returned in 1895 to use the external conventions of Wagner and Liszt (and in part, Strauss) to express his strategy of covert Czech assertion and populist realism.

Dvořák was therefore a peculiar sort of modern musical "realist." The photographic image was not merely the documentation of the real and familiar. As in the Erben poems, Dvořák's music was, rather, a sequence of related narrative photographic images in music. They illustrated and framed events clearly and unmistakably. At the same time they communicated a reflective picture of cultural norms and established taste distorted by the explicit perspective of the photographer. In the Erben symphonic poems, Dvořák, encouraged by his American experience, abandoned the symphonic framework and used the most evidently cross-cultural form—the folk tale—as a guide. The Czech element could then become more explicit. But by combining the fin-de-siècle audience's expectation of neo-Wagnerian musical narration with the discrete logic of sequential photographic frames, Dvořák made the reality of the story line and Czechness again subtly familiar.

The listener, like the observer of the photograph, could satisfy expectations of recognition—the ability to identify images easily. At the same time, the listener could glean a new and even unfamiliar point of view (as in the popular photographic travelogues about far-flung places of the 1890s), which the surface realism made welcome. Dvořák's modernism, like that of photography, was designed to gain the trust of the listener. The listener was brought into the circle of story telling without esoteric or confrontational barriers. In the direct, immediately comprehensible illustrative episodic frames of the late work, Dvořák communicated the human essence of the Czech folk tradition.

When German and English critics condescendingly praised Dvořák's gifts and contrasted his wealth of melodic ideas with his weakness in structural development, they hit the mark and also precisely missed Dvořák's intent. It was Dvořák's ambition to reach beyond them.[96] In this way he undercut the late nineteenth-century criteria of the distinction between high art and popular music. Dvořák helped set the stage for the breakdown of the link between aesthetic connoisseurship and aristocratic status, a link cherished by the nineteenth-century middleclass audience, which felt itself ennobled by its appropriation of the eighteenth-century high art, concert-music tradition.

It is this radical simplification and use of the expectations, conventions, and communicative meaning of instrumental music that sharpen the contrast with Mahler and Ives. Both integrated popular and native elements into symphonic and instrumental forms. But the photographic commitment to comprehensibility and the illusion of realism were rejected by both Mahler and Ives, who were ambivalent about Dvořák. Ives in particular recognized his debt to Dvořák, but was outraged by his usurpation of leadership in the definition of the "American," his seemingly affirmative and non-ironic use of the folk and native elements, and his refusal to generate a critique of surface sentimentality.[97]

In the case of Mahler, the divergence in aesthetic strategy can be explained in part by the differences in the late nineteenth century between assimilation and acceptance into Gentile society for Jews and the process of establishing cultural equality and social acceptance for Czech Catholics. For Mahler, a suspicion of the effort to achieve popular success was justified. The link between fin-de-siècle populist politics and anti-Semitism was too clear. The democratization of culture posed a threat to the exclusivity of cultural achievement. Loss of exclusivity, in turn, would deprive the Jew of a traditional route to security. Exceptional cultural achievement of the sort attained by Mahler held out the hope to individual Jews that they might be shielded from the undiscriminating brush of racial hatred evident in fin-de-siècle political and social movements.

In the case of Charles Ives, Dvořák's musical strategy directly forced a confrontation with a nineteenth-century American cultural insecurity vis-à-vis Europe. This insecurity led, ironically, to the invitation of Dvořák in the first place. In a musical world overwhelmingly dominated by the careful emulation of European strategies, as evident in the work of John Knowles Paine and MacDowell, Dvořák played a surprising role. In America Dvořák felt the freedom to articulate his strategy of reproduction and distortion through the integration of so-called native elements that seemed incompatible with the normative aesthetics of high art music.

Dvořák's advocacy of "Negro" and "Indian" elements becomes quite understandable. He quickly embraced the dimension in America most analogous to the Czech in the Habsburg Empire; the source that could most directly undermine and destabilize America's slavish imitation of a European aesthetic. Ives's anger was comparable to that of Smetana and his followers toward Dvořák. Ives thought he represented the "real" American. The outrage Dvořák committed was that of a foreigner advocating the supplanting of the more clearly European New England tradition by one seemingly stranger and clearly lower in social status. Ives preferred his own form of ironic rebellion. By embracing an esoteric modernism, Ives's work did not contain the powerful seeds of the radical populist transformation of norms evident in Dvořák's strategy.

The failure to recognize Dvořák's importance in a construct of modernism, and the link between Mahler, Ives, and Dvořák, was the consequence of a mistrust among advocates of twentieth-century modernism, from Schoenberg to Sessions, of the process of popularization, particularly through modern technology.[98] However, by distancing ourselves from this aspect of the inherited critical tradition, a plausible answer to Klaus Döge's framing of the Dvořák problem can be formulated.[99] Dvořák deserves to occupy a place "among the truly great composers of all time," as Rudolf Firkušný wrote in 1992—as an equal, as Hoffmeister claimed, to Brahms and Bruckner.[100] But he also deserves a place alongside Mahler, Schoenberg, and Ives.

Dvořák achieved a transformation of an aristocratic art form inherited by an elite, urban middle class in a manner adequate to the communicative possibilities of modern life mirrored in the enlarging audience. He achieved an aesthetic revolution within traditional boundaries by using a modern idea of imitation and reproduction and endowing it with a subjective individual vision without sacrificing comprehensibility. He led the way to a new kind of photographic convention in instrumental music. By exploiting a nearly realistic formalism and a comprehensible rhetoric, Dvořák innovated in the communication of content and in the significance of listening. The classical became acceptable to a wide audience, and new cultural elements were transformed from the commonplace into the classical.

The transcendence of social barriers in the audience was part of a project of aesthetic democratization. At the root of Dvořák's creation was not the celebration of any particular ethnic authenticity or uniqueness for its own sake but rather the destruction of inherited distinctions. A radical program of democratic aesthetic education (a cultural railroad system) could be furthered to the benefit of Americans, Britons, and Czechs alike.

The fact that German critics and their American, English, and Czech heirs have continued to denigrate Dvořák's work is a sign of a peculiar but revealing blindness. If one assesses the commercial music of our times and the contemporary musical theater, one might wish to conclude that Dvořák's project of populist classicism failed in the twentieth century. But perhaps that view simply underscores how difficult it has been to match Dvořák's achievement.

NOTES

1. Paul Bekker, *Musikgeschichte als Geschichte der musikalischen Formwandlung* (Berlin and Leipzig, 1926), p. 7.

2. Adolf Weissmann, *Die Entgötterung der Musik* (Berlin and Leipzig, 1928), pp. 13–14.

3. Robert P. Morgan, "Secret Languages: The Roots of Musical Modernism," in Monique Chefdor, Ricardo Quinones, and Albert Wachtel, eds., *Modernism: Challenges and Perspectives* (Urbana and Chicago, 1986), p. 41.

4. On twentieth-century divisions in Czech musical life see Rosa Newmarch, *The Music of Czechoslovakia* (New York, 1942; reprint, 1978), pp. 176–240; and Kurt Honolka, *Antonín Dvořák* (Reinbek bei Hamburg, 1974), pp. 118 and 124–35.

5. Karel Hoffmeister, *Antonín Dvořák* (edited from the 1924 Czech version), trans. Rosa Newmarch (London, 1928), p. 115. Honolka, in *Antonín Dvořák*, picks up this effort, as does the most recent (and excellent) German-language biography: Klaus Döge, *Dvořák* (Mainz, 1991).

6. See Hermann Kretzschmar, "Volksmusik und höhere Tonkunst" (1910), in *Gesammelte Aufsätze aus den Jahrbüchern der Musikbibliothek Peters* (Leipzig, 1911; reprint, 1973), pp. 461–63.

7. Goodrich (1847–1920) was a respected theorist; cited in Edward N. Waters, *Victor Herbert: A Life in Music* (New York, 1955), p. 214.

8. The denigration of the Ninth Symphony in terms of a gap between its striking accessibility and its presumed lack of formal musical virtues began with

the first European performances. See, for example, the selection of reviews from the first Vienna performance on 16 February 1896, in Manfred Wagner, ed., *Geschichte der österreichischen Musikkritik in Beispielen* (Tutzing, 1979), pp. 227–34.

9. Hoffmeister, *Antonín Dvořák*, pp. 112–20.

10. Richard Aldrich, "Antonín Dvořák and His Music," the *New York Times*, 8 May 1904.

11. Robert Hirschfeld, "Anton Dvořák," *Wiener Abendpost*, 4 May 1904, p. 2.

12. Hellmut Federhofer, ed., *Heinrich Schenker: Nach Tagebüchern und Briefen in der Oswald Jonas Memorial Collection* (Hildesheim, 1985), pp. 228–29.

13. See, for example, Joachim's letters from 1887 and 1898 to R. Barth and his nephew Harald Joachim, in Joseph Joachim, *Briefe*, vol. 3 (Berlin, 1913), pp. 305 and 482; also Hans von Bülow's comparison among symphonies by Dvořák, Karl Goldmark, and Robert Fuchs in 1889, in Hans von Bülow, *Briefe*, vol. 7 (Leipzig, 1908), p. 261.

14. Julius Korngold, *Die Korngolds in Wien. Der Musikkritiker und das Wunderkind. Aufzeichnungen* (Zurich, 1991), p. 31.

15. Christopher Fifield, *Max Bruch: His Life and Works* (New York, 1988), p. 198.

16. The polemical advocacy of Zdeněk Nejedlý was most notorious. It is ironic that in his effort to denigrate Dvořák, he compared Dvořák's role in Czech music to Mendelssohn's in German music; cited in Honolka, *Antonín Dvořák*, p. 141.

17. Theodor W. Adorno, *Einleitung in die Musiksoziologie* (Hamburg, 1968), pp. 178–79.

18. See Friedrich Nietzsche, *Aus dem Nachlass der Achtzigerjahre: Die Fröhliche Wissenschaft*, secs. 85–88; and letters to Carl Fuchs and Hans von Bülow from the summer of 1888 in *Werke*, ed. K. Schlechta (Munich, 1965), vol. 2, pp. 95–97, and vol. 3, pp. 793–94 and 1307–12.

19. Ottokar [*sic*] Hostinský, *Das Musikalisch-Schöne und das Gesammtkunstwerk vom Standpunkte der formalen Ästhetik* (Leipzig, 1877), pp. 154–55.

20. Ibid., p. 119.

21. Theodor W. Adorno in "Über den Fetischcharakter in der Musik und die Regression des Hörens," in *Dissonanzen* (Göttingen, 1963).

22. Quoted in Otakar Šourek, *Antonín Dvořák: Letters and Reminiscences* (New York, 1985), pp. 46–48, hereafter cited as *LR*.

23. W. H. Hadow, "Antonín Dvořák," in *Studies in Modern Music*, second series (New York, 1895), pp. 222–25.

24. See the fine Smetana biography by Brian Large, *Smetana* (New York, 1970; reprint, 1985).

25. Arthur Elson, *Modern Composers of Europe* (Boston, 1904), p. 107.

26. See, for example, the 1886 London interview with Dvořák entitled "From Butcher to Baton" in the *Pall Mall Gazette*, published in Döge, *Dvořák*, pp. 332–38.

27. Charles L. Graves, *Post-Victorian Music* (Port Washington, N.Y., and London, 1911; reprint, 1970), p. 50.

28. The explicit comparison to Eliza Doolittle was made (an act of irony, given George Bernard Shaw's contempt for Dvořák) in Alec Robertson, *Dvořák* (London, 1945), p. 84.

29. The words are Victor Herbert's, from a draft of a letter to Carl Engel quoted in Waters, *Victor Herbert: A Life in Music*, p. 88.

30. Richard Batka and Heinrich Werner, eds., *Hugo Wolfs Musikalische Kritiken* (Leipzig, 1911), pp. 158–60 and 335–37.

31. Gerald Abraham, "Dvořák's Musical Personality," in Viktor Fischl, ed., *Antonín Dvořák: His Achievement* (London, 1943; reprint, Westport, 1970), pp. 192–96; for a comparison regarding Victorian musical tastes see Derek Carew, "Victorian Attitudes to Chopin," in Jim Samson, ed., *The Cambridge Companion to Chopin* (Cambridge, 1992), pp. 222–29.

32. Gerald Abraham in Fischl, *Antonín Dvořák: His Achievement*, p. 193.

33. Carl Dahlhaus, *Nineteenth-Century Music*, trans. J. Bradford Robinson (Berkeley, 1989), p. 276.

34. See Frank Howes, "The National and Folk Elements," in Fischl, *Antonín Dvořák: His Achievement*, pp. 241–55.

35. See, for example Paul Stefan, *Anton Dvořák* (New York, 1941), pp. 206 and 238–39.

36. The citations from Darwin can be found in Bojan Bujic, ed., *Music in European Thought 1851–1912* (Cambridge, 1988), pp. 316–19.

37. Richard Wallaschek, *Ästhetik der Tonkunst* (Stuttgart, 1883), p. 277.

38. Richard Wallaschek, *Primitive Music: An Inquiry into the Origin and Development of Music, Songs, Dances, and Pantomimes of Savage Races* (London, 1893; reprint, New York, 1970), pp. 270 and 294.

39. Ibid., p. 280; see also pp. 60–61 and 279.

40. Ibid., p. 287; see also pp. 242–59.

41. Edward MacDowell, *Historical and Critical Essays*, ed. W. J. Baltzell (Boston, 1912; reprint, New York, 1969), p. 15.

42. Ibid., pp. 142 and 151.

43. This provocative metaphor and its consequences are indebted, clearly, to Henry Louis Gates, Jr., *The Signifying Monkey: A Theory of African-American Literary Criticism* (New York, 1988). An alternative would be to cite Hans von Bülow's reference to Dvořák as looking like Caliban, in *Briefe*, vol. 7, p. 271.

44. Hirschfeld, who corresponded with Dvořák in order to write the Vienna program notes for Dvořák's late symphonic poems, and who thought less of them, wrote in a review of the first Vienna performance of *St. Ludmila* that "Dvořák's talent is in this regard a unifying one, not one that separates people. His art is national, but transcends the boundaries of nationalism; it is world art. When we read his scores, we believe we recognize a classical disposition," in *Neue musikalische Presse* 47 (21 November 1897): 2.

45. In part, this argument, which identifies the late symphonic poems as innovative, is based on an effort to explain the negative critical response these works received, particularly from Dvořák's admirers, including Hirschfeld and Hanslick. Dvořák's abandonment of his earlier approach signaled a new attitude toward his Czech roots, one that did not sit well with his German de-

fenders. On Hanslick's views of late Dvořák (which reiterate the modifiers naive and childlike), see his review of *The Wood Dove*, in Eduard Hanslick, *Aus neuer und neuester Zeit* (Berlin, 1900), pp. 83–87.

46. Hugo Riemann, *Geschichte der Musik seit Beethoven 1800–1900* (Berlin and Stuttgart, 1901), pp. 531–32.

47. This difference in attitude, as played out in a Tchaikovsky-Dvořák contrast, was openly challenged in 1896 by Hanslick in his review of the "New World" Symphony. See Manfred Wagner, *Geschichte der österreichischen Musikkritik in Beispielen*, pp. 228 and 230.

48. *Die österreichisch-ungarische Monarchie in Wort und Bild: Böhmen*, vol. 1 (Vienna, 1894), p. 496.

49. Ibid., pp. 363–91 and 564–618.

50. For the cultural significance of the two Czech political camps see John Clapham, *Dvořák* (New York, 1979), pp. 54–55; and Brian Large, *Smetana*, pp. 233–51.

51. See Stanley B. Winters, "Austroslavism, Panslavism, and Russophilism in Czech Political Thought 1870–1900," in Stanley B. Winters and Joseph Held, eds., *Intellectual and Social Developments in the Habsburg Empire from Maria Theresa to World War I: Essays Dedicated to Robert A. Kann* (New York and London, 1975), pp. 175–202.

52. See John Clapham, "Dvořák's Visit to Russia," in *Musical Quarterly* 51 (1965): 493–506; and Large, *Smetana*, pp. 209–10.

53. *Wien im Lichte der Zahlen* (Vienna and Leipzig, 1900), table 6.

54. See, for example, an explicit case of this double standard in a review that compared symphonies by Tchaikovsky with Dvořák's Cello Concerto, in Hermann Kretzschmar, "Die für das Konzert bestimmte Komposition grossen Stils im Jahre 1896," in Kretzschmar, *Gesammelte Aufsätze aus den Jahrbüchern der Musikbibliothek Peters*, pp. 18–20.

55. One must be cautious in using the language of ethnicity and nationalism in the writing of history without accounting for the intellectual history of these terms, particularly vis-à-vis older terms such as race and folk heritage, which clearly separate political from social and cultural claims.

56. See Hermann Freudenberger, "Progressive Bohemian and Moravian Aristocracy," in Winters and Held, *Intellectual and Social Developments in the Habsburg Empire from Maria Theresa to World War I*, pp. 115–30.

57. A fascinating and somewhat benign example of the mix of admiration for the Czech native musicality and social snobbery can be found in the writings of the Austrian composer and critic Wilhelm Kienzl (1857–1941). He reported on the pronounced anti-Czech sentiment in Vienna during the mid-1880s that prevented performances of Dvořák's music. As late as 1902, he expressed surprise at the proficiency and musicality of the Bohemian Quartet. See Wilhelm Kienzl, *Meine Lebenswanderung* (Stuttgart, 1926), p. 284, and *Im Konzert* (Berlin, 1908), pp. 215–18.

58. See Hillel J. Kieval, "Jews, Czechs, and Germans in Bohemia before 1914," in Robert S. Wistrich, ed., *Austrians and Jews in the Twentieth Century* (New York, 1992).

59. Among the most compelling documents from the fin de siècle regarding the perspectives of German intellectuals on the culture and politics of Russia are Max Weber's writings on the Russian Revolution of 1905 and his views on the future of Russia from the vantage point of Germany and the Germans. See in particular the 1909 letter "Über die Erneuerung Russlands," in the volume that contains the entire range of Weber's writings on the subject: Wolfgang J. Mommsen and D. Dahlmann, eds., *Max Weber. Zur Russischen Revolution von 1905. Schriften und Reden 1905–1912* (Tübingen, 1989), pp. 691–92.

60. *LR*, pp. 159–62 and 163–69.

61. See, for example, Jarmil Burghauser, *Antonín Dvořák*, German trans. by Adolf Langer (Prague, 1966).

62. See Ernst Rychnovsky, "Etwas von Prager Publikum aus Vergangenheit und Gegenwart," *Der Merker* 1, no. 14 (1910): 606–8.

63. On the ambitions of the communist critical tradition see Döge, *Dvořák*, pp. 53–55.

64. *LR*, p. 194.

65. See Constantin Floros, *Brahms und Bruckner* (Wiesbaden, 1980), pp. 77–78.

66. Antonín Dvořák, *I. Symfonie c moll*, complete edition (Prague, 1961), p. xvii (preface by František Bartos); see also Robert Layton, *Dvořák's Symphonies and Concertos* (Seattle, 1978), pp. 8–13.

67. On the relationship between Dvořák and Janáček see John Tyrrell, *Janáček's Operas: A Documentary Account* (Princeton, 1992), and *Czech Opera* (Cambridge, 1988). On Dvořák and Ives see Stuart Feder, *Charles Ives: My Father's Song* (Yale, 1992), and "Homesick in America: The Nostalgia of Antonín Dvořák and Charles Ives," in John C. Tibbetts, ed., *Dvořák in America* (Portland, Ore., 1992), p. 175. The influence of Dvořák and Copland, transmitted through Copland's teacher, Rubin Goldmark, who was Dvořák's pupil, needs to be investigated, particularly with reference to Goldmark's orchestral scores. On Martinů's debt, see Brian Large, *Martinů* (New York, 1975); and Martinů's own words, cited in Honolka, *Antonín Dvořák*, p. 142.

68. Dvořák's famous comment in his 1904 interview with *Die Reichswehr* states this plainly, even though many biographers have doubted the importance of Dvořák's explanation. See *LR*, p. 223; and Döge, *Dvořák*, pp. 338–42.

69. See, for example, Bülow's letter dated 4 April 1889, in *Briefe*, vol. 7, p. 246.

70. Among the many discussions of the fin-de-siècle German view of America see the concise summary in Wolfgang J. Mommsen, *Max Weber: Gesellschaft, Politik, und Geschichte* (Frankfurt, 1974), pp. 72–96.

71. See *LR*, pp. 149–50; and the accounts of Dvořák's impressions of America in Clapham and Döge.

72. *LR*, pp. 151–52; see also John Clapham, "Dvořák's Visit to Worchester, Mass.," in Malcolm Brown and Roland Wiley, eds., *Slavonic and Western Music: Essays for Gerald Abraham* (Ann Arbor, 1985), pp. 207–19.

73. *LR*, pp. 192–93.

74. See, for example, Adolf Loos, "Die Frau und Das Haus" (*Neue Freie Presse*, 1898), in *Die Potemkinsche Stadt: Verschollene Schriften 1897–1933* (Vienna, 1983); and Adolf Opel, "Vorwort," in Adolf Loos, *Ins Leere Gesprochen* (Vienna, 1921; reprint, 1983), pp. 10–12.

75. See Oskar Schürer, *Prag: Kultur, Kunst, Geschichte*, 2d ed. (Vienna, 1935), pp. 325–40; and Elisabeth Lichtenberger, *Wien-Prag: Metropolenforschung* (Vienna, 1993), pp. 79–90.

76. See the collection of Dvořák's interviews and writings from America, in Tibbetts, *Dvořák in America*, appendix A.

77. See Dvořák's famous 1895 article "Music in America," in *Harper's*, pp. 428–34.

78. The argument that follows is based in part on Norbert Elias, *Power and Civility: The Civilizing Process*, vol. 2 (New York, 1982); Pierre Boudrieu, *Distinction: A Social Critique of the Judgment of Taste*, trans. Richard Nice (Cambridge, Mass., 1984); and Jonathan Crary, *Techniques of the Observer: On Vision and Modernity in the Nineteenth Century* (Cambridge, Mass., 1990).

79. As before, the comparison to Smetana is based on the account in Brian Large, *Smetana*.

80. See Michael Beckerman, "In Search of Czechness in Music," in *19th-Century Music* 10, no. 1 (1986): 61–73.

81. See the fascinating parallel discussion in Sidney Finkelstein, *Composer and Nation: The Folk Heritage in Music*, 2d ed. (New York, 1989), pp. 188–97, which stresses Dvořák's commitment to internationalism and egalitarianism.

82. Hans von Bülow, *Briefe*, vol. 7 (1886–94), p. 167; see also his account of tense concert appearances in 1886 in Prague, pp. 53–57.

83. Otakar Šourek, *The Chamber Music of Antonín Dvořák* (Prague, 1956), p. 156; and Large, *Smetana*, p. 283.

84. In 1884 Hugo Wolf noticed this aspect of the Scherzo. See Batka and Werner, eds., *Hugo Wolfs Musikalische Kritiken*, p. 32.

85. Layton, *Dvořák's Symphonies and Concertos*, pp. 22–25; see also Otakar Šourek, *The Orchestral Works of Antonín Dvořák* (New York, 1970), pp. 69–77.

86. Layton, *Dvořák's Symphonies and Concertos*, pp. 30–40; and Donald Francis Tovey, *Symphonies and Other Orchestral Works* (Oxford, 1989), p. 276.

87. Layton, *Dvořák's Symphonies and Concertos*, pp. 35–36.

88. Tovey, *Symphonies and Other Orchestral Works*, p. 268.

89. Bohumir Stedron, *Leoš Janáček in Briefen und Erinnerungen* (Prague, 1955), pp. 30–31 and 46–47; see also Charles Susskind, *Janáček and Brod* (New Haven and London, 1985), pp. 13–39.

90. See Gerald Abraham, "Verbal Inspiration in Dvořák's Instrumental Music," in *Studia Musicologica Academicae Scientiarum Hungaricae* 11 (1969): 27–34. This link between speech patterns and melodic structure is evident in the work of one of Dvořák's students, Rubin Goldmark, in the latter's *Requiem* for orchestra, where an excerpt from Lincoln's Gettysburg Address forms the basis of thematic material.

91. See Carl Dahlhaus, *Musikalischer Realismus. Zur Musikgeschichte des 19. Jahrhunderts* (Munich, 1982), pp. 122–25.

92. See Leoš Janáček's commentaries on the symphonic poems, in this volume.

93. See Michael Beckerman, "Dvořák's 'New World' Largo," in *19th-Century Music* 16, no. 1 (Summer 1992): 35–48; and "The Dance of Pau-Puk-Keewis and the Song of Chibiabos: Reflections on the Scherzo of Dvořák's Symphony 'From the New World,'" in Tibbetts, *Dvořák in America*.

94. Siegfried Giedion, *Mechanization Takes Command: A Contribution to Anonymous History* (New York, 1948; reprint, 1969), pp. 439–68.

95. See the unpublished 1992 paper "Christopher Columbus in Chicago," by Paul A. Miller, pp. 2 and 10. Miller describes in detail Steele MacKaye's career and his contact with Dvořák. See also the many advertisements of photographic entertainments in New York from the 1890s in the archive of the George Eastman House, Rochester, New York. In this connection, the work of Julie K. Brown on the place of photography in the 1893 World Exposition is helpful. See also the article by Nancy Bergh (assisted by Margaret L. Bergh), "The Live Model Illustrated Song America Style," in the *New Magic Lantern Journal* 2, no. 63 (February 1983, limited edition), of the Magic Lantern Society of Great Britain. I am indebted to James L. Enyeart, the director of the George Eastman House, for bringing this material to my attention.

96. *LR*, pp. 222–23. Dvořák's son recounted his father's ambition to be realistic in his plans for *Horymír*.

97. See Feder, *Ives*, pp. 148–50.

98. This is true particularly for Adorno. It had to do with Adorno's dispute with Walter Benjamin. See Ronald Taylor, ed., *Aesthetics and Politics* (London, 1979), pp. 100–141.

99. Döge, *Dvořák*, pp. 423–31 and 438.

100. Rudolf Firkušný, preface in Tibbetts, *Dvořák in America*, p. x.

Dvořák and Brahms:
A Chronicle, an Interpretation

DAVID BEVERIDGE

One of the most striking felicities in Antonín Dvořák's life was his long personal friendship with a man who was, after the death of Wagner in 1883, widely considered to be the greatest living composer in the Western world—Johannes Brahms. From late in 1877 until Brahms's death in 1897, Dvořák maintained a relationship with the German master that was important to both of them, even though they never lived in the same city.

One might expect this relationship to have loomed large in music historiography, especially because, for many influential musicians in Germany, the Austrian Empire, and the English-speaking countries at this time, the second rank among living composers was held by Dvořák himself. Attention seems warranted all the more by the fact that these two composers' attitudes toward each other were, as we shall see, far from straightforward. Rather, their friendship developed in the context of some underlying obstacles that reflect the cultural conditions of the era—and if we probe beneath the surface of their relationship, what we discover there is often fascinating.

Unfortunately, biographies of the two composers have tended to treat their friendship spottily, and the literature on Brahms, in particular, is riddled with errors. Meanwhile, in books addressing nineteenth-century music or Western music as a whole, the Brahms-Dvořák relationship has been slighted by the perennial placement of these composers in separate chapters, as representing the German "mainstream" and the peripheral "national schools," respectively.

I wish to thank Klaus Döge, Milan Kuna, Hartmut Schick, Otto Biba, and especially William Horne for their help with access to research materials used in the preparation of this essay.

Established early on by ethnocentric German musicologists, the mainstream/national dichotomy has recently come under attack by none other than the Germans themselves. Thus, for example, the Hamburg musicologist Peter Petersen delivered a telling critique of Dvořák reception-history in Germany, specifically as it affected perceptions of his relation to Brahms:

> The cause for the striking absence of a comparative study of Brahms and Dvořák . . . may lie in definite, long-established prejudices of German criticism regarding the music of Antonín Dvořák. Since these prejudices, which were in turn only the echo of a widespread chauvinistic way of thinking, were not shared by Johannes Brahms, the subject of Brahms and Dvořák could be treated only with difficulty . . . so the subject was ignored.
>
> Nevertheless a silent consensus set in within German-speaking areas regarding the difference in value between the two bodies of work. . . . [Brahms was regarded as] one of the "greats" of music history. By contrast the music of Antonín Dvořák was viewed in Germany as belonging to a nationally and qualitatively limited niche.[1]

Petersen helped to lay the groundwork for a more objective comparison of Dvořák and Brahms by pointing out that despite their different nationalities, the lives of the two composers exhibit a number of striking parallels:

Life span (Brahms, 1833–97; Dvořák, 1841–1904)
Origin in the lower middle class
Rise in social status, receipt of official honors, and so on
Middle-class existence maintained primarily by composing (secure positions, concertizing, and teaching activities remained relatively marginal)
First musical experiences in dance and entertainment music
Early musical education conservative and provincial
Achievement of world acclaim within lifetime, but both were humble characters not suited to the role of a "star"
Patriotism at a modest level of political reflection
Course of life quiet rather than eccentric
Life story fulfilled, rounded off, in comparison to those of Mozart, Mendelssohn, Schubert, Chopin
High volume of symphonies, concertos, and chamber music in the Viennese classical tradition
High volume of choral works

Against this background of similarities, we can better assess the significance of the substantial differences that Petersen also outlines:

Framework of composition influenced by different national histories, folk music, and languages (as well as different national prejudices to be overcome)

Urban childhood (Brahms) rather than rural (Dvořák)

Protestant (Brahms) rather than Catholic (Dvořák) upbringing

Bachelor adulthood (Brahms) rather than married family life with children (Dvořák)

Lack of interest in writing opera (Brahms) rather than prolific operatic output (Dvořák wrote eleven operas)

Abstinence from writing program music (Brahms), eventually embraced by Dvořák

It remains, however, to assemble systematically the relevant biographical information concerning the relationship between the two composers. There is a wide range of published source materials to draw on—some items issued long ago but never yet thoroughly utilized, others published only in the past few decades.[2] Based on these sources and others, it is possible to lay out for the first time a systematic chronology of the association between Brahms and Dvořák, and that will be part of our task here.

Chronology of the Relationship

Brahms and Dvořák each probably became aware of the other's music at around the same time, in the early to mid-1870s. From Dvořák's point of view, this was when Brahms's works first began to gain currency in Prague.[3] Dr. Ludevít Procházka, a man who was also important to Dvořák's career at this time, took a leading role in promoting Brahms's music in the Czech city. Procházka's wife, the soprano Marta Reisingerová, was known as a leading interpreter of songs by Brahms, and it was she who helped organize the concerts in which Dvořák received his own first performances in 1871 and 1872.

It was many years, however, before Brahms could have become a standard part of Dvořák's musical milieu. A performance of the E-minor Cello Sonata in 1876 marked the first occasion on which any of Brahms's larger works was received with real enthusiasm in Prague. In March 1877, the first complete performance of Brahms's *Requiem* in Prague made a sensation, and the D-minor Piano Concerto was received in December of that year, according to a letter from Dvořák to

Brahms, with great excitement. Yet as late as February 1880, when Brahms made his first and last concert appearance in Prague, a reviewer could report that "musical Prague gains knowledge of Brahms's compositions in public concerts only rarely and spottily."

A special factor in Dvořák's early exposure to the music of Brahms may have been his friendship with the young Leoš Janáček, who was an early advocate of Brahms in Brno. Janáček helped organize a performance there of the Brahms Piano Quintet in January 1877 and published an analytical article about the work at that time.

Unfortunately, we have no definitive record of Dvořák either mentioning or hearing of Brahms until late in December 1877, when Eduard Hanslick suggested that he write to the German composer. In the series of letters that Dvořák sent to Brahms soon afterward, he certainly implied a familiarity with and admiration for Brahms's music, though he may have exaggerated this a little in an effort to flatter the more established master.

Regarding Brahms's first encounters with the music of Dvořák, our knowledge is more precise. Dvořák submitted successful applications in each of five successive years, 1874–78, for an artist's stipend from the Austrian government for poor but talented artists. The head of the judging committee was Brahms's friend Eduard Hanslick, and, starting in 1875, Brahms became a committee member himself.[4]

It is conceivable that Brahms heard something about Dvořák before this, perhaps in the early 1870s when passing through Prague on concert trips or from Hanslick in connection with Dvořák's first stipend award based on his 1874 entry. Most likely, however, Brahms's first acquaintance with Dvořák came about when he became a judge on the stipend committee and helped to procure an award for Dvořák late in 1875. In a letter from September of that year, Brahms told Hanslick that "Dvořák and Reinhold thoroughly deserve the award by their accomplishments" and then went on to describe three more applicants in descending order of merit.[5]

Unfortunately, we do not know which pieces Dvořák submitted on this occasion, but they were probably his newest works, completed between mid-1874 (the date of his previous application) and mid-1875. Brahms probably never encountered the numerous works Dvořák had written before this time, for most of them were neither performed nor published until after both composers were dead.

For each of the next three years, Brahms again sat on the committee, and Dvořák was again awarded a prize. It was in 1877 that Dvořák submitted his Moravian Duets for soprano, contralto, and piano, which became the specific catalyst for a personal relationship between Dvořák and Brahms. These duets were settings of texts from Moravian folk songs for which Dvořák substituted his own music, in a fresh-sounding, relatively simple, folklike style.

On 30 November 1877 Hanslick wrote the following momentous letter to Dvořák:

.

Very honored sir!

It gives me special pleasure to inform you that at the meeting just held with Minister Stremayer you were by a unanimous vote awarded an artist's stipend of 600 florins. Johannes Brahms, who together with me has proposed this grant, takes a great interest in your fine talent and likes especially your Czech vocal duets, of which I too am exceptionally fond. The sympathy of an artist as important and famous as Brahms may be not only pleasant but also useful to you, and I think you should write to him (Vienna, Wieden, Karlsgasse 4) and perhaps send him some of your music. He has kept the vocal duets from your application materials in order to show them to his publisher and to recommend you to him. If you could procure a good German translation, he would certainly arrange for their publication immediately. Perhaps send him a copy, and something from your manuscripts in addition—after all, it would be desirable for your things to become known beyond your rather narrow Czech fatherland, which in any case does nothing for you.

In deep respect,
your most devoted
Professor Dr. Eduard Hanslick.[6]

.

Hanslick was correct in suggesting that Dvořák's music was not known outside his "Czech fatherland." And Brahms's intercession was indeed to alter this situation in short order: within two years, Dvořák would have an impressive list of works published by Simrock in Berlin, and his music would be heard at concerts in Austria, Germany, France, England, and even the United States.[7]

However, to say that Dvořák's fatherland had done nothing for him was an exaggeration, for he had accumulated a substantial list of publications and performances in Bohemia. Thus in this initial letter placing Dvořák on the path toward world fame we already find German ethnocentrism rearing its head. In Dvořák's letter to Brahms, which he dispatched forthwith on 3 December, he rather turned Hanslick's scenario on its head: he sought world fame not to escape his country but to honor it. On the other hand, the extreme servility of his language, according to Peter Petersen,[8] betrays his awareness of the superior position enjoyed by Germans over Czechs within the Austrian Empire. Like all the correspondence between the two composers, the letter was of course written in German:

Korntorgasse no. 10 [neu] II.   Prag 3.12.77

Highly honored sir!

I have just recently received a letter from the revered Herr Prof. Dr. Hanslick, in which he informs me that at the meeting held recently with His Excellency, Minister Stremayer, I was, on your esteemed (and the Herr Professor's) recommendation, awarded an artist's stipend.

Only through the invitation of the honored Herr Prof. Hanslick am I so fortunate as to address these few words to you, highly revered Master, to express to you my most deeply felt thanks for the kindness you have demonstrated to me.

But an even greater blessing is the sympathy which you, highly honored sir, let fall upon my modest talent and also the pleasure (as Herr. Prof. Hanslick writes to me) which Your Nobleness [Euer Wohlgeboren] has found in my two-voiced Czech songs. Now Herr Prof. Hanslick advises me that I should procure a German translation of the songs in question and that you, honored Herr Master, would be so kind as to recommend the same to your publisher. I have just this one more request to address to you, to be so good as to be helpful to me also in this matter which is so important for me. Truly, it would be of immeasurable worth not only for me but also for my beloved fatherland to be introduced by you, highly honored Herr Master, whose incomparable creations so highly delight the whole musical world, to that world.

In that I implore Your Nobleness once more for your highly prized favor, to preserve the same for me also in the future I ask at the same time for the gracious permission to be allowed to submit to you several of my chamber and instrumental compositions for your kind inspection.[9]

I have the honor to sign myself, in deepest respect to Your Nobleness most devoted

Anton Dvořák[10]

Just as Hanslick had predicted, Brahms wrote to his publisher Simrock to recommend the duets, and he answered Dvořák's letter apparently on the same day:

Very honored sir,

Permit me to thank you in all brevity for your words and many a pleasure that you have given me with your works that were sent to me.

I have taken the liberty of writing to Herr Fritz Simrock (Berlin W. Friedrichstraße 171) regarding the same, first of all regarding the Duets.

Judging by the heading, the duets appear to me to be still your property. In this case, you could sell them to Mr. Simrock. Only, to be sure, a good German translation must be attended to. Do you know how to go about that? Aren't some of the songs in Josef Wenzig's "Fairy Tale Treasure" (Leipzig: G. Senf, 1866)?

Do you know Herr Dr. Siegfried Kapper there, and would he perhaps attend to a translation?

In any case I should like to ask you not to hurry too much with this, to avoid harming the work. In the meantime, would you like perhaps to send the volume to Herr S. for his inspection? Then we'll see what happens next.

Please pardon my hurry today, but I didn't want to procrastinate in the matter. I hope I'll hear more news about it, and good news.

With deep respect,
very devoted
J. Brahms[11]
Wien IV, Karlsgasse 9.

Brahms's concurrent letter to Simrock reads as follows:

Dear S.,

Through my work with the state stipend I have already been enjoying for several years the things of Anton Dvořák (pronounced *Dvorschak*) from Prague. This year he sent among other things a volume of duets (10) for two sopranos with pianoforte, which seem to me all too pretty, and practical for publication. He seems to have had the volume printed at his own cost. The title and unfortunately also the texts are only in Czech.[12] I asked him to send you the songs! If you play through them, you will rejoice in them as I did, and as publisher especially rejoice in the piquancy. Only a very good translation must be sought judiciously! Perhaps some of the texts have already been translated by (the late) Wenzig. Otherwise perhaps one could enlist Dr. Siegfried Kapper in Prague. Dvořák has written everything possible.

Operas (Czech), symphonies, quartets, piano pieces. In any case he is a very talented man. And poor, besides! And I ask you to take that into consideration! The value of the duets will be obvious to you, and they might become a "good commodity." The address is: Prag, Korntorgasse no. 10, II. . . .

By the way, I have besides Dvořák a young Russian on hand [Ivan Knorr, according to Kalbeck] who has written excellent orchestral variations! But I'll bide my time and then some! But please know, and consider, that I don't make recommendations hastily, and have a look at the merry, fresh, Czech duets?

Best
your
J. Br.

Dvořák procured the translation in a remarkably short time and sent it to Brahms on the 19th, along with his reply to Brahms's letter:

Korntorgasse 10/II   Prag 19/12 77

Highly revered Master!

I beg your forgiveness for not having been able to thank you sooner for your highly esteemed letter, which I didn't receive until later owing to my absence for some days from Prague.

Allow me thus, very honored Master, to express once again my most humble thanks for all that you have done for me.

As regards the German translation of my songs, I can tell you that it is already completed, only I couldn't, as you advised, turn to Dr. Kapper, because he has been in Trieste for some time.

So I have found another translator [Josef Srb-Debrnov], and I believe I can suppose that he has performed his task well. Accordingly, I have taken the liberty of sending you a copy for your kind inspection.

Here and there some notes had to be changed on account of the declamation; thus particularly in the last duet, "The Wild Rose," the last measures: "so die Schönheit gedeiht."

I have also sent a copy to Mr. Simrock.

Should I get further news soon, I shall certainly not neglect to allow myself to give you, highly revered Master, a report.

May this action [letter?] of mine also be an auspicious one, and may I soon have the pleasure of telling you personally how sincerely I am your most devoted servant and your very obliged

Anton Dvořák

·

Dvořák received no immediate response from Brahms; apart from Brahms's oft-confessed aversion to letter writing, we should note that he was away on a concert tour from 1 January through 15 February. But Dvořák pursued this new relationship aggressively and had the audacity to send Brahms two more letters before receiving any reply. The first of them is dated 23 January 1878:

·

Korntorgasse Nr. 10/II   Prag 23/1 78

Honored Master!

About three weeks ago I set out on my intended journey to Vienna in order to render personally my thanks to Your Nobleness for all the kindnesses you have shown me. I was very sorry that I didn't have the pleasure of meeting you before your departure for Leipzig. On this occasion I also called on Herr Prof. Hanslick, who received me very cordially. At his request I left a number of my compositions with your housekeeper, and I would like to beseech you, honored Master, if you have already arrived back in Vienna, to be so good as to look through them a little. Also, I take the liberty of asking Your Nobleness whether you have received the duets with the German translation and whether it is good.

Mr. Simrock wrote to me recently. He will gladly publish the duets, only several more places must be changed for the sake of declamation. Thus particularly in the last song the last measures: "Pflücke mich nicht zur Maienzeit, wo die Schönheit gedeiht." Probably the first syllable of the word "Schönheit" should come on the downbeat. I beseech your advice as to how the relevant passage should sound.

Mr. Simrock also wishes me to send a copy to Mr. Siegfried Kapper; but that would be difficult, for his address is not precisely known to me; I know only that he is supposed to have been living in Trieste for a long time now.

I have further the honor to inform Your Nobleness that your splendid D-minor concerto was performed at a concert given recently here in Prague and was extremely successful. Mr. von Slavkovský played it, and very well indeed. The conductor was the tireless Dr. Lud. Procházka, to whom we also owe the greatest thanks that here, too, your wonderful creations have become known.

And now I venture to address another respectful request to you, highly revered Master. Permit me that I might offer you, out of gratitude and deepest respect for your incomparable creations, the dedication of my D-minor quartet. It would indeed do me but the greatest honor, and I would be the happiest of men, who has the honor to sign himself obliged to Your Nobleness in eternal thanks, and very devoted servant

Anton Dvořák

We cannot know what pieces Dvořák left with Brahms's housekeeper, except that they must have included the new D-minor String Quartet. Dvořák wrote yet again on 24 March:

Korntorgasse Nr. 10/II   Prag 18 24/3 87 [78]

Highly honored Master!

I beseech your forgiveness for once more taking the liberty of addressing a few words to you.

This happens in order to satisfy your recently expressed wish, in which you were good enough to ask me to report to you with something further and good [a reference to the end of Brahms's letter to Dvořák from early December]. Unfortunately this is a bit late, but I didn't receive the duets back from Mr. Simrock until last week, whereby he asks me to look over everything quite closely again, especially in regard to the German declamation, so that it conforms well to the music and also, primarily, sings well. I have indeed done all this already, and have also already sent the duets back to Berlin, and there is every reason to hope that the publication of the songs might take place soon, as Mr. Simrock assures me.

I have also been commissioned by Mr. Simrock to write some Slavonic dances.

Since, however, I did not know how to begin this properly, I have taken the trouble to procure your famous "Hungarian Dances," and I shall take the liberty of using these as an exemplary model for the arrangement of the corresponding "Slavonic."

In that I ask you once more, highly estimable Master, to accept from me my most deeply felt thanks for everything, and in that I will always strive to earn your high favor and sympathy through my further artistic deeds, I have the honor to remain in deepest respect

your very devoted servant
Anton Dvořák

This letter appears to have crossed in the mail Brahms's (undated) reply to the two previous letters:

Most honored sir,

I regret quite extraordinarily that I was away on a trip when you were here. All the more so in that because of my great dislike of writing, I can't hope to make up for it in the least through written correspondence. And so even today I say only that the study of your pieces gives me the greatest joy, but that I would also give a lot to be able to discuss some individual points with you. You write somewhat hurriedly. When you add the many missing ♯ ♭ ♮, however, perhaps look also now and then rather closely at the notes themselves, the voice leading, etc.

I hope you will forgive me; to express such wishes in these matters to a man like you is very presumptuous! For I also accept them very thankfully as they are, and the dedication of the quartet I would regard as an honor done to me.

It would seem to me very practical if you would immediately give me the two quartets I know. If Mr. Simrock should not be favorably inclined, might I try elsewhere?

The things entrusted to me I will, when you wish, send back.

For today, once more my best thanks for the communication and cordial greetings from your very devoted

J. Brahms[13]

Though Brahms does not reciprocate in Dvořák's obsequious language, he clearly views Dvořák with anything but condescension. And now he shows himself willing to recommend not just what was obviously salable but a more rarefied commodity—string quartets. Furthermore, he will not confine himself to his own publisher.

The two quartets that Brahms mentions are the new one in D minor and its immediate predecessor, the E-major quartet from 1876. Why he seems to request both quartets when he already has the one in D minor is perplexing; Dvořák's response of 1 April interprets this as meaning he should send the "the other quartet," presumably the E-major:

Prag 18 1/4 78

Most highly revered Master!

With feelings of the most joyful excitement I read the last letter, esteemed by me, from Your Nobleness, and the words so warmly felt that you spoke to me and the joy that you found in my works have moved me most deeply and make me quite extraordinarily happy. I can't find enough words to tell you, highly revered Master, everything that is happening now in my heart. I can only as much as say to you that you have already made me beholden to you in the greatest thanks for my whole life, in that you have toward me the best and most noble intentions, which are worthy of a truly great artist and man, and have the kindness to further me in my artistic aspirations.

The wishes that you have expressed to me I accept with the greatest thanks. You were so kind as to ask me for the other quartet as well. I have lent it to someone in the country, thus cannot serve you with it at the moment and therefore beseech your forgiveness; by all means I will not neglect to send it to you as soon as possible or take the liberty of bringing it with me on my next trip to Vienna.

Sincerely requesting the kind intercession with Mr. Simrock regarding the quartets, I permit myself, Your Nobleness, to express my most deeply felt thanks for the kind acceptance of the dedication of my work and the high honor that is thereby bestowed on it.

I have the honor to remain, Your Nobleness, in deepest respect most devoted and most thankful

Anton Dvořák

.

Again, Brahms was as good as his word and wrote to Simrock almost immediately [3 April 1878] with another general recommendation, but suggesting specifically that he have the quartets played for him:

> I would not have written this letter at all if I were not thinking about Dvořák.[14] I don't know what you want to risk further with the man. Also, I have no sense for business and how larger works really arouse interest. Moreover, I recommend reluctantly, because after all I have only my eyes and ears, and these are quite idiosyncratic. Perhaps have him send you, if you are interested at all in proceeding further, two string quartets in major and minor, and have them played for you. The best that a musician must have, Dvořák has, and is also in these pieces. I myself am a wicked Philistine—would prefer not to publish even my own things.[15]
>
> In short, I would rather say no more, than to recommend Dvořák in general. For the rest, you have of course also your ears and business knowledge, which after all has its say, too.

Simrock indeed procured the quartets and had them played, but he expressed strong reservations in his reply to Brahms of 18 June 1878:

"Invention he has indeed—but the working-out often gives the impression of something unspeakably tortured?"

To this Brahms responded diplomatically [25 June 1878], as though the complaints had been made not by Simrock himself but by others: "And the quartets? I can imagine how the people grumbled, and if they only should have so much music in themselves and be able to write it! But indeed, I too have wishes [i.e., criticisms]. I don't know Dvořák. If he lived in Vienna, perhaps I could also express my wishes." Brahms's last remark initiates a recurring theme in the relationship, for on a number of occasions up to the end of his life Brahms hinted at or asserted his desire that Dvořák move to Vienna (which the latter never did). It also indicates that as of mid-1878 the two composers had not yet met personally.

In the meantime, Dvořák had completed his first set of Slavonic Dances. One of the loveliest images of Brahms's appreciation for Dvořák comes to us from a report concerning these pieces, by Richard Heuberger: "The first time I heard him [Brahms, playing the piano] in an intimate situation was when I came to him one afternoon as he sat at the piano and played, glowing with enchantment, the just-published Slavonic Dances of Dvořák. He hardly broke off, then began immediately anew and played to me the blooming pieces with true rapture. Occasionally a word of wonderment escaped his lips" (pp. 131–32).

During this time Brahms apparently expanded his promotional activities on Dvořák's behalf to include arranging for performances. We find Simrock in letters of 14 November and 6 December 1878 asking Brahms's advice in getting the orchestral version of the Slavonic Dances placed on concert programs.

The long-awaited personal meeting occurred in Vienna in December 1878. According to the Prague music journal *Dalibor* of 1 January 1879, "Brahms received our composer with open arms."[16] Brahms reciprocated almost immediately with a visit to Prague, stopping there on his way home from an engagement at Leipzig. Dvořák's letter of 11 January 1879 to Simrock reports that during the Prague visit Brahms took a strong interest in his new String Sextet. Apparently he also discussed with Dvořák his "wishes" regarding the D-minor Quartet and other works.

During the year 1879 Simrock issued nine more works of Dvořák. Both composers initiated a pattern, maintained more-or-less continuously until Brahms's death, of sending messages to each other through the publisher, asking for news and requesting copies of each other's works.

Brahms commented very favorably to Simrock [June 1879] concerning the new Wind Serenade, recommending it also to his friends Joseph Joachim [May] and Theodor Billroth [June]. His letter to Joachim (in Berlin) suggests that there had been other communication between these two musicians regarding Dvořák, and it was probably through Brahms that Dvořák acquired this important new ally.

In Vienna, Brahms apparently recommended Dvořák to Josef Hellmesberger of the Hellmesberger String Quartet, occasioning the next correspondence between the two composers.[17] Brahms wrote to Dvořák in the first part of October 1879:

Most honored sir,

I should like to tell you only in all brevity, that through rehearsals of your newer works that have taken place you have won the sympathy of musicians here [in Vienna] to a quite extraordinary degree.

Thus yesterday with Hellmesberger through the Sextet and Quartet [Dvořák's newest string quartet, in E♭ major]. Hr. Hellmesberger now has the lively desire to be able to play through your two earlier quartets [probably those in D minor and E major], since this time his programs are not, as on earlier occasions, already fixed.[18]

If you can spare the score and parts now, would you be so kind as to send them to H.?

With best greetings your very devoted
J. Brahms[19]

Dvořák responded:

Prag 15/10 79

Most revered Master!

I thank you very much for your esteemed letter, in which I rejoiced quite extraordinarily, only I regret that for the moment I cannot send the score and parts of the quartets immediately, in that the publishing house Haslinger [now Schlesinger] in Vienna has obtained from me the quartet (already known to you) in D minor, which already will appear in print in a short while.

I have indeed already sent the parts for the D-minor quartet to Mr. H., but because I have revised the quartet in many places, I would thus beseech Mr. H. not to play from the handwritten parts until it is possible for me to send him the printed score and parts.

During your last stay in Prague [in January 1879] you were so kind as to draw my attention to some things in my works, and I must only be very thankful to you for it, for now I have really seen the many bad notes and have substituted others for them.

I saw myself all the more called upon to alter much in the D-minor quartet in particular, since you were so kind as to accept from me the dedication of the work; and so it was thus my sacred duty to offer to such a famous master a work that should satisfy if not all then at least (pardon my immodesty) many of the main demands that one can place on a work of art.

How happy I will be to see this confirmed by your perceptive eye! I hope for it!

And so I remain in boundless reverence for your genius,

> your ever thankful
> Anton Dvořák

·

We note here a continued tone of extreme respect but somewhat less obsequious posturing.

This is the last surviving letter between the two composers until fifteen years later, in December 1894. However, letters from Dvořák to Václav Zelený (January 1883) and Simrock (11 July 1889) make it clear that some correspondence in both directions has been lost.

During the decade from November 1879 through December 1889 we can document nine occasions on which the two composers met personally. There may have been further meetings, particularly in Prague, through which Brahms continued to pass frequently on concert trips, but the known visits during this period are as follows:

November 1879, Vienna. Dvořák's Third Slavonic Rhapsody is performed. Dvořák sits next to Brahms and is invited afterward to the home of Court Opera Director Franz Jauner, to whom Brahms warmly recommends him. (Letter of Dvořák to Alois Göbl, 23 November)

February 1880, Prague. Brahms and Joachim give a concert; Brahms spends some time with Dvořák.[20]

November 1880, Vienna. Dvořák makes the trip in order to show his new symphony (the Sixth) to Brahms and to deliver it to the Vienna Philharmonic for performance.[21]

February 1882. Travel together to Prague from Dresden, where Dvořák has apparently gone to hear Brahms play his new piano concerto.[22]

October 1883, Vienna.[23] Dvořák's letter to Simrock of 10 October: "Quite lovely days with Dr. Brahms. We were together every noon

and evening." Brahms plays Dvořák the first and last movements
of his new F-major symphony.[24]

December 1883, Vienna. Performance of Brahms's Third Symphony
and Dvořák's Violin Concerto.[25]

January 1884, Berlin. Brahms conducts his Third Symphony.[26]

December 1887, Vienna. Performance of Dvořák's Symphonic Variations. Brahms spent "the whole day" with Dvořák (Heuberger, p.
35).[27]

December 1889, Vienna. Brahms and Dvořák have an audience with
Emperor Franz Josef I, to thank him for honors they have
received.[28]

The substantial gap between January 1884 and December 1887 may
have resulted in part from Dvořák's trips to England, which he visited
on five occasions during that interval, staying at least two weeks each
time. To our knowledge he found time to visit Vienna only twice during the same period, and on both occasions Brahms was away from
home. The English trips could conceivably have contributed to a slight
cooling of Brahms's attitude toward Dvořák, for, as we shall see,
Brahms disliked England and disapproved of some of Dvořák's activities there.

Perhaps related to these matters is the resurfacing of Brahms's idea
about the desirability of Dvořák's living in Vienna. Brahms's friend
Hanslick proposed this to Dvořák in writing on 11 July 1882,[29] and
Brahms mentioned to Simrock much later [7 November 1887] that he
had earlier wished Dvořák would make the move. (But he never did.)

After December 1889, the two composers did not meet for six years.
In this period Dvořák traveled to England three more times, not including his passage through that country en route to America in September 1892. He also squeezed in a trip to Russia, but Vienna did not
appear on his itinerary. His stay in America, lasting from September
1892 to April 1895 with only a summer respite in Bohemia in 1894,
made visits with Brahms impossible, of course, but ironically it was
during Dvořák's American sojourn that the composers began to establish the truly cordial relationship they enjoyed in the last few years of
Brahms's life, as we shall see.

From this time period we have no surviving letters exchanged
between the two composers until December 1894, or any evidence
that correspondence has been lost. The apparent lack of communication may have been partly a consequence of the deterioration in
Dvořák's relations with Simrock, caused by disputes over the amounts
the composer should be paid and some questions of national pride.
Simrock published nothing by Dvořák between 1891 and 1893, and

virtually the entire year of 1892 passed without any communication between the publisher and the composer. It was the desire for Brahms's music—in particular his new piano pieces—that prompted Dvořák to break the silence with a humorous note to Simrock dated 10 December 1892:

Most revered sir!

Colleague Epstein [a pianist at the Vienna Conservatory] has received Opp. 118 and 117, and I not? Perchè sono in disgrazia?

Your very vexed
A.D.

In the following summer Dvořák and Simrock came into pleasant relations once more and agreed on publication of a whole list of works that Dvořák had written from 1891 through 1893. But sending proofs across the ocean seemed like an unwieldy idea to Simrock. Meanwhile Brahms, who had heard about Dvořák's ideas regarding inspiration from African-American music, expressed his approval of those ideas in a letter to Simrock [7 September 1893], and the publisher decided to ask Brahms if he would make the proof corrections for Dvořák's new works. Brahms readily agreed—"Please send me the Dvořák; that interests me naturally" [22 December 1893]—and commenced this work forthwith. (See his letter to Simrock [14 January 1894].) The works thus corrected in that year apparently included at least the *Dumky* Trio and the three overtures (*In Nature's Realm*, *Carnival*, and *Othello*), the "New World" Symphony, the "American" String Quartet, and the E♭-major String Quintet.[30]

Dvořák was overwhelmed by Brahms's generosity and his interest in his work, as witness his letters to Simrock (5 February 1894) and Alois Göbl (27 February). His rather tardy letter of thanks to Brahms, dated 28 December 1894, is the last and longest of all those exchanged between the two composers. Its tone departs dramatically from that of Dvořák's early letters to Brahms: now he seems much more a friend than a worshipful admirer or even a professional colleague. His failure even to mention the Cello Concerto, on which he was working at the time and about which he had written in detail to Göbl two weeks earlier, is puzzling. Dvořák's apologies for clumsiness of expression seem quite warranted—perhaps he was tired, having written at least three other letters on the same day, including a long one to Simrock with many musical citations from the Biblical Songs. Perhaps his command of German had slipped a bit during the years in America:

.

Highly honored Master and friend! New York 18 28/12 94

How and where should I begin today? I have not seen you for five years—I have been in America already two years—I was in Bohemia this summer—and didn't see you! How much I would have to tell you!—but how and where to begin? It is difficult for me!

I ought to have written to you long ago! Simrock told me that you were so very kind as to look through my things, and also Suk and Nedbal said that you told them in Vienna about the overtures, and much, much else tells me what an invaluable patron I have in you— and so today I can only say the simple words: thanks, heartiest thanks to you for all you have done unto me and for me!

How I looked forward to visiting you at Ischl this summer—but man proposes, God disposes—the illness of my daughter Anna interfered with my plans, and I couldn't leave Vysoká. Then in September I returned to Prague, and in October I had to set out on my journey back to America. Now I am sitting here again and doing just what I can. I left five children in Prague, and only my boy Otakar and my wife are here, and so we are often homesick, if I can write something, that is the only recovery for me. To be sure, there are musical pleasures enough here, but I avoid them as much as possible—only now and then do I go to the philharmonic or chamber music concerts, and they are very fine here. We shall hear your C-minor and soon your E-minor [symphonies] here—how glad I am—Seidl conducts. And how! Soon, also, all three of my overtures will be performed (but with explanations). I just read in the Vienna newspapers that Richter played the *Carnival* Overture on 9 December, and my composition was not—as so often—rejected.[31]

It's been a long time already since Mr. Simrock wrote to me; perhaps he will do it now, since I sent him the corrected proofs of my Biblical Songs today. What does Dr. Hanslick want to do now, since he has gone on pension? He remains anyway faithful to the *N.[eue] freie Presse*? How often I look for the initials E.H. in the *Presse*, but how seldom I find anything there! Why that is, I don't know.

Since only three days still separate us from the new year, I want to take this opportunity also to give you my heartiest good wishes, and ask you to preserve your friendship with me, which I so esteem. Please pardon most kindly that this letter is so ineffectual—but I consider writing letters to you to be very difficult, but above all when one has so much to say—but you know me too well, as nobody else, and so I believe for today I have acquitted myself of my task as well as possible, and I remain with heartiest greetings your most devoted

Antonín Dvořák

As a form of response, Brahms sent Dvořák his picture in March 1895, with a small musical quote from his own song "Über die See," Op. 69, no. 7, supplied with the words "Weit über das Meer" ("Far across the Ocean").[32]

Dvořák had various plans to visit Brahms after his return from America in April 1895—first in Berlin (letters to Simrock of 4 March and to Josef Bohuslav Foerster of 11 March), then in Ischl during the summer (letter to Adele Margulies of 31 July), then in Vienna in September (letter to Simrock of 28 August). But none of these plans were realized. He was, he said, tired of traveling.

By mid-December, however, he had regained his energy and made the trip to Vienna, initiating a period in which he visited that city with unprecedented frequency—five times within sixteen months. The first trip was for the express purpose of visiting Brahms; the last was for his funeral in April 1897, at which Dvořák was a pallbearer. On each of the other occasions he had performances and conducting engagements to attend to, but he also spent time with Brahms.

During the first of these visits Brahms wrote to Simrock [16 December 1895] saying how tremendously pleased he was to see his friend after such a long separation. Dvořák's letter to Göbl of 23 December reports that he and Brahms "were together almost constantly."

The next trip was for the Vienna premiere of the "New World" Symphony on 16 February 1896, at which Dvořák sat next to Brahms. (See Dvořák's letter to Simrock of 19 February 1896.) Brahms wanted to bring Dvořák with him to a party afterward at the home of his friend Viktor von Miller, and had written to the latter the previous day with a humorous but touching testimony to his friendship with Dvořák: "In case Dvořák comes to the concert tomorrow and is free, would you have anything against my giving him the pleasure of bringing him along to your house? I will give to him from my little plate and my little mug, and as far as I know he doesn't make any speeches!"[33] Apparently, however, Dvořák did not attend this gathering. He came to Vienna yet again in March 1896, when he conducted his dramatic cantata *Svatební košile* (The Specter's Bride), and attended concerts by Edvard Grieg as well as by the Czech Quartet.

We know that on at least one of these visits Brahms talked openly with Dvořák about his moving to Vienna for the sake of his career, and he had the impression that Dvořák would seriously consider it.[34] Apparently Brahms made an astonishing offer of his own financial assistance, in view of the great expense of Dvořák's maintaining his large family in Vienna.[35]

It was also during one or more of these visits that Brahms and Dvořák discussed religion:

> Brahms said that Dvořák was a fanatical Catholic. At Brahms's house recently, he had seen a book in his library by Dr. Thode—*St. Francis*—and taken it with him immediately. Brahms said that Dvořák was quite happy, quite pious, when he had the book. He told Brahms then that he read every day in the Bible. "I don't find that comical at all," said Brahms. "A man so industrious as Dvořák by no means has time to get stuck on doubts; rather all his life he stands by what he was taught in his childhood." (Heuberger, 24 February 1896, p. 95)

Around the same time, Brahms referred somewhat less politely to the difference between his views and Dvořák's, when discussing the oratorio *St. Ludmila*: "The text, to be sure, is too silly for me! Miracles! Pure nonsense! Dvořák believes in that, he can do it!" (ibid., 31 March 1896, p. 101).

When next Dvořák saw Brahms, the German composer was on his deathbed. Having heard about Brahms's illness, Dvořák somewhat surprisingly found it necessary to ask Simrock on 22 October 1896 whether he thought Brahms would like a visit.[36] Without knowing Simrock's reply we cannot fathom Dvořák's motives, but he postponed the trip for five months. After traveling to Vienna in March 1897, he reported to Simrock that he had seen "how sadly it is all true, what I heard from you. But we want to hope that all is not yet lost! God grant it!"[37]

Brahms died on 3 April.

On the Nature of the Personal Relationship

It must be granted that the personal relationship between Dvořák and Brahms was not fully balanced. For instance, Dvořák seems to have made the effort to visit Brahms much more often than the latter visited him. Nevertheless, there is no doubt that their affection was mutual. The extremely deferential tone of Dvořák's first letters moderated greatly over time, and the two men came to regard each other with something closer to equal respect. We have many testimonies to the pleasure each found in the other's company. A particularly revealing example comes from Dvořák, in a letter to Simrock of 10 October 1883:

> The intimacy with me seems to have pleased him, and I am truly so enchanted with his charm as an artist and a man that I can love

him! What heart and soul hide in the man! You know how he is very reserved even toward his dearest friends and musicians, especially where his composition is concerned, but he was not that way toward me. Upon my request to hear something from his new symphony [the Third], he was immediately ready and played me the first and last movements.

Brahms, for his part, described his encounters with Dvořák as being pleasant, at a minimum:

1883: "Dvořák was here for several days and was very nice." (Letter to Simrock [13 October 1883])
1887: "Very agreeable and nice were the hours with him." (Letter to Simrock [9 December 1887])
1895: "His visit was a great joy to me." (Letter to Simrock [16 December 1895])

Brahms seems to have appreciated Dvořák's deep and genuine humanity: "He gushed over Dvořák when I was with him and described him as a 'succulent [vollsaftig] fellow'" (Heuberger, 31 March 1896, p. 101).

Once Brahms wrote to Simrock [21 October 1883] contrasting the value he found in Dvořák's friendship with what apparently seemed like the emptiness of his everyday life: "That the symphony [the Third] pleases Dvořák so much is of course a great joy to me, whereas naturally it interests me but little how many articles you have and acquire in the season." He sometimes felt compelled to defend Dvořák against his friends' criticisms. Aware of Dvořák's relative lack of knowledge about literature, he not only justified it but also downplayed its importance: "Dvořák is endlessly industrious [i.e., always turning out new compositions], which is why he knows only a little literature. He knows quite little even of the literature of music. Of other education, likewise, he has only a little, but talent and eminent ability!" (Heuberger, 16 February 1896, pp. 92–93).

Perhaps the most telling remark Brahms ever made about Dvořák's person was also the briefest, made not long before his own death, prior to a performance of the Cello Concerto: "You will hear a piece today, a piece by a man!"[38]

Dvořák's Debt to Brahms in His Career Advancement

All Dvořák's letters to Brahms express gratitude for the latter's help in his progress toward world fame—gratitude whose sincerity is affirmed by his comments, no less effusive, to others. For example, as Tchaikovsky recalled from his meeting with Dvořák in 1888, "Dvořák told with tears in his eyes how much understanding and sympathy Brahms had shown toward him, when he got to know his, Dvořák's, compositions, which no publisher wanted to accept and no artist wanted to perform, and how energetically and effectively he saved him from being forgotten."[39]

Such testimonies, however, tell us more about Dvořák's humility than about the true extent of his debt, for he is understating the level of success he had achieved prior to Brahms's intervention. As of December 1877 Dvořák had seen two operas produced, with a third already scheduled for January 1878, and his concert performances had included a complete symphony, among other orchestral works, a choral work with orchestra, many chamber works, and many songs. Czech publishers, meanwhile, had issued the Moravian Duets, a string quartet (in parts only), a number of songs and piano pieces, and the String Serenade in four-hand piano arrangement. Had Brahms never entered Dvořák's life, the latter's fame would certainly have continued to grow, and he would have achieved at least some degree of international renown on his own or with the help of other benefactors.

Dvořák's Debt to Brahms in Musical Style

The early letters between the two composers reveal both that Brahms was willing to give Dvořák advice regarding his compositions and that Dvořák was glad to accept it. This relationship apparently continued for many years, and one might even say that in a sense Dvořák "studied" composition with Brahms.

Regarding his Sixth Symphony in D major, Dvořák wrote to Simrock (on 24 September 1880) that upon finishing it he would "lay the work first of all before Meister Brahms for his inspection." And of the Seventh in D minor he wrote (again to Simrock, in February 1885) that "the new 'symphony' has occupied me already for a long, long time, but something respectable should result, for I don't want to prove wrong the words Brahms spoke to me: 'I imagine your symphony to be something quite different again from this D-major one!'"

Undoubtedly, Dvořák took Brahms's own music as an example to some extent. He was always requesting Brahms scores from Simrock, and his comments were always appreciative—the most common adjective is "splendid" (*herrlich* or *großartig*).

The only Brahms work on which we have detailed commentary from Dvořák is the Third Symphony, regarding which he wrote to Simrock after Brahms played him the outer movements at the piano (10 October 1883):

> I say without exaggeration that this work surpasses his first two symphonies, if perhaps not in greatness and powerful conception then certainly in—beauty!
> There is a mood in it that one does not often find with Brahms! What splendid melodies one finds there! It is pure love, and it does one's heart good! Think about my words and, when you hear the symphony, you will say that I have heard well. But enough of that.
> This work is a credit to art, and I congratulate you in advance.

In at least two cases, Dvořák cited works by Brahms as specific models for himself. One was the Hungarian Dances, taken as a model for the Slavonic. The other was the "Academic Festival" Overture, cited in a letter to Simrock of 31 December 1881: "I'm also writing something new now: music for a play, *Kajetan Tyl*. It consists of several pieces, an overture (in which Czech songs are elaborated), melodrama, entr'actes, etc. Should it be allotted to me to write such a work as the 'Academic' of Brahms, I would thank God for that." Indeed, the referenced overture (known commonly as *My Home*) employs preexisting Czech tunes in much the same manner as the "Academic" employs student songs.

In the absence of specific support from the composers' testimony, writers have described, more-or-less plausibly, numerous further instances of Dvořák works alluding to particular works of Brahms by way of structural modeling, thematic similarity, or especially strong stylistic reminiscence.[40] Some have made the risky move of tracing Brahmsian influences in the works Dvořák composed before he knew Brahms personally. The trouble with this, of course, is that Dvořák probably was not very familiar with Brahms's music up to this time. In some cases where a Brahmsian style has been convincingly described, we must conclude that Dvořák arrived at that style independently, based on other influences and his own creativity. Thus, Dvořák's Piano Concerto has strong affinities with Brahms's D-minor Piano Concerto—yet, as Šourek has shown, it was written at a time when Dvořák most likely had only a passing familiarity with Brahms's music, and almost certainly had not encountered the concerto.[41]

In general, there has been a tendency to exaggerate Dvořák's stylistic debt to Brahms. This pattern was established long ago primarily by Germans, but once again the most systematic exposé of the practice comes also from a German, of a younger generation. Hartmut Schick, in his *Studien zu Dvořáks Streichquartetten*, makes a direct indictment of the conventional wisdom: "The common view that Antonín Dvořák, eight years younger than Brahms, developed his productivity in these fields [symphony and chamber music] only as a follower of Brahms . . . is an error grown out of reception-history." And Schick's book brims with analyses that illuminate Dvořák's achievement independently from Brahms, even in advance of him, in aspects of style for which Brahms is often lauded. (Developing variation and rhythmic intricacy loom large.)

Dvořák himself made it clear enough, in an article he wrote about Schubert in 1894, that for him Brahms was only one bright star within a whole constellation of composers who could provide inspiration. In this article he discusses twenty-four composers as they compare with Schubert in their varied achievements. Brahms plays a fairly prominent role but certainly not an overwhelming one.[42]

If the influence of Brahms on Dvořák is essentially limited to a certain chronological phase of his life—beginning in 1878 and, most writers agree, tapering off after 1885—we must also keep in mind that it pertains almost exclusively to certain types of pieces, namely chamber and orchestral works in the classical forms. And these works are by no means the whole of Dvořák's output. No serious attempts have been made, and none would likely succeed, to describe Brahmsian influences in the many works written throughout Dvořák's life in genres of composition quite foreign to his mentor: operas, Catholic liturgical works, choral works with Czech texts on Czech subjects, and symphonic poems.

Šourek claimed that "Dvořák was an individual just as outstanding and just as distinctive and rich as Brahms, nay even more distinctive and rich."[43] Perhaps this sounds strange, given our critical tradition in which the superiority of Brahms is taken for granted. But Šourek's claim can be validated in objective terms: whatever one thinks of the consistency of Dvořák's workmanship or his average level of profundity or sophistication as compared to Brahms, it is indisputable that his output was broader, more varied, and in many ways more interesting than that of Brahms. And though Brahms made an important contribution to Dvořák's stylistic development, we must acknowledge that Dvořák's achievement was in large measure his own.

Brahms's Musical Debt to Dvořák

Whereas most authors have been attentive to the influence of Brahms on Dvořák, the possibility of a reciprocal relationship has scarcely occurred to them. But careful consideration of the respect that Brahms accorded Dvořák certainly makes it plausible that the influence was exerted in both directions.

Brahms followed Dvořák's career keenly up to the end of his own life, at first partly to help the struggling Czech composer but later mainly for his own interest. He frequently requested copies of Dvořák's music from Simrock, just as Dvořák did of his; and upon Brahms's death, his library contained more scores by Dvořák than by any other of his contemporaries, and roughly as many by Dvořák as by Schubert, Schumann, or Mendelssohn.[44]

And just as Dvořák stated his desire to emulate the "Academic Festival" Overture, so Brahms once described a Dvořák work as something he might himself have imitated. Unfortunately it was not until the last full year of his life, when his composing days were nearly over, that he encountered Dvořák's Cello Concerto in B minor, calling it "a great and excellent work" (letter to Simrock [27 January 1896]) and confessing on another occasion that "had I known that such a violoncello concerto as that could be written, I could have tried to compose one myself!"[45]

Were there instances in which Brahms actually did draw inspiration from Dvořák in his own music? Some possibilities have been suggested just in the past few years.[46] The String Quartet in B♭ major, often cited for its stylistic divergence from Brahms's earlier works, shows striking similarities to earlier chamber works of Dvořák. The unusual practice of setting biblical texts as songs with piano accompaniment, as Brahms did in his late Serious Songs, may have been inspired by the Biblical Songs of Dvořák. And the Third Symphony in F major, whose anomalies have led writers to seek precedents in music of the New German School, actually has more in common—the anomalous features, precisely—with Dvořák's Fifth Symphony in the same key.

Unfortunately we have no record of Brahmsian commentary on the particular Dvořák works that, according to the hypotheses just mentioned, may have inspired him. But his preserved remarks on many other works of Dvořák are extensive (much more so than Dvořák's commentary on Brahms), thanks to his generally free expression in letters to Simrock and to the efforts of Heuberger, who recorded so many of his verbal utterances. And as we shall see, this record provides much food for thought quite apart from the question of musical influences.

How Brahms Viewed Dvořák

The Cello Concerto turns out to be unique among Dvořák works for which we have recorded commentary from Brahms, in that Brahms seemed to consider it comparable to his own music. More often, the qualities he found in Dvořák's music were of a quite different sort. Here is a fairly complete synopsis of Brahms's preserved comments on Dvořák works that he praised with no explicit reservation:

Moravian Duets: Merry, fresh, piquant, pretty. (Letter to Simrock [December 1877])

Piano Concerto: He was very pleased by it, referring to "easily shaping fantasy" [*leicht gestaltende Phantasie*].[47]

E-major and D-minor String Quartets: "The best that a musician must have, Dvořák has, and is also in these pieces." (Letter to Simrock [3 April 1878])

D-major Slavonic Rhapsody: "Oh, that is so musical." (Heuberger, 1882/83, p. 149)

Wind Serenade: "A more lovely, refreshing impression of real, rich and charming creative talent you can't easily have . . . I think it must be a pleasure for the wind players!" (Letter to Joachim [mid-May 1879])

Slavonic Dances, first set: He played them "glowing with enchantment." (Heuberger, 1882/83, p. 149)

String Sextet: "Brahms gushed again and again: 'It is endlessly beautiful. I always have the feeling that people don't admire this piece enough. This splendid invention, freshness and sonorous beauty . . .'" (Ibid., 28 March 1896, p. 99)

Legends for piano, four hands: "A charming work, and enviable the fresh, merry, rich invention." (Letter to Simrock [8 August 1881])

Works proofread while Dvořák was in America: "I rejoice in his cheerful [*fröhlich*] creations." (Letter to Simrock [17 January 1894])

Carnival Overture: "Merry"; "music directors will be thankful to you." (Letter to Simrock [17 January 1894])

The words Brahms chose to describe these works—"merry," "charming," "fresh," and filled with "invention" (*Erfindung*)—are not often thought of in connection with his own music. And indeed, in Dvořák's Legends Brahms finds the "invention" to be "enviable."

The clear differentiation that Brahms made between his own strengths and those of Dvořák becomes even more evident when we consider those works of Dvořák on which his recorded verdict is mixed. On the Symphonic Variations, he equivocated. According to Heuberger, "Brahms gushed over the splendid piece of music that he had heard: 'It is wonderfully beautiful and yet never refined, so natural!'" (5 December 1887, p. 35). Then, in a letter to Simrock [9 December 1887], "It's a shame that he hasn't been able to meaningfully rework the whole exciting and vivacious piece!"

The "New World" Symphony occasioned a particularly revealing critique following its performance in Vienna:

> Brahms praised the E-minor symphony and its wonderful timbre. When Kalbeck raised objections, he said: "Don't forget, I know the symphony by heart and could here or there find something to criticize. Had I written it one day after breakfast, so I would thereupon look it over, to see what could possibly be made from it. But just as it stands, it is so unspeakably gifted, so healthy, that one must rejoice in it." (Heuberger, 16 February 1896, pp. 92–93)

Interpretation: if Brahms had written the piece he would have made many changes—but he hadn't written it, indeed couldn't have written anything possessing the particular beauties of this work, which Dvořák seemed miraculously to have produced with such ease.

Even more telling is Brahms's commentary on the Eighth Symphony:

> Too much that's fragmentary, incidental, loiters about in the piece. Everything fine, musically captivating and beautiful—but no main points! Especially in the first movement, the result is not proper. But a charming musician! When one says of Dvořák that he fails to achieve anything great and comprehensive with his pure, individual ideas, this is correct. Not so with Bruckner, all the same he offers so little! (Ibid., 6 January 1891, p. 47)

Bruckner has greater constructive power, then, but Brahms prefers Dvořák anyway. He seems to be saying that pure melodic invention is more valuable than compelling formal structure!

Brahms's statements elsewhere regarding the importance of melodic invention, and his own perceived deficiencies in this area, are well known. Aware of his own worth but also his own limitations, Brahms consciously valued in Dvořák precisely those qualities—and for the most part *only* those qualities—that he felt were lacking in his own music. Klaus Döge was right to conclude in his recent Dvořák biography that from Brahms's point of view the relationship was largely based on an attraction of opposites.[48]

But *were* they in fact opposites? Should we view Dvořák as Brahms did? Before answering this question, we must make a further, rather astonishing observation about the record of Brahms's commentary on Dvořák's music. The works critiqued are of course a small subset of the works Dvořák composed, but they are not a random subset. Nor do they represent the most important works, regarded by critics as Dvořák's greatest achievements. Amazingly, it is precisely the greatest works that are missing! On the Sixth and Seventh Symphonies and the C-major String Quartet we have no comment from Brahms, nor on *any* of the chamber works with piano. (What would Brahms have thought about the famous Piano Quintet, or the equally great F-minor Trio?) For such pieces as these, the image of Dvořák's music as fresh, charming, and melodious might be less appropriate, or these characteristics might be less clearly their chief distinguishing feature.

If Brahms meant his comments regarding the Eighth Symphony— that Dvořák failed to make anything substantial out of his melodic inspirations—to apply to the composer's music in general, he must have simply blocked many works out of his mind. When Donald Tovey wrote of the opening movement of Dvořák's Seventh Symphony, it was the development section that he singled out for special tribute—"It is impossible to over-praise [its] mastery and tragic power"—as helping to make this work one of the greatest symphonies composed since Beethoven.[49] And most careful analysts have found that, in general, Dvořák's music realizes impressively his own professed philosophy of composition, which actually placed emphasis not on melodic ideas but on their "working-out": "To have a beautiful idea is nothing special. The idea comes from itself and if it is beautiful and great, man can take no credit for that. But to develop the idea well and make something great from it, that is the most difficult, that is—art!"[50]

Could there have been an external factor that caused Brahms, despite his great admiration for Dvořák, to overlook some of his strongest assets? The answer is far from obvious, but we can begin to perceive it through an examination of Brahms's comments on those works of Dvořák that he roundly condemned. In the preserved record, there are only three of them.

Regarding one of Dvořák's choral works, Brahms wrote to Simrock [27 January 1896] that "the *Te Deum* is no doubt intended for the 'Celebration of the Destruction of Vienna and Berlin by the Czechs' and seems to me well suited for that." Of course Brahms was joking. But why would it occur to him to characterize a piece in this way?

Regarding the *Hussite* Overture, a work using Czech patriotic tunes to commemorate the Hussite Wars, in which Czech religious reformers struggled against the power of German landowners in Bohemia, Brahms protested to Simrock [18–19 August 1884] as follows:

[That piece] I hate in manuscript and in print . . . [He complains about printer's errors] . . . I would not want to have published it—I wish Dvořák had not given you the opportunity to do so! . . . Dvořák would probably not stand for it, if you wanted to be publisher and critic, and with just cause. So if you become Royal Bohemian Court and National Composer, then I can at most regret that less good things by Dvořák have also contributed to that. You know and believe, that I only wish Dvořák to give you always such quality as he can. (The overture is unfortunately bragging, insolent, and bad.) But you are concerned with business, and I know, concerning you, to say nothing.

But he really has said quite a lot, hasn't he? Modern biographers of Dvořák have called this overture "a noble work," "a glorious piece of music . . . powerful."[51] In Brahms's own time, his friends Hanslick and Bülow liked it very much. Bülow in fact insisted for some time on conducting it in virtually every concert he directed—but he encountered opposition from German nationalists. Apparently Brahms was one of them.

The remaining work that Brahms castigated is the oratorio *St. Ludmila*, commissioned by the Leeds Festival in England. We have already observed his impatience with the religious miracles in this work. But Brahms had more to say about a planned performance of a part of it in Vienna in 1897: "*St. Ludmila* I would rather not perform at all! It is an occasional piece for an English music festival, and weak. If one wants to do something of Dvořák, let it be one of his works that belong to him. His *Stabat Mater* or some such. But let's have nothing of the English occasional pieces!" (Heuberger, 22 February 1897, p. 122). Though condemned here as an "English piece," this oratorio is actually on a Czech subject and exuberantly glorifies the Czech nation. Along with the *Hussite* Overture, it is one of the very few pieces by Dvořák that make an explicit political statement of Czech nationalism beyond merely evoking the stylistic traits of Czech folk music.

Can it be a coincidence that the only three works of Dvořák seriously censured by Brahms in the recorded commentary all pertain, or were linked by him, to overt nationalism?

Brahms's Nationalism

Brahms's patriotic fervor for Germany has been well documented; it was in fact probably greater than Dvořák's Czech patriotism. Robert

Schauffler has given ample evidence of Brahms's dislike for the French, the English, and the Americans,[52] which he manifested to the point where one suspects a degree of xenophobia. And in Vienna during the late nineteenth century, xenophobia among the German-speaking population was rampant, what with a growing threat to their supremacy posed by the other nationalities—including the Czechs—in the Austro-Hungarian Empire.

Brahms was associated in Vienna with the "liberal" party, consisting of the German educated middle class, liberal indeed in its social values for Germans but not when it came to extending those values to other nationalities. From 1879 on, the liberals were on the defensive in Vienna thanks to the regime of Prime Minister Eduard Taaffe, which drew its support from a coalition of German, Czech, and Polish conservatives.[53] According to Kalbeck, Brahms hated Taaffe and his Slavic leanings.[54] It was in this context that he wrote sarcastically to Simrock [25 February 1883] that "I think we will yet experience the catastrophe—but in the meantime, we are founding Czech schools in Vienna." There was even a rumor that Brahms wanted to leave Vienna, based, according to Kalbeck, on the composer's mutterings that life there was hardly bearable any longer for a German. Elisabeth von Herzogenberg referred to this rumor in a letter to Brahms of 1 October 1883, suggesting that the reason must be the Slavic leanings of the Empire and even mentioning Dvořák as someone who could profit—at Brahms's expense—from the political climate.[55]

Although there is no evidence of professional jealousy in Brahms's statements regarding Dvořák, he did confess in two different letters to Simrock ([7 November 1887] and [9 December 1887]) that he had suspected Dvořák of being a "fanatical Czech." Ultimately, he recognized that this was not the case, yet he remained hypersensitive to Dvořák's nationality to the end. As Heuberger relates, only a little more than a year before Brahms died, "When Dvořák got carried away, with the strange remark that Wotan was a Slavic name, Brahms said: 'The fellow will yet claim the whole trilogy is "bemmisch" ' [i.e., böhmisch, meaning Czech]" (15 December 1895, p. 89).

The relevance of all this to Brahms's views on Dvořák's music derives from the fact that his political attitudes were linked to strong prejudices about the character of particular nationalities, including the Czechs. Just as Brahms's last utterance regarding Dvořák was one of the most telling—that his music was composed "by a man"—so perhaps was one of his first comments, made in a letter to Simrock [10 December 1877]: "Dvořák seems to me to be a typical Czech."

Brahms did not explain in this letter what he meant by "a typical

Czech," nor are the implications clarified explicitly anywhere else in his preserved commentary. But in this matter the record of Simrock's views helps greatly because Simrock, another German nationalist, disguised his prejudices thinly at best in comments about Dvořák to Brahms, and even to Dvořák himself. And Simrock's overall attitude toward Dvořák seems to have paralleled that of Brahms very closely. His adjectives of praise—merry, fresh, melodious, filled with invention—were precisely those used by Brahms. The difference is that Simrock also made many criticisms. As a rule, Brahms failed to endorse explicitly these criticisms, but he did not contradict them, either.

Ironically, the national character of Dvořák's music was something that Simrock prized—its folklike (*volkstümlich*) and even "*national-poetisch*" qualities apparently enhanced its marketability in the publisher's eyes (letter from Simrock to Brahms of 28 December 1877). But Simrock's arrogant attitude toward the Czechs was such as to force Dvořák on one occasion to plead, "Don't make fun of my Czech brothers" in a reply (22 August 1885) to a letter from Simrock that is unfortunately lost. True artistic refinement, Simrock seemed to think, was a little beyond the capacity of a Czech like Dvořák. Regarding some of Dvořák's songs he wrote, "There is something really crude in them— but not without charm and original musicality" (2 June 1879). And when it came to the more cerebral task of thematic development, "Invention he has indeed—but the working-out often gives the impression of something unspeakably tortured?" (18 June 1878).

Such pronouncements echo chauvinistic attitudes that were already evident among German music critics in the late eighteenth century. As Mary Sue Morrow has shown, such critics often dismissed the whole Italian nation as being incapable of thematic development.[56]

The context of such judgments within a cultural pattern of German ethnocentrism has been described clearly, once more, by modern German scholars. Manfred Jähnichen has shown how, in the sphere of literature, Germans of the late nineteenth century regarded the Czechs as congenitally uncultivated, with an inherently lower potential for achievement.[57] And Peter Petersen observed that in the realm of music, a composer like Dvořák could be dealt with most comfortably as a "Bohemian *Musikant*"—implying rustic natural talent while avoiding any suggestion of greatness. The basis for such a stereotype, he adds, was thoroughly established in the attitudes promulgated by the German liberal and national press.[58] It is against this background that we must understand Brahms's description of Dvořák as a "typical Czech."

Our analysis of Brahms's attitude toward Dvořák began with the observation that he admired specifically those qualities he himself lacked. But we must now add that these qualities were precisely what a German nationalist would be expected to find in a Czech composer—raw natural talent, without refinement. In one respect, then, the views of Petersen cited at the outset of this study were wrong: the national prejudices that have distorted perceptions of the Dvořák-Brahms relationship through history were in fact shared, to some extent, even by Brahms himself. It is instructive to learn, from our survey of Brahmsian pronouncements on Dvořák's music, just how high a premium Brahms placed on raw talent. But we must realize also that, in perceiving this kind of talent as Dvořák's chief attribute, Brahms was operating under the influence of subjective prejudices.

Though intended as a comprehensive overview, this essay obviously cannot claim to have delivered the last word on the relationship between Dvořák and Brahms. Indeed, if it has raised more questions than it has answered, that would befit its purpose. This musical and personal relationship was a complex one that unfolded over the course of many years, ebbing and flowing irregularly, and it was influenced by external circumstances in ways that may not be obvious but are important nevertheless, forming significant links to larger historical issues. Further exploration will doubtless yield rich rewards.

NOTES

1. Peter Petersen, "Brahms und Dvořák," in *Brahms und seine Zeit: Symposion Hamburg 1983*, Hamburger Jahrbuch für Musikwissenschaft, vol. 7, ed. Constantin Floros et al. (Hamburg, 1984), pp. 125–26.

2. Among the older publications, paramount are the letters from Brahms to his publisher Simrock, edited by Max Kalbeck, in vols. 9–12 of the *Johannes Brahms Briefwechsel* (Berlin, 1919). Important sources published comparatively recently include the letters from Simrock to Brahms, edited by Kurt Stephenson, in *Johannes Brahms und Fritz Simrock: Weg einer Freundschaft* (Hamburg, 1961), and the collected letters of Dvořák written through 1895, edited by Milan Kuna et al., in *Antonín Dvořák: Korespondence a dokumenty*, vols. 1–3 (Prague, 1987–89). In this essay, all citations from these letters will be by date only, from which the letters can be located easily enough in the appropriate volumes. Dates given in square brackets rather than parentheses represent estimates by the editors of the letters. Such estimates are usually necessary for Brahms, who rarely dated his letters.

Also invaluable are the diary entries of Brahms's friend Richard Heuberger, *Erinnerungen an Johannes Brahms*, 2d ed. (Tutzing, 1976), referenced here by page number and, if known, the date of the described event or conversation.

3. Unless otherwise noted, the information about Brahms performances in this and the following two paragraphs comes from Zdeněk Nouza, "Beobachtungen zu Brahms' Stellung im tschechischen Musikleben seiner Zeit," in *Brahms-Kongress Wien 1983: Kongressbericht*, ed. Susanne Antoniček and Otto Biba (Tutzing, 1988), pp. 405–12.

4. Much new information concerning Dvořák's applications for and receipt of the stipends, which rectifies some widely circulated errors, is presented in Milan Kuna's article "Umělecká stipendia Antonína Dvořáka," *Hudební věda*, n.s., 4 (1992): 293–315.

5. Hanslick printed this letter in his article "Johannes Brahms. (Erinnerungen und Briefe.) II.," in the *Neue freie Presse*, 29 June 1897.

6. John Clapham, "Dvořákovy vztahy k Brahmsovi a Hanslickovi," in *Hudební věda* 10 (1973): 214.

7. John Clapham, *Dvořák* (New York, 1979), p. 44.

8. Petersen, "Brahms und Dvořák," p. 127.

9. Dvořák probably did not send music along with his letter; rather, he delivered the music personally to Brahms's house in Vienna about a month later. In Brahms's reply to this first letter, he acknowledges the pleasure he derived "durch Ihre übersandten Werke," by which he apparently means the works that had been sent to him as a member of the judging committee.

10. The known extant correspondence between Dvořák and Brahms includes seven letters from Dvořák and three from Brahms, thus ten altogether, of which all but one come from the early years of the relationship—1877–79. All have been published previously, though several had to wait until 1971, to appear in John Clapham's article "Dvořák's Relations with Brahms and Hanslick," *Musical Quarterly* 57 (1971): 241–54. The present essay marks both the first time they have all been assembled in one place and the first time they have all been translated into English with no excisions. I have made new translations for all the letters in this essay (as well as for all the other material quoted, unless noted otherwise), partly for consistency in style but also to rectify small errors in previous renditions.

11. "Antonin Dvořák im Verkehr mit Fritz Simrock," in *N. Simrock Jahrbuch II*, ed. Erich H. Müller (Berlin, 1929), p. 86.

12. It is curious that Brahms recommended the duets apparently without having any knowledge of the meaning of the words! They must have appealed to him purely because of their musical charm.

13. Max Kalbeck, *Johannes Brahms*, vol. 3 (Berlin, 1904–14), p. 156n.

14. Here Brahms, to whom the Czech language was a mystery, jokingly decorates Dvořák's name with a plethora of random diacritical marks above and below the letters, as he also did on a number of subsequent occasions.

15. Kalbeck interprets this remark, plausibly, as meaning that he could recommend Dvořák's things as little as his own; measured against his ideal, both were imperfect.

16. As cited in Otakar Šourek, *Život a dílo Antonína Dvořáka*, 3d ed., vol. 2 (Prague, 1955), p. 62. Šourek refers (on p. 61) to the autograph manuscript of

Dvořák's Five Choruses for Men's Voices, on which the composer wrote, "Composed on the trip from Prague to Vienna, 12 December 1878," and states that Dvořák took this trip for the purpose of finally meeting Brahms.

17. See also Brahms's letters to Simrock of [8] and 13 October 1879.

18. This implies that Brahms had perhaps already suggested works of Dvořák to Hellmesberger on a previous occasion.

19. Altmann, "Antonín Dvořák im Verkehr mit Fritz Simrock," p. 88n.

20. Nouza, "Beobachtungen zu Brahms' Stellung im tschechischen Musikleben seiner Zeit," p. 412; Šourek, *Život a dílo Antonína Dvořáka*, vol. 2, p. 109; and Kalbeck, *Johannes Brahms*, vol. 3, p. 235; also Dvořák's letter to Leoš Janáček [19 February 1880].

21. See Dvořák's letters to Simrock, 24 September and 26 November 1880; also Brahms's letter to Simrock [23 November 1880].

22. Letters from Dvořák to Simrock, 2 January and 25 February 1882.

23. Dvořák had intended to make a trip to Vienna much earlier in the year 1883, but his plans seem not to have materialized. See his letters to Václav Zelený [January] and to Eduard Hanslick (23 February).

24. See also Brahms's letter to Simrock [13 October 1883].

25. Brahms to Simrock [7 November 1883]; Šourek, *Život a dílo Antonína Dvořáka*, vol. 2, p. 188; and Kalbeck, *Johannes Brahms*, vol. 3, p. 413. The Brahms letter to Simrock says that Dvořák will conduct his symphony in Budapest after the concert and implies that he will travel there in Dvořák's company, but Dvořák did not in fact travel to Hungary at this time.

26. Dvořák to Simrock, 1 January 1884. Also Šourek, *Život a dílo Antonína Dvořáka*, vol. 2, p. 189, and Florence May, *The Life of Johannes Brahms*, 2d ed. (London, n.d.), p. 575.

27. See also Dvořák's letter to Simrock of 6 December and Brahms's letter to Simrock [9 December 1887].

28. Dvořák to Simrock, 28 June 1889; also Šourek, *Život a dílo Antonína Dvořáka*, vol. 2, p. 337.

29. Clapham, "Dvořák's Relations with Brahms and Hanslick," p. 249.

30. There is no record of further Dvořák proof corrections by Brahms in 1895, but early in 1896 (curiously, after Dvořák's return to Europe) Brahms corrected the *Te Deum* and the Cello Concerto (see his letter to Simrock [27 January 1896]), and it appears that he corrected some further unspecified music of Dvořák later in the same year (see letters to Simrock [17 April 1896] and [28 September 1896]).

31. Brahms had given Simrock a glowing report on this performance in a letter of 21 December 1894. It is unclear here whether Dvořák means that the piece was not rejected, as his compositions often were; or that, as so often with his pieces, it was not rejected. The original German: "Ich lese soeben in den Wiener Zeitungen, daß Richter die 'Karneval' Ouvertüre am 9. Dezember gespielt hat und nicht wie so oft—meine Komp[osition] abgelehnt wurde." Dvořák's reception in Vienna had had its ups and downs.

32. As described in Dvořák's letter to Simrock of 29 March 1895. See also Heuberger (18 March 1895), p. 78.

33. Brahms's letter to Viktor von Miller, 15 February 1896, in Kalbeck, *Johannes Brahms*, vol. 4, p. 427. Facsimile in *Ein Brahms Bilder-Buch* (Vienna, 1905), p. 59.

34. Brahms reported this in his letter to Simrock [16 December 1895], and on 30 December Johann Fuchs wrote to Dvořák saying he had heard from Brahms that Dvořák intended to move, and offering him a position as teacher of composition at the Vienna Conservatory. See the letter cited by Klaus Döge in *Dvořák: Leben, Werke, Dokumente* (Mainz, 1991), p. 291, from unpublished material.

35. The source usually cited for this information is a reminiscence by Josef Suk, "Aus meiner Jugend: Wiener Brahms-Erinnerungen," in *Der Merker* (1910). Suk's account contains some important discrepancies with known facts, but Eduard Hanslick published a cryptic anecdote in 1899 that seems to confirm the gist of the story. See Hanslick's "Memories and Letters," trans. Susan Gillespie, in *Brahms and His World*, ed. Walter Frisch (Princeton, 1990), p. 181.

36. Altmann, "Antonín Dvořák im Verkehr mit Fritz Simrock," p. 147. Dvořák's letters from after 1895 have not yet been published in the collected *Korespondence a dokumenty*.

37. 19 March 1897. Altmann, "Antonín Dvořák im Verkehr mit Fritz Simrock," p. 147.

38. Related to his friend Gänsbacher as they entered the concert hall on 7 March 1879, where Brahms's own Fourth Symphony was to be played as well! In May, *The Life of Johannes Brahms*, p. 282. The word "man" is according to May's translation; Brahms probably used the word *Mensch*, which more literally would mean "human being."

39. As cited by Döge, *Dvořák: Leben, Werke, Dokumente*, p. 172.

40. See especially Hartmut Schick, *Studien zu Dvořáks Streichquartetten* (Heidelberg, 1990), vol. 17 of the *Neue Heidelberger Studien zur Musikwissenschaft*, ed. Ludwig Finscher and Reinhold Hammerstein; and David Beveridge, "Romantic Ideas in a Classical Frame: The Sonata Forms of Dvořák" (Ph.D. dissertation, University of California, Berkeley, 1980).

41. Otakar Šourek, *Život a dílo Antonína Dvořáka*, vol. 1, 3d ed. (Prague, 1954), p. 287.

42. "Franz Schubert," by Antonín Dvořák (in cooperation with Henry T. Finck), in John Clapham, *Antonín Dvořák: Musician and Craftsman* (New York, 1966), pp. 296–305, reprinted from the *Century Illustrated Monthly Magazine* (July 1894).

43. *Život a dílo Antonína Dvořáka*, vol. 1, p. 317.

44. See Alfred Orel, "Johannes Brahms' Musikbibliothek," in Kurt Hofmann, *Die Bibliothek von Johannes Brahms* (Hamburg, 1974).

45. Related in person to the cellist Hausmann, who then conveyed it independently to Florence May and Donald Francis Tovey. These two writers reported it in almost the same words; the version here is from May, *The Life of Johannes Brahms*, p. 663.

46. See Michael Beckerman, "Dvořák and Brahms: A Question of Influence," *American Brahms Society Newsletter* 4, no. 2 (Autumn 1986); David Bev-

eridge, "Vliv Antonína Dvořáka na Johannese Brahmse," trans. Jitka Slav-íková, *Hudební rozhledy* 44, no. 3 (April 1991): 35–37; and David Beveridge, "Echoes of Dvořák in the Third Symphony of Brahms," in *Musik des Ostens*, vol. 11 (Marburg, 1989), pp. 221–30.

47. Louis Ehlert's letter to Dvořák expressing his own and Brahms's opinion, 31 July 1883. See *Antonín Dvořák: Korespondence a dokumenty*, vol. 1, p. 359, n. 4.

48. *Dvořák: Leben, Werke, Dokumente*, p. 179.

49. *Essays in Musical Analysis*, vol. 2 (London, 1936), p. 96.

50. From his pupil Josef Michl, as cited by Klaus Döge in *Dvořák: Leben, Werke, Dokumente*, p. 178. Döge points out that this philosophy essentially dupli-cates that expressed by Brahms himself to his friend Georg Henschel.

51. Clapham, *Antonín Dvořák: Musician and Craftsman*, p. 113; Hans-Hubert Schoenzeler, *Dvořák* (London, 1984), p. 106.

52. *The Unknown Brahms: His Life, Character, and Works* (New York, 1933), p. 74.

53. Kann, Robert A., *A History of the Habsburg Empire, 1526–1918* (Berkeley and Los Angeles, 1974), p. 361.

54. Kalbeck's annotations to letters from Brahms to Simrock [25 February 1883] and from Elisabet von Herzogenberg to Brahms of 1 October 1883. For the latter, see *Johannes Brahms in Briefwechsel mit Heinrich und Elisabet von Her-zogenberg*, vol. 2 (Berlin, 1907), p. 8.

55. Ibid.

56. See "Discussing the Indisputable: Taste and Nationalism in Late Eighteenth-Century German Music Criticism," an unpublished paper read at the annual meeting of the Southern Chapter of the American Musicological Society, New Orleans, 27 February 1993.

57. "Zur Vermittlung und Aufnahme des tschechischen Literaturguts im deutschsprachigen Gebiet in der 2. Hälfte des 19. Jahrhunderts," *Zeitschrift für Slawistik* 7 (1962): 7–23, as cited by Peter Petersen, "Brahms und Dvořák," p. 126.

58. Petersen, ibid.

Dvořák and the New World:

A Concentrated Moment

JOSEPH HOROWITZ

Though little remembered today, even by musicians, Dvořák's New York was a world music capital. A century ago, the New York Philharmonic enjoyed unprecedented artistic and financial prosperity. The Metropolitan Opera had entered its "Golden Age." New York was inundated with phenomenal vocalists and instrumentalists. Its orchestras and opera houses eagerly presented important premieres. As never since, music was central to the city's intellectual culture at large. Concert-giving and operagoing were, more than rites of habit, a necessary response to aesthetic urges and emotional needs.

Three individuals—Anton Seidl, Jeanette Thurber, and Henry Edward Krehbiel—collectively suggest the reasons that New York stirred and seduced Dvořák.

Seidl, born in Budapest in 1850, was one of the leading conductors of the late nineteenth century. For a dozen years following his arrival in 1885, he was New York's most influential musician. At the Metropolitan Opera, he presided over six historic German-language seasons, during which the German ensemble arguably surpassed any in Europe. With the New York Philharmonic, at the Brooklyn Academy, at Coney Island's Brighton Beach resort, he was also New York's leading concert conductor. The most important musician ever to visit the United States and stay, he became an American citizen, bought a country house in the Catskills, and would not be addressed as "Herr." His "America-mania" included a fondness for mixed drinks and excited approbation of the prospective Spanish-American War. He befriended Edward MacDowell, and—in an excess of partisanship for the Wagner

The author wishes to thank Michael Beckerman for referring him to pertinent articles and letters of Dvořák and Henry Krehbiel.

cause he extolled—called the American composer greater than Brahms. He championed opera in English as a necessary step toward the production of important American operas. He called for an elaborate system of musical education to counteract the harmful influence of itinerant foreign artists. A suitable opera school, he wrote, "would keep at home those young musicians"—not only singers but conductors and instrumentalists—"who annually go abroad to study."[1] Seidl himself embarked on a Wagnerian music drama, to a libretto in English, based on the Hiawatha legend. His goal for the United States was a "national music," "an individual musical art."

If Seidl's opera school never materialized, its nearest equivalent was Jeanette Thurber's New York–based National Conservatory of Music, where Seidl taught conducting. Thurber was a visionary. No less than Seidl, she dreamed of rescuing American music from possessive European parents. Her wealthy husband, the food merchant Francis Beattie Thurber, sympathized. With his financial help, she had in 1885 established the American Opera Company—an opera-in-English venture designed to subvert the snob appeal of Old World divas and foreign tongues. Emphasizing American singers, affordable ticket prices, and integrated musical theater, the American Opera Company survived for two hectically administered yet artistically rewarding seasons. Much longer-lived was the National Conservatory, begun the same year. Having attended the Paris Conservatory herself, Thurber poured time and money into creating a thorough music school for Americans. In addition to Seidl, the faculty included the pianist Rafael Joseffy (himself a student of Moscheles and Tausig), the composers Horatio Parker (later dean of the School of Music at Yale) and Rubin Goldmark (later head of the composition department at Juilliard), and the influential critics James Gibbons Huneker (who taught piano) and Henry Finck (who taught music history).

Thurber's agenda stressed the self-sufficiency of an American musical education. She espoused an American idiom based on native sources. She offered scholarships for women, minorities, and the handicapped. African-Americans were prominent students at every level of study. Campaigning for a Congressional charter, she gave a concert of works by Americans, including Dudley Buck and John Knowles Paine. Enactment of this unusual legislation, in 1891, was heralded as a landmark commitment to American art. Thurber's personal charm played no small role in winning these and other victories. "She was a picturesque woman," Huneker would recall. "She spoke French like a Parisian, and . . . I confess that her fine, dark eloquent eyes troubled my peace more than once."[2]

New York's central arbiter of musical taste, and the acknowledged dean of American music critics, was Henry Krehbiel of the *Tribune*. He was one of Anton Seidl's few intimate friends. Like Seidl, with whom he conversed in German, he paid complex dual allegiance to the Old World of Beethoven and Wagner and a new world of American musical prospects. Like Seidl and Thurber (whose opera company he accurately faulted for poor management and for the "impudent exaggeration" of its "claims to excellence"), he advocated opera in English as one component of an integrated musical theater contradicting meretricious vocal glamour. Opera in the United States, he wrote, would remain "experimental" until "the vernacular becomes the language of the performances and native talent provides both works and interpreters"; it would remain "an exotic" until "it becomes a national expression in art, using the vernacular and giving utterance to national ideals."[3]

In common with Seidl and Thurber, Krehbiel embraced contemporary notions of cultural nationalism. He maintained that a nation's highest expression in art, music, and literature was to some degree a function of "race": "Like tragedy in its highest conception, music is of all times and all peoples; but the more the world comes to realize how deep and intimate are the springs from which the emotional element of music flows, the more fully will it recognize that originality and power in the composer rest upon the use of dialects and idioms which are national or racial in origin and structure."[4] An autodidact of vast erudition, Krehbiel made himself a virtual ethnomusicologist. Documenting the relationship of folk song to national schools of composition, he researched and wrote about the folk music of Magyars, Slavs, Scandinavians, Russians, Orientals, and Native Americans. Of special interest are his findings regarding "Afro-American folk songs," which he began publishing in the *Tribune* in 1899 and which in 1914 generated a 155-page book—not a vague armchair rumination but a closely argued report packed with scrutiny of modes, rhythms, and the like. Krehbiel hoped America's composers would appropriate plantation songs and other such tunes, and he rebuked as "ungenerous and illiberal" those culture-bearers who balked at equating "negro" and "American."[5]

Enter Dvořák. Jeanette Thurber was the agent of his coming. The first director of the National Conservatory, the baritone Jacques Bouy (who created the role of Escamillo), had returned to Paris in 1889. Thurber needed an eminent replacement. Dvořák was not only eminent; with his rustic roots and egalitarian temperament, he was the kind of cultural nationalist to inspire Americans. She offered him $15,000 for each of two years. When Dvořák declined she went into high gear, besieging him with letters and emissaries until he capitulated. Dvořák arrived in New York on 27 September 1892, the most prominent composer ever to take up a teaching post in the United States. He proved inquisitive and empathetic, as eager to learn as to teach. His aspirations for American music resonated with the hopes of Thurber, Seidl, and Krehbiel. A concerted mandate was mutually pursued.

.

The climactic moment in Dvořák's American career came on 16 December 1893—the premiere of his "New World" Symphony at Carnegie Music Hall, with Seidl leading the New York Philharmonic. The concert was the most famous the Philharmonic gave during Seidl's tenure. The symphony is the most famous encapsulation of Dvořák's agenda for America.

As early as September 1892—the month Dvořák arrived aboard the S.S. Saale—Krehbiel wrote in *Century Magazine*: "In Dvořák and his works is to be found a twofold encouragement for the group of native musicians whose accomplishments of late have seemed to herald the rise of a school of American composers . . . There is measureless comfort in the prospect which the example of Dvořák has opened up."[6] The following month, at Carnegie Music Hall, the National Conservatory honored Dvořák at a concert including Liszt's *Tasso*, conducted by Seidl, and Dvořák's *Te Deum*, conducted by Dvořák. Krehbiel wrote in the *Tribune* that Dvořák "found ready to greet him an assemblage that crowded the splendid concert room and entered with fervor into the spirit of the unique occasion. . . . nearly all of the musicians of note in the city were present." Krehbiel's American pride, which frequently suffered outrage in the face of European neglect, spurred him also to observe that

> the eminent musician who has cast his lot temporarily with us had no cause to question the sincerity and heartiness of the welcome which was extended to him and less to be dissatisfied with the manner in which his music was performed. It is a question whether he has ever stood before an orchestra that was quicker in understanding his wishes, or more willing and able to fulfil them than the eighty men in the band last night, the great majority of whom belonged to Mr. Seidl's metropolitan organization. In respect of ability to read and grasp the contents of new music, the orchestral players of New-York may truthfully be said to be without peers.[7]

In fact, no less than Seidl before him, Dvořák swiftly absorbed what musical New York had to offer. In subsequent concerts, twice leading his Symphony no. 7 in D minor (Op. 70), he had occasion to test Seidl's conviction that New York's pool of superb orchestral musicians surpassed that of any European city. He also led his *Requiem* with Artur Nikisch's magnificent Boston Symphony. Meanwhile, his frequent visitors at his home on East Seventeenth Street included the twenty-five-year-old Harry Burleigh. Attracted by Jeanette Thurber's scholarships for African-Americans, Burleigh had enrolled at the National Conservatory in mid-1892. Dvořák eagerly absorbed the spirituals and Stephen Foster songs Burleigh sang for him; his favorites included "Swing Low, Sweet Chariot," which he seemingly adapted in the E-minor symphony he was then composing in sympathy with Thurber's suggestion that he "write a symphony embodying his experiences and feelings in America."[8] The principal subject of the slow movement—a tune so resembling a spiritual that it later, as "Goin' Home," became one—was entrusted to the English horn, whose reedy timbre, it has been suggested, resembled Burleigh's voice.

On 21 May—three days before he completed the "New World" Symphony—Dvořák was extensively quoted in the *New York Herald* in "On the Real Value of Negro Melodies." "'I am now satisfied,' he said . . . , 'that the future music of this country must be founded upon what are called the negro melodies. This must be the real foundation of any serious and original school of composition to be developed in the United States. When I first came here last year I was impressed with this idea and it has developed into a settled conviction.'" The same article cited Thurber's declaration that "The aptitude of the colored race for music, vocal and instrumental, has long been recognized, but no definite steps have hitherto been taken to develop it, and it is believed that the decision of the conservatory to move in this new direction will meet with general approval and be productive of prompt and encouraging results." On 28 May, in a letter to the *Herald*, Dvořák added, "It is to the poor that I turn for musical greatness. The poor work hard; they study seriously. . . . If in my own career I have achieved a measure of success and reward it is to some extent due to the fact I was the son of poor parents and was reared in an atmosphere of struggle and endeavour." (Krehbiel later commented that Dvořák's life had been "a story of manifest destiny, of signal triumph over obstacle and discouraging environment," that Dvořák had triumphed "by an exercise of traits of mind and character that have always been peculiarly the admiration of American manhood."[9])

On 3 June, Dvořák left New York for Spillville, Iowa, a Czech settlement where he encountered visiting Native Americans—possibly Kickapoo or Iroquois—who danced and sang. He returned to the National Conservatory the following September. In November, Seidl secured permission from Dvořák to give the first performance of the "New World" Symphony and scheduled the premiere. In preparing the piece, Seidl formed the opinion that the second movement expressed homesickness for Bohemia. And his languid tempo may have been the reason Dvořák changed the marking from "Larghetto" to "Largo."

Krehbiel hailed the new symphony in a 2,500-word article in the *Tribune* on 15 December. At the time (as Michael Beckerman has ascertained), Krehbiel and Dvořák were constantly in touch. Krehbiel spoke for them both when he wrote, in his article,

> That which is most characteristic, most beautiful and most vital in our folk-song has come from the negro slaves of the South, partly because those slaves lived in the period of emotional, intellectual and social development which produces folk-song, partly because they lived a life that prompted utterance in song and partly because as a race the negroes are musical by nature. Being musical and living a life that has in it romantic elements of pleasure as well as suffering, they gave expression to those elements in songs which reflect their original nature as modified by their American environment.[10]

In the ensuing exegesis, Krehbiel explored "negro" and "American" traits of the new work. He also remarked that "if there is anything Indian about Dr. Dvořák's symphony it is only in the mood inspired by the contemplation of Indian legend and romance, and that is outside the sphere of this discussion." By this he apparently meant that Dvořák relied on no vernacular specimens. An article in the *Herald* the same day cited Dvořák's own testimony that his second and third movements were influenced by Longfellow's *The Song of Hiawatha*, which he had first encountered, in translation, thirty years before. He also indicated that he envisioned composing a Hiawatha opera or cantata. (In fact, Thurber secured permission from Alice M. Longfellow for Dvořák to use the poem.[11] But Dvořák progressed less far on his Hiawatha project than Seidl did on his; according to Huneker, Seidl managed to finish one act of music before his death.[12])

A "public rehearsal" (actually, a first performance) of the "New World" Symphony took place on 15 December. For the formal premiere the following evening, Dvořák was present. After the second movement, the packed house erupted in applause. Seidl turned to gesture toward Dvořák's box. "Every neck was craned so that it might be discovered to whom he was motioning so energetically," reported the *Herald*:

> Whoever it was, he seemed modestly to wish to remain at the back of the box on the second tier.
>
> At last a broad shouldered individual of medium height, and as straight as one of the pines in the forests of which his music whispered so eloquently, is descried by the eager watchers. A murmur sweeps through the hall. "Dvořák! Dvořák!" is the word that passes from mouth to mouth. . . .
>
> With hands trembling with emotion Dr. Dvořák waves an acknowledgement of his indebtedness to Anton Seidl, to the orchestra, to the audience, and then disappears into the background while the remainder of the work goes on . . . At its close the composer was loudly called for. Again and again he bowed his acknowledgements, and again and again the applause burst forth.
>
> Even after he had left his box and was walking about in the corridor the applause continued. And finally he returned to the gallery railing, and then what a reception he received! The musicians, led by Mr. Seidl, applauded until the place rang again.[13]

The critic—presumably Albert Steinberg, like Krehbiel a close friend of Seidl—called the work itself "a great one" and distinctively American in flavor. Krehbiel, in the *Tribune*, decreed it "a lovely triumph" and wrote of the new symphony's indebtedness to African-American song. A signature trait of both reviews—and of others in the daily press—was the detailed description of musical content. Of the *Herald* critic's twenty-six paragraphs, twelve analyzed Dvořák's idiom (the flatted seventh tone of his scale, etc.), his folk sources, and his rhythms and harmonies, instrumentation, and structure. To the performance of the new work, the *Herald* critic allotted a single sentence, terming it "most poetical." He dispatched the remainder of the program with a sentence reading: "The orchestra played the 'Midsummer Night's Dream' music, and Henri Marteau played Brahm's [*sic*] violin concerto with an original cadenza by himself." This eager concentration on new music documents a moment, a century ago, when composer and audience were one.

Dvořák's example focused a debate that had grown vigorous, sophisticated, and dense. The general intellectual discourse of newspapers and magazines already routinely scrutinized America's concert and opera life, stressing issues of taste and identity. Wagnerian progress toward unified musical theater, and away from gaudy vocal display, was one frequent topic. Another concerned the proper sources of a native compositional idiom: should it be consciously nationalistic, or would some ineffable folk essence ultimately inflect American music without special effort? Rejecting Dvořák's advocacy of the first strategy, genteel critics like Boston's William Foster Apthorp and genteel composers like Boston's John Knowles Paine dismissed cultural nationalism as quasi-barbaric. In cosmopolitan New York, where Native American and African-American influences seemed more picturesque, less exogenous, the response was more favorable. Of America's composers, the prominent Indianist Arthur Farwell considered himself "the first composer in America to take up Dvořák's challenge . . . in a serious and whole-hearted way."[14] Farwell also revered Seidl, who helped guide his musical education.

Dvořák returned to Bohemia in May for the summer. He resumed his duties in New York the following October, then left the United States for good in April 1895. In addition to the "New World" Symphony, his American output included his best-known string quartet, in F major, and his best-known concerto, for cello in B minor. The latter was partly inspired by the Second Cello Concerto of Victor Herbert. Dvořák heard the premiere, performed by the composer with Seidl conducting the New York Philharmonic, in March 1894. Herbert was Seidl's principal cellist and sometime assistant conductor. He eventually wrote an opera, *Natoma* (1911), on Native American themes. As an important conductor of the Pittsburgh Orchestra and of his own Victor Herbert Orchestra, he was a Seidl protégé.

To what degree Dvořák's compositional style was influenced by his American stay is a good question. Though his kinship to Brahms is often contemplated, in New York Dvořák did not seem Brahmsian. Seidl, who dismissed Brahms much as Hugo Wolf did in Vienna, renewed Dvořák's interest in Wagner. Michael Beckerman argues that the "New World" Symphony, with its programmatic complexion, represents a turning point toward the tone poems and operas Dvořák later composed. Like the "American" String Quartet, this last Dvořák symphony eschews the denser motivic and contrapuntal interplay of earlier, more Brahmsian works. It was in America, too, that Dvořák, assisted by the Wagnerite critic Henry Finck, authored an essay on Schubert whose seven references to Wagner compare to only three to Brahms. Here, he favorably compares the "weird" harmonies of "Der Döppelgänger" to Ortrud's scenes in *Lohengrin*; he stresses the "deep pathos" of Schubert's Fourth Symphony (!), anticipating "the anguish of Tristan's utterances; nor is this the only place wherein Schubert is prophetic of Wagnerian harmonies"; he comments that Schubert likewise anticipates Wagner for employing "the brass, not for noise, but, played softly, to secure rich and warm tints"; he likens the "powerful emotional effects" of Schubert's modulations in his "later songs," and the aversion to "word-repetitions," to Wagner; and—citing *Tannhäuser* and, especially, *Parsifal* (which Seidl considered Wagner's magnum opus)—he ranks Wagner with Palestrina and Bach as one of the three composers "who have been most successful in revealing the inmost spirit of religious music."[15]

Dvořák's final thoughts about "Music in America" were published in *Harper's* in February 1895. He praised musical Americans for their aptitude and enthusiasm but lamented the absence of governmental support for musical instruction and performance. He castigated the Metropolitan Opera as a company that "only the upper classes can hear or understand" and called for "opera companies where native singers can be heard, and where the English tongue is sung." Seidl, Krehbiel, and Thurber equally understood that, otherwise, no important American operas would be written. No less than Dvořák, who avoided the Met as a rich man's preserve, Seidl, Krehbiel, and Thurber impugned operatic tinsel and glamour. Krehbiel complained of the "domination of fashion instead of love for art," Seidl of "the rich who [regard] music as a mere diversion.[16] Both Seidl and Krehbiel profoundly comprehended, with Dvořák, that reliance on vast individual wealth ultimately acted to discourage an indigenous musical high culture.

That this mattered to Dvořák—that, like Seidl, he was no mere interloper—was a crucial source of American gratitude and affection. Far more typical was the case of the next major European composer to take an American position: Gustav Mahler, who during his years with the Met and the New York Philharmonic (1907–11) summered at home in Europe, and for whom the composition of a "New World" Symphony would have been unthinkable. In decades to come, an army of important Europeans followed, ranging in attitude from Ernst Křenek, who held American culture in something like contempt, to Kurt Weill, who refused to speak German from the day he arrived. Most of the prominent immigrant composers were modernists for whom cultural nationalism—and, concomitantly, the search for an American idiom—was passé. Few and far between were such New World portraits as Ernest Bloch's *America: An Epic Rhapsody* (1928), Paul Hindemith's "Pittsburgh" Symphony (1958), and Darius Milhaud's *A Frenchman in New York* (1962). Even had they been more musically distinguished, these contributions could not possibly have made such a formidable impact as had Dvořák's famous symphony. After World War I, classical music in the United States was increasingly marginalized by popular culture. At the same time, a democratized new audience for classical music preferred canonized European masters to contemporary or American creators.[17] The quest for a distinctly American musical high culture would never again be the consolidated priority it seemed to Dvořák, Seidl, Krehbiel, and Thurber, and their readers, listeners, and students.

Seidl did not long survive Dvořák's leave-taking from America; he died in 1898 at the age of forty-seven. His final season with the New York Philharmonic included performances of the "New World" Symphony. He had earlier repeated the work with the Philharmonic in 1894 and had introduced it to Brooklyn to great acclaim. Krehbiel once wrote to Dvořák that he had "had no greater happiness from 20 years of labor on behalf of good music than has come to me from the consciousness that I may have been to some degree instrumental in helping the public to appreciate your compositions, and especially the ["New World"] Symphony."[18] Following Seidl's death, and the onset of twentieth-century fragmentation, Krehbiel gradually lost enthusiasm for New York's world of music; he died dispirited in 1923.[19] Thurber wrote in 1919 that "in looking back over my 35 years of activity as President of the National Conservatory of Music of America there is nothing I am so proud of as having been able to bring Dr. Dvořák to America."[20] Her school never regained the dominant role it enjoyed during Dvořák's directorship. It was declared officially defunct in 1952, six years after Thurber's death at the age of ninety-five.

For general background, see Joseph Horowitz, *Wagner Nights: An American History* (Berkeley and Los Angeles, forthcoming). For background on Anton Seidl, see Henry Finck, ed., *Anton Seidl: A Memorial by His Friends* (New York, 1899; reprint, 1983). For background on Jeanette Thurber, see Emanuel Rubin, "Jeanette Meyers Thurber and the National Conservatory of Music," *American Music* (Fall 1990).

NOTES

1. Anton Seidl, "The Development of Music in America," reprinted in Henry Finck, ed., *Anton Seidl: A Memorial by His Friends* (New York, 1899; reprint, 1983), pp. 206–9.

2. James Gibbons Huneker, *Steeplejack*, vol. 2 (New York, 1925), pp. 65–66.

3. Henry Krehbiel, *Chapters of Opera* (New York, 1909; reprint, 1980), pp. 44 and 207.

4. Henry Krehbiel, "Antonín Dvořák," *Century Magazine*, September 1892.

5. Henry Krehbiel, *Afro-American Folksongs: A Study in Racial and National Music* (New York, 1911), p. vii. Krehbiel deplored ragtime, however, as a gross popularization that nevertheless proved "that a marvelous potency lies in the characteristic rhythmical element of the slave songs." He came to associate jazz with "negro brothels of the south" and affirmed that it encouraged instrumental techniques—"unnatural contortion of the lips and forcing of the breath"—unsuited to the higher purposes he wished African-American music to serve. See ibid., p. v.

6. Krehbiel, "Antonín Dvořák."

7. *New York Tribune*, 22 October 1892. Seidl's "metropolitan organization" is presumably the Metropolitan Orchestra, as his free-lance ensemble was sometimes called—a group whose membership overlapped that of the German-wing Metropolitan Opera Orchestra that Seidl also conducted.

8. Jeanette Thurber, "Dvořák as I Knew Him," *Etude*, November 1919.

9. Henry Krehbiel, "Antonín Dvořák."

10. This article, with commentary, has been reprinted in "Henry Krehbiel, Antonín Dvořák, and the Symphony 'From the New World,'" *Notes* 49, no. 2 (December 1992): 447–73. [Ed.]

11. Thurber, "Dvořák as I Knew Him."

12. *Musical Courier*, 6 April 1898. Following a suggestion by Krehbiel, Seidl's opera started not with Longfellow's version of the Hiawatha story but with the Iroquois legend connecting Hiawatha with the founding of the Confederacy of the Five Nations. The result would be an operatic trilogy, an "American *Nibelungenlied*." Seidl procured examples of Indian music from Krehbiel. His librettist was Francis Nielson, later the stage manager at Covent Garden. Curiously, in his article "Wagner's Influence on Present-Day Composers" (*North American Review*, January 1894), Seidl commented regarding the United States that "this country is so young that its history does not afford material for great conceptions as do the European countries, rich in legend and tradition. One might go for material back to the Indians, but it would be pretty thin; it would be lacking in those majestic elements which Wagner found in the Norse legends."

13. *New York Herald*, 17 December 1893.

14. Evelyn Davis Culbertson, "Arthur Farwell's Early Efforts on Behalf of American Music," *American Music*, Summer 1987.

15. Antonín Dvořák, "Franz Schubert," *Century Magazine*, July 1894. Also suggestive is Krehbiel's comment, in the *New York Tribune* of 13 January 1894, that the Op. 96 Quartet and Op. 97 Quintet were composed in a transparent style "in order that the composers, who may undertake to work on the lines which [Dvořák] has marked out, may have the clearest model before them."

16. Krehbiel, *Chapters of Opera*, p. 207. Finck, ed., *Anton Seidl: A Memorial by His Friends*, p. 209.

17. For the impact of a "new audience," see Joseph Horowitz, *Understanding Toscanini: How He Became an American Culture-God and Helped Create a New Audience for Old Music* (New York, 1987).

18. Letter from Krehbiel to Dvořák, 16 December 1893, cited in Michael Beckerman's "Dvořák's 'New World' Largo," in *19th-Century Music* (Summer 1992).

19. Krehbiel's swan song for the *New York Tribune*, on 11 February 1923, was "The Curse of Affectation and Modernism in Music."

20. Thurber, "Dvořák as I Knew Him."

Dvořák: The Operas

JAN SMACZNY

Dvořák and Opera

In an interview given two months before his death, Dvořák expressed the view that his "main inclination was towards dramatic composition."[1] He also stated that he was turning down requests for chamber works from his publisher, Simrock, and that he had demonstrated years before that his main interest was in opera rather than in symphonic music. This was not the maverick boast of a composer secure in his reputation wanting to surprise the musical public; Dvořák spoke in such terms only slightly more than three weeks before the premiere of his eleventh opera, *Armida*.[2] He had been engaged in operatic projects since the completion of *Alfred* (at that stage unknown) in 1870 and was, by the end of the century, the most popular Czech opera composer after Smetana.

The view that he was principally an instrumental composer had been promulgated as early as 1879. In a survey of Czech music in the periodical *Dalibor*, the critic V. V. Zelený advanced the opinion that "although Dvořák has augmented the number of Czech operas in this period with *Vanda* and currently, in particular, the comic opera *The Cunning Peasant*, and will doubtless contribute more, his particular strength lies in instrumental composition."[3] Emanuel Chvála echoed Zelený in a more extensive survey of Czech music in the twenty-five years from the opening of the Prague Provisional Theater.[4] Concentrating mainly on Dvořák's instrumental music, he concluded that the composer represented the "prototype of the absolute musician" whose gifts were ideally suited to chamber and symphonic music, as opposed to Smetana, who was "a poet, a composer of program music, a composer for words, of poetic notions; an artist and a tone poet."[5] This clear division between the absolute and the programmatic and poetic is reflected in later writing on Dvořák.

Dvořák's personality may account in part for this anomaly. At a time when the consideration of the nature of national opera was rife and polemic on the subject, a regular part of the musical life of Prague, Dvořák remained silent. He was not by inclination a writer, and he made no journalistic contribution to Czech musical periodicals. Even his letters reveal a minimal discussion of the nature of opera. Nor was he politically inclined. Although Dvořák was prepared to state that he "considered opera to be the most suitable form for the nation"[6] his enthusiasm seems to have arisen from the breadth of the audience available rather than from the belief that opera made a specific statement.

Dvořák's choice of subject matter in his serious operas must also have looked a little strange. Although his comic operas fit more-or-less into the tradition that emerged after Smetana's *The Bartered Bride* and Vilém Blodek's *In the Well*,[7] Dvořák's grand operas stand oblique to the work of many of his contemporaries. Where Šebor, Bendl, Smetana, and Fibich were prepared to take the subject matter for a number of their serious operas from Czech history and mythology—in the case of Smetana, all his serious operas derive from this source—Dvořák searched beyond the bounds of his native land. Thus his first two grand operas, *Vanda* and *Dimitrij*, look to Poland and Russia respectively, while *Armida*, his last, eschews even Slavic subjects in favor of the exotic and oriental. Dvořák's belief in and love for his nation cannot be held in any doubt. His correspondence with his Berlin publisher, Fritz Simrock, offers abundant evidence of a profound affinity for his native land that is best exemplified by the following, which amounts almost to a personal artistic credo:

> Still what have we two to do with politics—let us be happy that we can give our service in the cause of beautiful art!
>
> And nations which possess and represent art will, we hope, never perish, no matter how small they are!
>
> Forgive me but I wanted to tell you that an artist also has a native land in which he must have faith and a warm heart.[8]

For some, however, warmth of feeling for his native land did not make up for an apparent lack of involvement with the national cause. Born a generation after Smetana, Dvořák harbored aspirations that are best described as national rather than nationalist. A virtuoso ability to handle an eclectic operatic style coupled with a refusal to adopt wholesale a progressive stance, unlike his younger contemporary Fibich, put Dvořák beyond the pale for some influential authorities. The important critic Zdeněk Nejedlý's kindest comment on Dvořák is to be found in the preface to a book entitled *Modern Czech Opera*: "The operas of A.

Dvořák are, however, such a complicated phenomenon that it is necessary to exclude them entirely, since detailed comment alone would occupy an entire book."[9] Elsewhere Nejedlý was less circumspect, stating baldly that "Dvořák negates the development of Czech opera."[10]

Less virulent, though still somewhat puzzled, was the reaction of Otakar Hostinský, who produced the first extensive consideration of Dvořák's operas.[11] From the perspective of slightly more than five years after Dvořák's death, the composer remained unclassifiable as an opera composer in the Czech tradition. Hostinský concluded that despite the musical virtues of Dvořák's operas, they lacked a true dramatic sense—although he did concede that this was in part because of the nature of the libretti he used. Doubtless, part of the problem perceived by commentators was that Dvořák did not follow a predictable path in his operatic output, nor did he respond to contemporary trends in Czech opera. As has been noted, Dvořák was the only major composer working in the Provisional and National Theaters who did not compose a serious opera to a subject from Czech history or mythology. In the 1890s, when Bendl and Rozkošný, two composers of the older generation who had worked in the Provisional Theater in the late 1860s and 1870s, were turning to *verista* subject matter, Dvořák stayed aloof.[12] His use of material from folklore in *The Devil and Kate* and *Rusalka* in the late 1890s was also atypical of the contemporary repertoire, as was the use in *Armida* of the archaic conventions of grand opera. Dvořák's independence from contemporary fashion did not, however, necessarily imply that he did not have a consistent approach to opera. Hostinský was an avowed progressive who had supplied Fibich with the libretto of *The Bride of Messina*,[13] the first and only thoroughgoing attempt at a Czech Wagnerian music drama, and his view of Dvořák was compromised by his inability to locate him in a progressive context. For the Czech critical establishment Dvořák was an awkward anomaly who stood outside the norm: whereas program music was the expected path for orchestral music after Smetana, Dvořák produced some of the finest abstract symphonies and chamber works of the century; whereas Smetana glorified Czech dance, Dvořák cast more broadly through the Slavonic repertoire; and when Dvořák did explore the symphonic poem in later years he did not turn to the mythologically heroic but took his inspiration from the heartwarming, occasionally sinister ballads of Erben. For those inclined to scoff—and Nejedlý turned his antipathy toward Dvořák almost into a career—there was the inescapable fact that Dvořák was sensationally popular both during his life and after. His operas may not have been the most obviously, nationalistically Czech of the late nineteenth century, but a handful were enormously popular in their day and have remained an intrinsic part of the repertoire in his native land. Nejedlý could fulminate to his heart's content about Dvořák's *Rusalka*, but his critical efforts could not prevent the work from rivaling Smetana's *The Bartered Bride* as the most popular Czech opera ever composed. *The Jacobin* and *The Devil and Kate* are also frequently performed, and even *Armida* and *Dimitrij* are beginning to show signs of returning to the repertoire. Dvořák's operatic Odyssey may be a personal one that owes only sporadic allegiance to native tradition, but it makes a fascinating and individual story, rising from obscurity, progressing steadily toward the heights of achievement, and ending equivocally with the unsatisfactory debut of *Armida*.

The Operas

Opera was the natural vehicle for a Czech composer in the 1860s and 1870s. The opening of the Prague Provisional Theater[14] on 18 November 1862 for the performance of plays and operas in Czech was the crucial factor in initiating the operatic wing of the national revival. Embarrassingly, there was no obvious Czech opera of sufficient grandeur available for the opening of the Provisional Theater. Thus, the first opera to be given in the new theater was Cherubini's *Les deux journées*.[15] This was followed some three weeks later by František Škroup's modest Singspiel *The Tinker*.[16] The first opera to be given in the Provisional Theater by a living Czech composer was Skuherský's *Vladimír, God's Chosen One*,[17] and yet originally this had been written to a German libretto.

The native repertoire developed slowly, and it was not until the second half of the 1860s that it gained a sure foothold with the works of Šebor and Smetana. Šebor's *The Templars in Moravia*[18] was premiered on 19 October 1865 and was the first serious opera by a Czech composer to a Czech libretto to be given in the theater. *The Templars* was given five performances over the next year but was eclipsed in popularity by Smetana's first opera, *The Brandenburgers in Bohemia*,[19] which was premiered on 5 January 1866 and received thirteen performances in its first year alone. Smetana had written his opera in response to a competition set up by Count Jan Harrach in 1861, designed to create new works for the Provisional Theater. Harrach's competition must have seemed a disappointment. Apart from Smetana's *Brandenburgers*, the only entry to appear on the Provisional Theater stage was a libretto by František Šír, *Drahomíra*, which was eventually set by Šebor and premiered on 20 September 1867. By then the *Templars* and *Branden-*

burgers had been joined by Smetana's *Bartered Bride*[20] and Jan Nepomuk Škroup's *The Swedes in Prague*.[21] Over the next few years the Czech repertoire grew steadily, fortified by works from Blodek, Bendl, Vojáček, Měchura, Rozkošný, and Hřímalý, as well as new operas by Smetana, Šebor, and Skuherský. By the time Dvořák and Fibich made their debut in the Provisional Theater—Fibich beat Dvořák to the draw by some six months[22]—the credentials of the Czech repertoire were well established.

As a viola player in the Provisional Theater orchestra from its inception in 1862 to the end of the season in July 1871, Dvořák was, of course, aware of the nature and deficiencies of Czech opera as it developed. He also fell under the influence of the many non-Czech composers whose works made up the vast majority of the repertoire.

Translations of Italian, French, and German opera into Czech had been common enough in Prague even before the opening of the Provisional Theater. In the years leading up to its opening, performances of plays and operas in Czech were allowed in the German Theater[23] at Sunday matinees and occasionally on weekdays, usually Thursdays. In the first fourteen months of the Provisional Theater's existence there was a marked trend toward Italian opera, starting with two performances of Bellini's *I Capuletti e i Montecchi* in December 1862 and January 1863. Rossini and Donizetti took the lead, however, during 1863 with *Il barbiere di Siviglia* and *Otello*, and *Lucrezia Borgia* and *Belisario*, respectively. French opera was represented by a broader range of composers, including Auber, Halévy, Méhul, Meyerbeer, Boieldieu, and Offenbach. Balfe's *Bohemian Girl* enjoyed a brief vogue in 1863–64 with nine performances, although its title was discreetly changed to *Cikánka* (The Gypsy Girl). German opera was represented by Mozart, Weber, Lortzing, and Flotow. Verdi had entered the repertoire in 1863 with *Il trovatore*, which was joined in 1864 by *Rigoletto*, affirming a slight bias that year toward Italian opera (sixty-two performances, as opposed to only fifty-five performances of French operas). Seven of these were of Offenbach's *Orphée aux enfers*. In 1865 Italian opera maintained its hold on the repertoire, with Verdi outstripping his countrymen with twenty performances to Donizetti's seventeen, Bellini's eleven, and Rossini's five. French grand opera had been growing in popularity, and the eleven performances of operas by Meyerbeer rose to sixteen in 1865. Performances of the operettas by Offenbach and Hérold were also on the increase.

The arrival of Smetana as musical director of the Provisional Theater, in succession to Jan Maýr, in September 1866 secured the position of French grand opera, and even after his withdrawal from the theater in 1874, as a result of deafness, it remained an important element in the repertoire: Meyerbeer's *Les Huguenots* and *Robert le diable*, Auber's *La Muette de Portici*, Halévy's *La Juive*, and Rossini's *Tell* led the field. Of the 196 performances of opera and operetta given in the Provisional Theater in 1882, its last complete year, 31 were French grand operas; only 23 were by the Italians Bellini, Donizetti, and Verdi. Twenty-four of the performances were accounted for by Beethoven, Flotow, Gluck, Lortzing, Mozart, and Tchaikovsky. Thirty-nine performances were of operas by Czechs. The remaining 79 were of operetta, and if Anger's *Záletníci* and Hřímalý's *Zakletý princ*, both billed as operettas, are included, close to half the performances of this last complete year of the Provisional Theater's existence were given over to operetta. This was not a novel trend. In 1872, a year in which Smetana was still musical director, 70 of the 176 performances were billed as operettas. In fact between 1870 and 1874 the most popular composer in the Provisional Theater was not Smetana or even Verdi, but Offenbach.

Italian and French opera were important to Dvořák throughout his composing career, and the background of light comic opera cannot be ignored. After all, Dvořák, along with Fibich and a number of other musicians, was prepared to put his name to a statement in support of Smetana, part of which read, "with *The Bartered Bride* he blazed a trail for Czech light opera; indeed we may say he is the creator of that genre."[24] Conspicuous by his absence from the repertoire of the Provisional Theater was the composer who remained a powerful influence on Dvořák throughout his composing career—Wagner. The presence of his harmonic style and other aspects of his musical language run like a leitmotif through the fabric of Dvořák's compositional development. At times the impact of Wagner is crystal-clear—specifically at the beginning and end of Dvořák's operatic journey—at others, however, he seems to have all but disappeared—notably in the comic operas *The Stubborn Lovers*, *The Cunning Peasant*, and the first version of *The Jacobin*.

A focus for Dvořák's early experience of Wagner was a concert conducted by the German composer on 8 February 1863 in which Dvořák played, which included the overtures to *Die Meistersinger* and *Tannhäuser* and the prelude to *Tristan*. Whether Dvořák did or did not see any of Wagner's operas in the German Theater in Prague—either is more of a possibility than a certainty—the impact of his musical style is clear in the Czech composer's first two operas. *Alfred*, his first, is also one of Dvořák's most mysterious works. There is a near-complete lack of written evidence of the work during the composer's lifetime, and although he may have shown the score to Smetana, few if any of Dvořák's friends were aware of its existence. Indeed, Dvořák seemed happy to allow the impression to be made public that *The King and the Charcoal-Burner* was his first opera.[25] The reason for this secrecy must remain a matter of speculation. It is possible, though unlikely, that Dvořák intended to offer the work to a house in Austria or Germany, though the librettist, Karl Theodor Körner (1791–1813), was a controversial figure as far as the imperial authorities were concerned. The fact that the opera's libretto was German did not necessarily disqualify it from consideration for performance in the Provisional Theater. Both the brothers Škroup had written operas in German, and three of Skuherský's German operas had been translated and performed in the theater.[26] Dvořák himself petitioned Rudolf Wirsing, the director of the Provisional Theater, in 1876 for a loan to assist in the translation of a libretto from German to Czech by the author Eduard Rüffer.[27]

Dvořák's decision to set the work of a writer who had died nearly sixty years before needs some explanation. Libretti in Prague in the late 1860s were in very short supply, and for all its archaic qualities, Körner's text contains copious instructions for the layout of the singing parts. For Dvořák, the guiding hand of a writer who was prepared to offer an "opera-by-numbers" scheme may have seemed irresistible. The subject matter of the opera, in which the gallantry and ingenuity of the oppressed Britons, led by King Alfred, turns Danish victory to defeat by the end of the third act, had genuine resonance for a Czech composer. The subject matter of a number of Czech operas had much to do with the sufferings of the Czech nation under foreign yoke.[28] As a metaphor for the oppressed Czechs, the story of *Alfred* presents few problems. Dvořák may also have been fired toward such subject matter by recent developments in the repertoire of the Provisional Theater. Verdi's *Nabucco* had been premiered on 7 December 1868, and Auber's *Gustave III* on 26 January 1869, but if any event was decisive it was most likely the revival of Smetana's *The Brandenburgers in Bohemia* in 1869, followed by a single performance on 30 January 1870.

Dvořák's willingness to follow Körner's prescription for structure in *Alfred* is tempered by a firm hand with regard to important aspects of form. The most significant of these was Dvořák's decision to bring the first act to a close at the end of the fourth scene, thus making Körner's two-act original a three-act opera.[29] The alteration makes the most of the change of scene in the original act 5, and with Dvořák taking full advantage of Körner's direction to include a "characteristic dance" in act 1, scene 3, it must have been clear to the composer that had the first act continued, it would soon have become unwieldy. On a smaller scale, there are a number of places where Dvořák made intelligent decisions regarding the dramatic impact of the text; for instance, in the first scene of the opera he elides a fragment of recitative for the Danish noble Gothron to bring it in during the arrival of the triumphant

Danish army, thus increasing the dramatic effect of the passage (example 1).

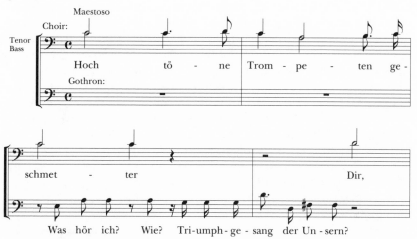

Example 1. *Alfred*, act 1, scene 1

Although Dvořák frequently resorts to Wagnerian harmony and occasional Wagnerian melodic turns, *Alfred* is not music drama. The orchestration, made perhaps with a view toward the limited resources of the Provisional Theater, is lighter than that of Wagner, and the texture does not convey the seamlessness cultivated by the German composer in his mature music dramas. Dvořák's adherence to Körner's libretto to the letter would have precluded a genuinely modern approach to the structure of the whole, but there are times when he clearly reveals a desire to unify exended passages. This tendency is strong in the first scene, in which the concluding figure of the introduction to the act is taken up as an accompaniment to the first chorus and then emerges as a punctuating and pivotal feature in the succeeding recitative for Gothron (example 2).

Example 2. *Alfred*, act 1, scene 1

Dvořák's natural tendency to think symphonically, already exercised in two symphonies and a number of chamber works before he began work on *Alfred*, is well to the fore, although it does not conceal a clear commitment to number opera. Dvořák's operatic symphonism may at times conceal the joints between the steady tread of accompanied recitative, aria, ensemble, and chorus, but even a superficial scrutiny of the score reveals the presence of clear divisions. The paragraphs are well constructed musically and are often broad, but they remain paragraphs. Many features, particularly recitative conventions deriving from early nineteenth-century practice with its impressive chords, tense accompaniments, and spiraling punctuating figures, were fixed for Dvořák in *Alfred* and remained part of his operatic language until his last work in the genre, *Armida*. But the framework for these details of style remained a personal variation of number opera. For a composer of Dvořák's melodic skill, the scale of the aria and ensemble was the most appealing: *Rusalka*, of all his operas, may approach the Wagnerian ideal most closely, but it moves in a steady sequence of numbers, many of which may be excerpted without doing too much violence to the texture of the whole.

Beyond its formative structural nature, *Alfred* shows Dvořák well aware of contemporary operatic convention: at the end of the third act (Körner's second) the librettist supplied a "canon" for Alwina, Rowena, Dorset, Harald, and Sieward. Placed in a moment of crisis before the Britons' happy resolution of the opera, Dvořák treats it as an *a capella* "pezzo concertato" almost in the manner of Rossini or Verdi. Elsewhere, Dvořák's handling of convention is less successful: the finale of the second act—in which Alfred's identity is revealed, to the consternation of the Danes—is rendered chaotic by overemphasis and the overlaying of parts; Dvořák also miscalculated in the finale of the first act a duet between Harald and Alwina, in which widely divergent emotions are expressed in music better suited to lovers. In fact, Dvořák later salvaged the duet, which includes some of his most characteristic melodic lines, for just this purpose in the first act of *Vanda*.

Dvořák's treatment of voice types does not go much beyond the conventional. Alfred, while nominally a bass, moves into the baritone range and anticipates the grave nobility that Dvořák cultivated for such figures as the King in *The King and the Charcoal-Burner* and Bohuš in *The Jacobin*. In the other parts, the characterization is somewhat hit-and-miss. The neurosis of Gothron and the arrogance of the temporarily victorious Harald are well captured in the first act but not always convincingly sustained. A great deal of *Alfred* is founded on the principle of recurrent motifs, which at times clash with the set-piece nature of the libretto. Except for the first version of *The King and the Charcoal-Burner*, Dvořák tended to employ motifs mainly as reminiscences up to and including *The Jacobin*. The handling of motifs in *Alfred* bears comparison more suitably with the *Erinnerungsmotiv* practiced by Wagner in *Tannhäuser* and *Lohengrin* than with the leitmotif of the mature music dramas. But even here the situation is too fluid to fit convenient theoretical definition. Motifs are used freely for reminiscence and, in the case of Alfred's theme, as symbols anticipating the appearance of the subject. Dvořák was never entirely consistent in his treatment of motifs in later operas, and a slight uncertainty over their handling in *Alfred* is symptomatic of this later tendency.

Alfred may be unsatisfactory from many points of view, but it reveals considerable qualities, not least a basic musical technique and an ability to handle aspects of Wagnerian musical style unrivaled among Dvořák's contemporaries. Had *Alfred* reached the stage of the Provisional Theater,[30] its many failings would doubtless have led to its demise. Perhaps the most disappointing aspect of the work is its melodic writing. Apart from Alfred's own motif and the duet for Harald and Alwina at the end of act 1, much of the melody employed is terse, underdeveloped, and at times even antilyrical. This, more than anything, may have prompted Dvořák's secrecy about the work in later years. Even so, lyrical deficiency was never a problem for Dvořák again.

The Early Comedies up to *The Jacobin*

Dvořák completed the full score of *Alfred* on 19 October 1870.[31] His career as a composer of comic operas began the following year with work on Bernard Guldener's (1836–77; Guldener kept the pen name of B. J. Lobeský through the publication of the libretto in 1875) *The King and the Charcoal-Burner*, completing the whole opera on 15 October 1871 and finishing the orchestration of the overture on 20 December of the same year. Dvořák's debut as a composer of comic opera was less than successful. Late in 1873, when the opera was in rehearsal at the Provisional Theater, its complexity and general difficulty proved too much for the company, and with Dvořák's agreement the work was withdrawn. The lesson was well learned, and Dvořák's complete recomposition of the opera revealed a decisive change of style. The second version, to entirely new music, occupied Dvořák for a little under eight months—17 April to 3 November 1874—and was rewarded by an approving if not exactly ecstatic critical response.

Interestingly, many of the commentators of the first performance noted the work's "national tone." The critic of *Národní listy* singled out the scenes involving the charcoal-burners and bagpipe-player as being from "the pen of someone who truly knows how to paint the happiest pages from the life of the people."[32] "National tone" can be identified in many ways, and certainly the appearance and consequent musical depiction of a bagpiper, a potent national symbol,[33] was an obvious rallying point. This aside, the plot of *The King and the Charcoal-Burner* and its setting is somewhat distant from the world of the typical Czech village as portrayed in Smetana's *The Bartered Bride* and Blodek's *In the Well*. The sources of the libretto are to be found in the puppet plays of Prokop Konopásek (1775–1828), who produced a conflation of myths and history based on the figures of Oldřich and Božena. The setting of *The King and the Charcoal-Burner* was the Bohemia of 1612, a long way from the pseudopresent of *The Bartered Bride*. Indeed, the combination of deep forest glade and courtly magnificence in Dvořák's first comedy anticipates the milieu of his greatest opera, *Rusalka*. There is a concentration on the kindness and homely qualities of the charcoal-burner Matěj and his family, and the lovers Liduška and Jeník could be transposed as types to any Czech village comedy, but the resolution of the plot, through deliberately mistaken identity and lavish profession of friendship from the King to the charcoal-burner, who looked after him when he was lost in the forest, is delivered in unmistakably courtly surroundings.

In his next three comic operas, Dvořák proceeded to a greater simplicity of outline, and in *The Stubborn Lovers* and, most of all, in *The Jacobin* to an image of village life that approaches Smetana's ideal, although Dvořák never abandoned a fondness for courtly goings-on: *The Cunning Peasant*, *The Jacobin*, and *The Devil and Kate* all involve the nobility and their dwellings. Dvořák's third comic opera, composed in the late summer and early autumn of 1874, was the single-act *The Stubborn Lovers*. Set in and around the public gardens of a small country town, the opera, in which the problems of a silly pair of headstrong lovers are sorted out, has a plot that begins to approach the idealized countrified world of the Smetana operas to libretti by Eliška Krásnohorská. The strategies involved in the plot and many of the characters in Dvořák's fourth comic opera, *The Cunning Peasant*, equate well with the models developed by Krásnohorská, but the setting has retreated to

South Bohemia in the late eighteenth century, although the presence of a castle and nearby farm would have been a familiar part of any rural Bohemian landscape in the second half of the nineteenth century. In fact the background to Josef Otakar Veselý's libretto seems to have been Mozart and Beaumarchais's *Le Nozze di Figaro*. There are obvious parallels between the Count and Bětuška in *The Cunning Peasant* and the Count and Susanna in *Figaro*. Beyond this, things are rather more confused. The main difference in terms of character is that Jeník, the young lover of Bětuška, for whom the Countess wrings a farm from the erring Count, is no sort of parallel to Figaro since he is not the object of anyone's attentions except Bětuška's. The fact that this is the object of parental disapproval places the plot of the opera more in the realm of *The Bartered Bride* and *The Kiss* than that of *Figaro*.

At first sight, *The Jacobin*, set as it is in "the time of the French Revolution, 1793," might seem still farther from the rural model. But the location of Marie Červinková-Riegrová's excellent libretto, by far the best Dvořák had set up to that time, is a country town in Bohemia, and its plot has less to do with the echoes of revolution in a faraway country than with the reconciliation of a father with his son through the intervention of the schoolmaster, Benda, and the wife of the prodigal, Julie. Besides exploring the sadness of the old man and the integrity of the son, the opera comes most vividly to life in the scenes of town life: a marvelously rich image of the comings and goings after church on Sunday in the first act, and a magical evocation of a musical rehearsal in the second. Alongside the understated dignity of the main pair, Bohuš and Julie, is the more wholeheartedly provincial warmth of the young lovers Jiří and Terinka, which develops in a superb sequence of duets in the second act.

The distance Dvořák traveled between the first version of *The King and the Charcoal-Burner* and *The Jacobin* not only touched on the nature of the plot and its setting. Musically, the two operas stand at either end of a dramatic change in style. Apart from its complexity—there are times when the musical texture goes into eight separate parts—much of the score of the first *The King and the Charcoal-Burner* feels inflated. Dvořák responded to the story with music that far outstrips the modest intentions of the librettist. Wagner is certainly present at times in the music, but there is also a poetry in many passages that is captivating and wholly individual, not to mention prophetic for 1871, as in an extract from the introduction to the first act (example 3). Dvořák also looks forward to the ostinato-based style of Janáček at the beginning of the third act.

[Allegretto grazioso]

Example 3. *The King and the Charcoal-Burner* (first version), introduction

In some ways, the music of the second version of *The King and the Charcoal-Burner* seems a little tame after the spiraling brilliance of Dvořák's first effort, but there is no denying that its modesty suits the libretto far better. The fragile comedy of the scenes between the lovers Liduška and Jeník is well reflected in the musical setting, and there is a persuasive logic to the progress of the drama, such as it is, with Dvořák responding with contiguous closed units. There are many points in the first version of the opera where Dvořák seems to have been moving toward a simpler style; with the aid of the model of, in particular, Lortzing's *Czar and Zimmermann*, popular in the Provisional Theater and clearly influential in ensembles, Dvořák produced in the second version an attractive score that understandably won critical approval.

Dvořák's move toward a simpler, more symmetrical, and less experimental style was confirmed in *The Stubborn Lovers*. As V. J. Novotný noted in his review of the first performance, not given until 2 October 1881, the libretto of *The Stubborn Lovers* was poor, "frankly speaking, the least good"[34] that Dvořák had set. The music, however, is far superior in rendering bearable such disastrous dramatic decisions as a reflective ensemble for the three older protagonists placed on the heels of the brisk overture. *The Cunning Peasant*, with its greater range of characters and richer situations added flexibility to Dvořák's operatic armory. There is also clear evidence that he was taking greater note of Smetana's model, especially in the first act. This may well have reflected a libretto that, with its choruses of peasants and artful simplicity, does tend to favor the national tone prevailing in comic opera in Prague at the time. Moreover, the sequence of events, including a duet for the lovers Bětuška and Jeník near the start of the first act, has many parallels with the sequence of events and musical material of the opening of *The Bartered Bride*, a fact that did not escape Eliška Krásnohorská when she noted in a letter to Smetana about *The Cunning Peasant*: "The things he borrowed from you are not just from *The Kiss*; for the rest there are many of the strengths of *The Bartered Bride*."[35] Krásnohorská's position was, on Smetana's behalf, defensive, and what she failed to note was the benefit of the influence on Dvořák of the older composer. Smetana's example was important in clarifying Dvořák's approach at a time when his musical style was moving toward the directness of his most obviously nationally inflected stage; *The Cunning Peasant* was written in 1877, a matter of only a few months before the first set of Slavonic Dances (completed 7 May 1878), the third of which was added by the management of the Provisional Theater to the opera as an extra ballet from 27 September 1878.

Ten years elapsed before Dvořák made use of the experience gained in his early comic operas. A perceptible classicism in his musical language had successfully meshed with the national tone cultivated in the works of the later 1870s. Dvořák had maintained his interest in larger forms with the cantata *The Specter's Bride* (1884) and the oratorio *St. Ludmila* (1886); if not opera, these works required a vivid imagination, and *The Specter's Bride*, in particular, was among Dvořák's most consciously dramatic compositions.

Dvořák's other great advantage in *The Jacobin* was that he had, at last, acquired the comic libretto he deserved. He may have had doubts about the provincial nature of the subject matter, but when he eventually began work on the opera he soon saw the sterling merits of the story. Červinková-Riegrová's libretto, in the first two acts at least, has both logic and convincing dramatic impetus; the characters are well drawn, and the language has an affecting quality that captures the relief, worry, and inherent nobility of the returning exiles, Bohuš and Julie, as well as the intrigues of the townsfolk.

Although the libretto tends to move in the set-piece divisions Dvořák favored, there is more than enough flexibility to render the steady tread of the scenes as credible dramatic development. Dvořák's ability to create smooth transitions also increases the impetus of each act. The conclusions of the first two acts required considerable control on Dvořák's part, and he did not disappoint. Conflicting emotions are present in both finales, and Dvořák accommodated them with skill. Underlying the power of these finales is the composer's experience of Verdi and French grand opera put to work with fine effect in the conclusions of acts in the two grand operas *Vanda* and *Dimitrij*. The presence of the style in *The Jacobin* does much to enhance the work. Although there are many comic scenes in the opera and it has a radiantly happy outcome, there is a much more serious demeanor: the background to the Steward's courtship of Terinka has the unpleasant odor of *droit de seigneur*, and Bohuš stands to lose not only the love of his father but also his freedom.[36] Far from raising the stakes too high, the weighty nature of the finales in the first two acts is a focus for the gravity of the drama, and each adds a point to the sustained rejoicing at the end of the third act.

Much as Dvořák responded to Červinková-Riegrová's ordering of the drama, he was able to let his imagination take flight with her characterization. In early comic operas, where a strong character emerged, and this was rare where Lobeský, Štolba, and Veselý were concerned, Dvořák responded with appropriately vivid music. The busy affability of the charcoal-burner Matěj, particularly in the second version of *The King and the Charcoal-Burner*, is well conveyed, and with an eye toward such models as Janek in Blodek's *In the Well* and Kecal in *The Bartered Bride*, Dvořák had dealt most effectively with the comic figures Řeřicha in *The Stubborn Lovers* and the overbearing Martin in *The Cunning Peasant*. Dvořák was also developing a successful way of dealing with dignified baritone leads, originating in the role of the King in the second version of *The King and the Charcoal-Burner*. Dvořák's depiction of the Count in *The Cunning Peasant* may have been a touch off-kilter given his duplicitous role, but no less an authority than Krásnohorská noted that his was "the most thoroughly and consistently drawn character. . . . he has a certain noble sentiment, an almost Chopinesque nature."[37] The beneficiary of these developments is Bohuš in *The Jacobin*. His contributions are unfailingly commanding, rich in sentiment and melodic content; Dvořák's blend of recitative and lyrical arioso provides an effective medium for the evocation of his dignified character.

Given that Dvořák's last comic opera, *The Devil and Kate*, has no love interest, a situation almost unique in Czech comic opera, the pair of young lovers in *The Jacobin*—Jiří and Terinka—are the composer's final treatment of the type. They are also the most winning example. Dvořák traces the development of their love during a stolen moment in the second act in a ravishing duet that combines lyricism with a telling suggestion of yearning (example 4).

The studied academicism of the music teacher Benda is also superbly captured in short, often repetitive phrases; the scene in which he rehearses his serenade with Jiří, Terinka, and the choir is one of the most vivid in all Czech opera. Filip, the Count's steward, is also a splendidly

Example 4. *The Jacobin* (revised version), act 2, scene 2

observed caricature. Dvořák had employed a certain element of classical pastiche in his depiction of Řeřicha in *The Stubborn Lovers* and for the first-act finale of *The Cunning Peasant*, but he deploys it to much more wicked effect at the start of the third scene of the first act of *The Jacobin* for Filip's egregious and oleaginous approach to Benda and his daughter (example 5).

Example 5. *The Jacobin*, act 1, scene 3

As a whole, *The Jacobin* is a marvelous demonstration of what Dvořák could do with suitable material. Much of the weakness of his earlier comedies derives from limp humor, underdeveloped characterization, and contrived situations. Dvořák's music in these works is rarely less than captivating, and where drama raises its head, he responds with conviction. Červinková-Riegrová's libretto has certain derivative features, but its compromise with the kind of rural comedy developed by Smetana and Krásnohorská is wholly beneficial. As a type *The Jacobin* could not be described as mold-breaking; indeed its very conventional features allowed Dvořák to explore a fuller image of characterization within the constraints of a norm. Czech opera does not offer a wealth of clear developmental trends. One of the few traditions that developed in the four last decades of the nineteenth century is the village comedy, poised on the knife-edge of tragedy, happy in conclusion, and fundamentally warmhearted. *The Bartered Bride* initiated the type, and Dvořák's *The Jacobin* is its most convincing later manifestation.

The Jacobin was a major success for Dvořák and supplanted *The Cunning Peasant* in public esteem. But while it was undeniably popular in its original form, there were problems with the third act. In the first version of *The Jacobin* (1887) the ballet comes at the end of an allegorical play in act 3, scene 2, before the main drama of the exposure of Adolf's perfidy. In 1894 Červinková-Riegrová suggested to Dvořák various changes to the shape of the act, comprising the removal of the allegorical play, an interruption of the revelation of Adolf's villainy with the arrival of the chorus, and the curtailment of the celebration so as not to slow the plot unnecessarily. In a letter, she added that the end of the opera might be the most suitable place for a "happy and lively chorus and ensemble in national spirit."[38] In the revised version of *The Jacobin*, Benda's serenade is duly curtailed when it occurs in scene 7, and the *Écossaise* from the original is removed and placed with some newly composed dances before the final chorus of the opera. Effective as these changes are—and there can be little doubt that they shape the act much more convincingly—they have a precedent in an earlier opera. In February and March 1887, Dvořák, with the aid of V. J. Novotný, revised the untidy third act of the second version of *The King and the Charcoal-Burner*. Apart from the removal of an irrelevant episode with the extra characters Eva and Jindřich, Dvořák and Novotný further tightened up the action by putting the hitherto separated dances of the ballet together at the end of the act just before the final rejoicing that concludes the opera. This successful rationalizing of the action may have been at the back of Dvořák's and Marie Červinková-Riegrová's minds when they recast the final act of *The Jacobin* in August 1894.

The Grand Operas:
Vanda, Dimitrij, and *Armida*

Dvořák's three grand operas have had a distinctly mixed impact on the public. In the cases of *Vanda* and *Armida*, an unjustified reputation for being unwieldy and unsuccessful has led to a certain indifference on the part of performers and public. The fate of *Dimitrij* has been rather

different: although it was an undoubted success during Dvořák's lifetime, its progress in the twentieth century has been dogged, in part, by
Dvořák's own revisions[39] and latterly by the unavailability of a reliable
edition.[40]

A damagingly poor reputation has had perhaps the worst effect on
Vanda, which has enjoyed only four stagings. No less an authority than
Hostinský praised the work in the following terms: "*Vanda* involves
such interesting and impressive features and is so important for understanding Dvořák's development in the field of drama, that it is deplor-
able that it was missing from the repertoire during the commemorative
cycle of Dvořák's operas in 1901."[41] The wonder of *Vanda* is that
Dvořák managed to invest such a poor libretto[42] with so much good
music, and in such a short time. The opera was composed in just over
three months in 1875, a veritable *annus mirabilis* in which Dvořák also
wrote the Fifth Symphony and the E-major Serenade, along with much
else. His lyrical imagination, having crystallized after his acutely experimental early phase, was in full flood and occasionally looked forward
to his late maturity, as in the B-major romance for Slavoj in act 1, with its
clear resemblance to the lovely second subject of the B-minor Cello
Concerto composed in 1895 (example 6).

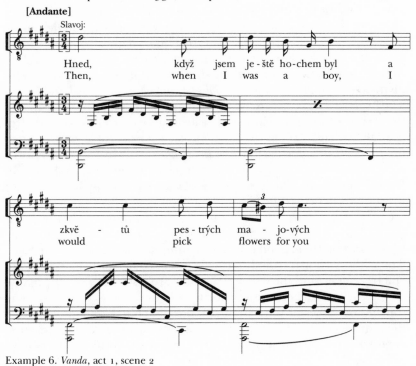

Example 6. *Vanda*, act 1, scene 2

Dvořák did not let his superabundant lyricism blind him to the need for motivic integrity. Slavoj's romance is used superbly as a reminiscence during Vanda's last farewell to him. The motif associated with Vanda's coronation oath[43] is used with great subtlety throughout. Not only does it impart unity to the coronation scene and the conclusion of the first act but it is used with dramatic insight throughout the opera, most notably as a pastorally inflected ostinato at the start of the last act. Dvořák's symphonic instincts were also well to the fore in much of the opera, uniting scenes and, in the case of the third act, even larger units by freely developing melodic ideas. A similar tendency is visible in such effective transitions as the progress from the battle, where uncertainty reigns, to the triumphant march of the Poles in act 4.

Elsewhere, there is sure evidence of Dvořák's developing a convincing operatic style. Vanda's magnificent aria in the first act, "Great Gods" ("*Bohové velci*"), anticipates both the style and the rhetoric of Rusalka's second-act aria "O Useless It Is" ("*Ó Marno to je*"). Similarly, Vanda's threatening call to the evil German Prince Roderich to guard himself before battle in the fourth act was used, only slightly transformed, for Armida's demand for vengeance in act 2 of the later opera.[44] Vanda herself is Dvořák's strongest operatic character to date. Aside from her role in fixing the characterization of Dvořák's later operatic heroines, his depiction of Vanda was important in determining the nature of the eponymous hero of his next grand opera, *Dimitrij*.

Vanda was billed at its first performance as a "Grand Opera in Five Acts,"[45] and in many ways it stands apart from Smetana's historical-mythological operas: *The Brandenburgers in Bohemia*, *Dalibor*, and *Libuše*. The broad, loose structures of French grand opera, with their capacity for lyrical expansion within separate numbers, clearly appealed to Dvořák. As late as 1903, Dvořák expressed considerable excitement at the prospect of a performance of *Les Huguenots*.[46] In 1875, the experience of playing in a range of French grand operas was still fresh in Dvořák's mind, and the lesson was well learned. The finales of three of the acts, in particular the first, benefit from Meyerbeer's example; and the composer's knowledge of Gounod's *Faust*, premiered in the Provisional Theater in 1867 when Dvořák was still a viola player in the orchestra,[47] is put to good use in the triumphal march of the fourth act. The soldiers' chorus from *Faust* act 4, no. 14, is similar in temperament and treatment, and the development toward a statement of the march theme for full orchestra and chorus in both works is very close. The concluding sallies of the march also owe much to Gounod. Although these influences tended to reinforce a natural tendency toward number opera, they were also important in diverting Dvořák from an image of music drama that may have subverted his individuality still further. There are miscalculations in *Vanda*—not least at the start of the second act and in the wildly inappropriate dance of the sorceress Homena's followers in act 3—but at no point do they outweigh the real qualities of this absurdly neglected masterpiece.

Dvořák's next grand opera, *Dimitrij*, has the signal advantage of a fine libretto. The first destination of Červinková-Riegrová's libretto had been Karel Šebor, but the star of this once-significant figure in Czech opera had been fading since the failure of *Blanka* in 1870, which received only four performances. Šebor made no progress with *Dimitrij*, even though he had suggested the subject to the librettist, and at the prompting of her father, the Old-Czech politician František Rieger, the librettist offered it to Dvořák. Having recently revised *Vanda*, for performances in 1880 and with a view to publication, Dvořák may well have felt ready to set to work on another grand opera. *Dimitrij* occupied Dvořák from the middle of 1881 to nearly the end of September 1882, and the premiere on 8 October 1882 was a notable success. It is interesting to contrast the popularity of *Dimitrij*, with its old-fashioned four-act formula, with the relative lack of success of Fibich's *The Bride of Messina*, an attempt to provide the Czech repertoire with a thoroughgoing music drama. By the end of the century, *Dimitrij* had been given fifty-five times, whereas *The Bride of Messina* received only sixteen performances and was not performed at all between 1889 and 1900. Dvořák was criticized for his adherence to the forms of grand opera in *Dimitrij*, and yet the logic of its structure, external brilliance, and sure movement toward effective finales brought out the best in him. In revising the opera in late 1894 and early 1895, Dvořák was responding to criticism of his word setting and his own worries about the opera's relative lack of success on tour in Vienna during 1892. The result much increased the naturalism of the word setting and was a valuable experience in advance of his last operas. Along with the naturalism that, among much else, turned the bright, ear-catching introduction to the fourth act into a brooding, quasi-Wagnerian prelude, Dvořák cut much fine music: choruses were reduced in length, and the marvelous chorus with solo quintet just before the opera's tragic denouement—one of the composer's finest inspirations—was excised. The unsatisfactory nature of the revision highlights the virtues of the original version; monolithic it may be, but it has a breadth of design and melodic spaciousness, whereas the revision seems ungenerous, in some ways an unhappy compromise with a poorly absorbed image of Wagnerism.

Dimitrij's public scenes encompass a surprising range. In the first act Dvořák captures the uncertainty of the crowd after the death of Boris

Godunov, their hysterical support of Fedor Godunov, and their subsequent change of heart with compelling virtuosity. The first part of the opera builds impressively toward the appearance of Dimitrij himself, whose greeting of the Kremlin is the lyrical, still center of the first act (example 7).

Example 7. *Dimitrij*, act 1, scene 5

Dvořák was equally effective in depicting the rival Russian and Polish soldiery in the second act. Nearly all the roles are strongly characterized and build on earlier models. The one who emerges most strongly, however, is Marfa, the widow of Ivan the Terrible and the figure on whom the identification of Dimitrij as her son depends. Her quandary at the end of the opera results in the work's finest music. Nor does Dvořák disappoint us in the final pages. The climactic cries of the crowd to Marfa to swear that Dimitrij is the rightful czar, Dimitrij's assassination by Šujský, and the hushed mourning of the crowd after his death are all handled brilliantly in a memorably paced finale.

Alongside the palpable success of *Dimitrij* Dvořák's third grand opera, *Armida*, cuts a curious figure. The composer had already to some extent bucked the trend in Czech opera toward *verismo* in the 1890s with his fairy-tale operas *The Devil and Kate* and *Rusalka*; even so, *Armida*'s old-fashioned demeanor[48] looked out of place in the early twentieth century. Dvořák's desire to find an opera with an effective female role for Růžena Maturová, the highly successful first Rusalka, led him to a libretto that gave him considerable problems. The period of composition for *Armida*, seventeen months from March 1902 to August 1903, is well out of line with those for *The Devil and Kate* and *Rusalka*, which took eight and seven months, respectively. The sketch of *Armida* also shows that Dvořák had problems with the work. Unlike the fluency of *The Devil and Kate* and *Rusalka*, the continuous sketch of *Armida* reveals hesitancy, with two false starts to the first act and three different versions of its conclusion.

Nevertheless, where the libretto moved with fluency, Dvořák responded with music of convincing sweep. All four finales are impressive—especially that of the first act, where Armida's anticipation that she will see the man she loves and Ismen's and the Hydraot's triumphalism acquire a sinister dimension as the music veers from a radiant G major to a wild G minor with the call of the Muezzin. The major characters—Ismen, Armida, and Rinald—are drawn effectively; Ismen and Armida, in particular, have some fine arias. A major problem, however, is the low temperature of the love music between Armida and Rinald. The baritone Bohumil Benoni, the first Ismen, attributed this to Dvořák's being "too naive and religious a Christian."[49] The duets for Armida and Rinald in the second, third, and fourth acts are undoubtedly beautiful, but they lack the passionate qualities of those in *Dimitrij* and *Rusalka*; nor do they have the frank eroticism that Fibich cultivated in the second act of *Šárka*. There are many points at which Dvořák seems to be cultivating a new style of harmonic coloring, almost impressionist in effect (example 8), but this tendency is counterbalanced by the conventional demeanor of some of the recitative.

Example 8. *Armida*, act 3, introduction

The melodic writing also seems routine at times, certainly well below the quality of *Rusalka*. Had Dvořák lived for any length of time after the premiere of *Armida* on 25 March 1904 he most probably would have revised the opera, given his track record with earlier works. During composition Dvořák had asked its librettist, Jaroslav Vrchlický, to condense the four acts into three, but the poet had not cooperated. This suggests that Dvořák was aware of at least some of the libretto's deficiencies and could well have considered a thorough revision after what was less than a successful premiere; unfortunately he died only a little over a month later, on 1 May 1904.

The Fairy-Tale Operas:
The Devil and Kate and *Rusalka*

Dvořák's two stays in America did not pass entirely without bearing operatic fruit. Apart from the revisions to *Dimitrij*, Dvořák made sketches for a setting of Longfellow's *Song of Hiawatha*. Other melodies sketched in America found their way into the composer's next two completed operas, *The Devil and Kate* and *Rusalka*. Both works reflect Dvořák's developing interests during his last decade. Disillusion with abstract composition, and with the symphony in particular, led to the fascinating series of symphonic poems based on the ballads from K. J. Erben's *Kytice*. These highly characteristic works, with their close connection with Erben's words,[50] anticipate the musical language of the two operas. With their command of atmosphere and almost neo-primitivist use of ostinato they provided a springboard for the vivid and poetic world of the operas, neither of which is typical of Czech opera in the 1890s.

The Devil and Kate, composed between 5 May 1898 and 27 February 1899, has affinities with the Erben tales although the opera is based on a story from Božena Němcová's *Fairy Tales* of 1845. With its lack of love interest and robust characterization, the opera is a winning, uncomplicated comedy that results in a feudal princess's freeing her serfs. The three central figures—Jirka, Káča, and the devil Marbuel—are among Dvořák's most convincing. The word setting in the parts of Káča and Marbuel have a telegraphic realism that at times anticipates Janáček (example 9).

Example 9. *The Devil and Kate*, act 1

Ballet had been important in Dvořák's operas up to this time; all but the one-acter *The Stubborn Lovers* include one. As an ornamental feature, ballet had been a major constituent of Czech opera and was reflected in the favored foreign repertoire in Prague since the 1860s. In *The Devil and Kate* Dvořák employs it as both ornament and an active part of the plot. After a long ballet in the second act, Káča, whose passion for dance is well-nigh insatiable, is projected out of hell during a climactic polka. For all the occasional Wagnerisms of the score, national features, present in all Dvořák's earlier comic operas, are well to the fore in *The Devil and Kate*. In *The King and the Charcoal-Burner*, Dvořák had taken the pioneering step of putting that symbol of Czech national music, the bagpiper, on stage. In *The Devil and Kate* he emulates Smetana's use of the bagpipe idiom in the introduction to the first act of *The Bartered Bride*, by interrupting the buildup to the first chorus entry with a similar bit of bagpipe coloring. Beyond this, the prevalence of symmetrical musical phrases seems a deliberate attempt to echo the rural simplicity of the village characters. By contrast, the Princess, who appears in the third act, has conspicuously more flexible vocal lines.

The successful premiere of *The Devil and Kate* was well deserved, as was the prize later awarded it by the Czech Academy of Sciences and Arts. Dvořák considered, and made sketches for, Karel Pippich's *The Death of Vlasta*; interesting as these sketches are, it is probably just as well that Dvořák, at the prompting of the director of the National Theater, František Šubert, took a much more fruitful interest in Jaroslav Kvapil's retelling of Hans Christian Andersen's *The Little Mermaid* in a Bohemian woodland setting, *Rusalka*. In language of great delicacy and poetry, Kvapil transformed the characters of the original story to archetypes of Czech folklore familiar to Dvořák from the ballads of Erben and the tales and surroundings of his own childhood. Dvořák's continuous sketch of the work reveals the extraordinary fluency with which he worked on the score, beginning on 21 April 1900 and completing the entire work by 27 November.

Not only was *Rusalka* a triumph at its premiere but it has continued to be the composer's most popular opera by far, for reasons that are not difficult to fathom. Undoubtedly the clarity and poetry of Kvapil's libretto had much to do with the work's success—notwithstanding Dvořák's qualms at the idea of cursing God! Beyond this, the characters have a depth that transcends those with which Dvořák had dealt in *The Jacobin* and *The Devil and Kate*. The Water Goblin and the witch Ježibaba are allowed to go beyond their more jocular demeanors to become threatening demiurges with consummate ease; both aspects of their characters are rich and convincing. The comic characters, the Gamekeeper and Turnspit, whose music rattles along to a credible imitation of a bagpipe song, are effective both in setting the scene for the appearance of Rusalka and the Prince in the second act and as a way of initially reducing, then precipitating, tension in the third. The ballet in the second act is also drawn into the drama by emphasizing Rusalka's alienation from the wedding guests.

Had Dvořák's music for the Prince in the first act been less convincing than it is, Rusalka's dumbness, a condition of her transformation into a human being, might have been a problem. Dvořák manages to convey in the music both tenderness and passion for the Prince, which obviates the need for a duet and produces, through a gradual series of rhythmic diminutions, one of the most breathtaking finales in the Czech repertoire. The Prince is equally persuasively portrayed as a disillusioned lover in the second act and a fevered penitent in the third. Many examples of Dvořák's superb word setting in the work may be cited, but none is finer, in terms of the ability to marry realistic declamation to the lyrical requirements of the style Dvořák had built by the time of *Rusalka*, than the death of the Prince in the third act (example 10, next page).

Whereas the depiction of Rusalka herself takes something from the dignity of Vanda and Julie and the tenderness of Xenie, she again is a more complete figure than any other women in earlier operas. Dvořák gave her the most memorable melody of the opera and some of the finest arias. In addition to the well-known "Song to the Moon" ("*Měsíčku na nebi hlubokém*") there is the marvelously evocative aria addressed to Ježibaba, "Your Ancient Wisdom" ("*Staletá moudrost*"), in the first act, and the exquisite lament at the start of the third, "My Youth Is Gone" ("*Mladosti své pozbavena*"). But as with the Prince, her finest moment is at the end, when she passes a benediction on the human she loved before returning to her woodland lake to face a bleak future.

The context for all this fine characterization is a command of atmosphere that transcends anything in Czech opera before Janáček's evocation of the forest in *The Cunning Little Vixen*. The presence of Wagnerian harmony and occasionally orchestral coloring aids rather than weakens the articulation of a score that has a fluid, seamless quality for all the excerptability of separate numbers.

At the end of his career, Dvořák managed more effectively than ever to reconcile his symphonic instinct with the lyrical and dramatic requirements of opera. The only small cause for regret regarding *Rusalka* is that, as with Smetana and *The Bartered Bride*, the transcendent excellence of the opera has tended to obscure the virtues of his other works in the genre.

Example 10. *Rusalka*, act 3

NOTES

1. From an interview with Dvořák in *Die Reichswehr*, 1 March 1904, reprinted in Otakar Šourek, *Dvořák ve vzpomínkách a dopisech* (Prague 1938), pp. 180–81; English trans. in Otakar Šourek, *Antonín Dvořák: Letters and Reminiscences*, trans. R. Finlayson Samsour (Prague, 1954), p. 223.

Example 10. (*Continued*)

2. 25 March 1904, National Theater, Prague.

3. V. Zelený, "Přehled české hudební produkce," *Dalibor*, January 1879.

4. Emanuel Chvála, *Čtvrtstoletí české hudby* (Prague, 1888).

5. Ibid., p. 24.

6. Antonín Dvořák in *Die Reichswehr*; see Otakar Šourek, *Dvořák ve vzpomínkách a dopisech*.

7. Titles are given here in English throughout. The dates of the first performance of *The Bartered Bride* and *In the Well* (*V studni*) are 30 May 1866 and 17 November 1867, respectively.

8. Otakar Šourek, *Dvořák ve vzpomínkách a dopisech*, pp. 74–75; p. 98 in R. Finlayson Samsour's English translation.

9. Zdeněk Nejedlý, *Česká moderní zpěvohrá* (Prague, 1911), introduction, p. i.

10. Zdeněk Nejedlý, *Zdenko Fibich; zakladatel scénického melodramatu* (Prague, 1901), p. 172.

11. Otakar Hostinský, "Antonín Dvořák ve vývoji naší hudby dramatické," in *Antonín Dvořák, Sborník statí o jeho díle a životě* (Prague, 1912), pp. 208–26.

12. See Jan Smaczny, "Czech Composers and *Verismo* in the 1890s," in *Proceedings of the International Conference on Janáček and Czech Music*, ed. Michael Beckerman and Glen Bauer (Stuyvesant, N.Y., 1993).

13. *Nevěsta messinská*, first performed on 28 March 1884, National Theater, Prague.

14. *Králové zemské prozatímní divadlo*, 1862–83. The fullest and most compre-

hensive discussion of Czech opera in this period is to be found in John Tyrrell's *Czech Opera* (Cambridge, 1988).

15. *The Water-Carrier*, or *The Two Days*, 20 November 1862.

16. *Drateník*, 8 December 1862.

17. *Vladimír, Bohův zvolenec*, or *Der Apostat*, 27 September 1863.

18. *Templáři na Moravě*.

19. *Braniboři v Čechách*.

20. *Prodaná nevěsta* (see n. 7).

21. *Švedové v Praze*, 22 April 1867.

22. Fibich's *Bukovín* was premiered on 16 April 1874, and Dvořák's *The King and the Charcoal-Burner* (*Král a uhlíř*) on 24 November 1874.

23. The Estates Theater, formerly the Tyl Theater and originally the Nostitz Theater.

24. See B. Large, *Smetana* (London, 1970), p. 239.

25. In 1888 Dvořák worked closely with V. J. Novotný on a revision of *The King and the Charcoal-Burner*; he would certainly have had the opportunity to correct Novotný's published statement that "it is well known that *The King and the Charcoal-Burner* is Dvořák's first operatic work," from V. J. Novotný, "O nové upravě Dvořákovy komické opery 'Král a uhlíř,'" in *Nedělní listy* (the Sunday supplement to the newspaper *Hlas národa*), 27 March 1887, later reprinted as an introduction to the first edition of the revised libretto of *The King and the Charcoal-Burner* (Prague, 1887).

26. *Vladimír, Lóra*, and *Rektor a generál*.

27. Eduard Rüffer (1837–78) wrote libretti used by Šebor and Rozkošný. See Milan Kuna, ed., *Antonín Dvořák: korespondence a dokumenty*, vol. 1 (Prague, 1987), pp. 124–25.

28. Outstandingly, *The Brandenburgers in Bohemia* and *The Swedes in Prague*.

29. There is no record of a three-act version of Körner's *Alfred der Grosse*. The two settings of the text by J. B. Schmidt and Flotow are in two acts.

30. Its first and hitherto only performance was in Czech translation, in the Olomouc City Theater on 10 December 1938.

31. The full score of *Alfred* is extremely neat and contains very few alterations. It seems probable that the manuscript represents only the final part of a chain of preparations that may well have extended back into 1869.

32. *Národní listy*, supplement no. 324, 26 November 1874.

33. See John Tyrrell, "Švanda and His Successors: The Bagpiper and His Music in Czech Opera," in *The Smetana Centennial*, International Conference, San Diego, 29–31 March 1984, ed. J. Mráček (in preparation).

34. V. J. Novotný, "Tvrdé palice," *Dalibor*, October 1881, p. 227.

35. See M. Očadlík, *E. Krásnohorská–B. Smetana, Vzájemná korespondence* (Prague, 1940), p. 112.

36. His cousin Adolf has him imprisoned and seeks to prevent his father from realizing that Bohuš is alive.

37. M. Očadlík, *E. Krásnohorská–B. Smetana, Vzájemná korespondence*, p. 112.

38. See Otakar Šourek, *Episoda z osudů Jakobína* (Prague, 1939).

39. At the prompting of Hanslick, Dvořák persuaded Červinková-Riegrová

to alter act 4, scene 4, in order to remove Xenie's assassination. This was followed by slight revisions before publication in 1885. Dvořák made still more radical revisions between 28 March and 31 July in New York and Prague, and early in 1895 in Prague.

40. The 1885 edition of the opera is something of a rarity. Karel Kovařic produced his own, altered performing edition of the work (printed in 1912) for a revival in 1906. This version formed the basis of subsequent performing editions. Recently Milan Pospíšil has produced a thorough revision of the full score, which is slated to become part of the Dvořák complete edition.

41. Otakar Hostinský, "Antonín Dvořák ve vývoji naší dramatické hudby," in *Antonín Dvořák sborník statí o jeho díle a životě* (Prague, 1912), p. 215.

42. The provenance of the libretto is not at all clear. The main candidates for the work are Václav Beneš-Šumavský and František Zákrejs, who may have based their work on material from Julian Surzycki. See pp. 53–68 of Alan Houtchens's excellent study of *Vanda, A Critical Study of Antonín Dvořák's "Vanda"* (Santa Barbara, 1987).

43. Otakar Šourek identified this as Vanda's personal motif in *Antonín Dvořák: život a dílo*, vol. 1 (newly revised 3d ed., Prague, 1954), pp. 254–55; I dispute this in Jan Smaczny, *A Study of the First Six Operas of Antonín Dvořák: The Foundations of an Operatic Style* (Oxford, 1989), pp. 361–68.

44. See Antonín Dvořák, *Armida*, vocal score (Prague, 1941), p. 136.

45. *Velká zpěvohra v pěti jednáních.*

46. See Otakar Šourek, *Antonín Dvořák: Letters and Reminiscences*, pp. 219–20.

47. *Faust* was given 119 complete performances in the Provisional Theater, until the opening of the National Theater. Its closest rivals were Smetana's *The Bartered Bride*, which received 114 performances, and Verdi's *Il trovatore*, which received 106.

48. The poet Jaroslav Vrchlický had been commissioned by Karel Kovařic to produce a libretto for *Armida* in 1888. Kovařic did not get beyond the first act.

49. See B. Benoni, *Moje vzpomínky a dojmy*, vol. 1 (Prague, 1917), p. 308.

50. A number of the themes in these four works are derived from setting lines of Erben's poetry.

The Master's Little Joke:

Antonín Dvořák and

the Mask of Nation

MICHAEL BECKERMAN

Dvořák's secretary in the United States was an American-born Czech violinist named J. J. Kovařík. While Otakar Šourek was compiling his groundbreaking four-volume Dvořák biography, in the late 1920s he began to write to Kovařík for information about the composer's American years. Their correspondence, still largely unpublished, is quite a beautiful one, with Šourek treating Kovařík somewhat like a spy master treats a treasured informer.[1] One of the most tantalizing passages in this correspondence is the following description of the manner in which Dvořák's Symphony in E minor got its nickname:

> [On the following day] Seidl told the Master that the Symphony would be presented at the next concert of the N.Y. Philharmonic, around the 15th of December, and he asked the Master to send him the score as soon as possible, because he wanted time to study it, and to get the parts copied. The same evening, before I started off with the score, the Master at the last minute wrote on the title page "From the New World"! Before it had only said "Symphony in E Minor, No. 8."
> The title "From the New World" caused at that time, and keeps causing, at least here in America, a lot of stir and debate; there were many, and there still are, who believed and still believe that this title means "An American Symphony," and that with this title the Master somehow attached to his work an "American seal." This is an erroneous interpretation. The fact that the Master wrote, at the last moment, the title "From the New World" onto the title page was simply one of his innocent jokes—and does not mean

anything more than "Impressions and greetings from the New World," as he declared more than once. When at last the symphony was performed, and when on the following morning the Master read all those different views served up by the reviewers to their readers concerning the title "From the New World," he smiled and said: "It looks as if I got them confused quite a bit" and added, "Back at home they'll know at once what I meant." But I think that even in this the Master was a bit mistaken—and that "at home"—in Bohemia—there were many and, perhaps, still are those who misunderstood the Master's little joke and still misunderstand it.[2]

A full century has passed since Antonín Dvořák put the finishing touches on his symphony. The full score was completed on 24 May 1893, and the work was first performed in December of that year. It has become one of the most popular and enduring works in the concert repertoire. Perhaps, in honor of its hundredth anniversary, we should ask whether or not we have come to understand what Kovařík called "the Master's little joke." To explore the problem it is necessary to pose broad questions about the way Dvořák constructed himself as a national composer. But first we must review the circumstances under which Dvořák came to this country and the role he played in the debates on American music that were taking place at that time.

Dvořák arrived in New York in September of 1892, brought to the United States by Jeannette Thurber as director of her ambitious National Conservatory. To many he was, after Brahms, the greatest living composer. Thurber had an agenda of monumental scope. She hoped that Dvořák, as a professional of the first rank, would apply his considerable compositional skills to the creation of an American school of composition, and she was one of several people suggesting that he use American themes and contexts in his work. In the vernacular we might consider that Dvořák was a "ringer" brought in to "jump start" American music.

Some might find it peculiar, fifty years after Foster's "Old Susannah," Gottschalk's "Bamboula," and Heinrich's *Manitou Mysteries—The Voice of the Great Spirit: Gran sinfonia misteriosa Indiana*, that there would be any doubts about the possibility of an American music that drew on indigenous elements. But we must understand that the New York Dvořák encountered was a place of astonishing cultural vitality, bent on redefining and reshaping the past, present, and future of the nation. Also, it was the four hundredth anniversary of Columbus's voyage, and this lent a special edge to the consideration of national identity.

Though the rhetoric of the time was conspicuously less contentious than that of our own time, the issues being raised concerning multicultural identity have a truly contemporary ring.

We can capture the flavor of the time in this account of an event held in Dvořák's honor shortly after his arrival in the United States: "There took place a concert which had been specially arranged to introduce him to the public of New York. He appeared in the two-fold capacity of composer and conductor, and while he gave the audience an opportunity to study him, he had in turn an opportunity to learn something about the extent and character of the musical culture of the metropolis."[3]

There were massed choruses and a series of ceremonies. The writer, probably Henry Krehbiel, goes on: "The welcoming exercises . . . opened with 'America' sung by the choir, while the listeners stood in their places and Mr. Warren wielded the baton. Afterward came the oration of Colonel Higginson, in which he discussed a subject announced as 'Two New Worlds: The New World of Columbus and the New World of Music.'"

If all this was supposed to inspire the new arrival to create something in an American spirit, it was successful. Either just before or shortly after this event Mrs. Thurber gave Dvořák a copy of Longfellow's *The Song of Hiawatha*; it was her fervent wish that the composer write the Great American Opera, based on that poem. Dvořák took the suggestion to heart and tried to write a dramatic work, and the story of his unsuccessful attempt to write such a work is a fascinating one.[4] He did get to work on a symphony just over a month later, at least in part under the influence of the poem, and perhaps he remembered the title of Higginson's speech when he scribbled "From the New World" on the title page as Kovařík was running out the door.[5]

It was just after the completion of the symphony, in the spring of 1893, that Dvořák began to write about issues relevant to national music and to articulate his basic philosophy and approach.[6] We might note that there are two main difficulties in distinguishing what, precisely, is Dvořák's voice. First, most of his utterances had to be translated from either German or his own rather rustic English. (A charming example of this is from an unpublished letter to Jeannette Thurber: "As you know, I am a great admirer of Longfellow's *Hiawatha*, and I get so attached to it that I cannot resist the attempt to write an opera on this subject, which would be very good fitted for that purpose."[7]) Thus it is only rarely that we hear the composer speak in his natural idiom. Also, there were many critics and intellectuals—people like Henry Finke, Henry Krehbiel, and James Huneker—who had their own agenda and would have been perfectly happy to subvert Dvořák's meaning at least slightly to their own.

Yet there are several reasons that I believe we can trust the general character of these writings. We know that Dvořák read newspapers fervently, and his understanding of written English was perfect. There are times when he comments on a particular review that he finds congenial, and other times when he objects to something about one of his works that has appeared in print. The notion that he would have allowed substantial articles to appear under his name without verifying their contents is preposterous. Finally, I have never found anything attributed to him that turned out later to be false, even when a particular statement seems unusual. (For example, he states in one interview that he has known *The Song of Hiawatha* for several decades, which seemed suspicious.[8] It turns out, however, that the Czech translator of the poem was a close personal friend and that the composer surely was familiar with Longfellow's work in his own language.) In two articles and a letter Dvořák offers something akin to a recipe for American music:

1. There is such a thing as nationality in music.
   "This proves to me that there is such a thing as nationality in music in the sense that it may take on the character of its locality." (Letter to the editor, *New York Herald*, 28 May 1893)[9]

2. Americans should have their own music.
   "The new American school of music must strike its roots deeply into its own soil. There is no longer any reason why young Americans who have talent should go to Europe for their education. It is a waste of money and puts off the coming day when the Western world will be in music, as in many others, independent of other lands . . . I am convinced that when the youth of the country realize that it is better now to stay at home than to go abroad we shall discover genius, for many who have talent but cannot undertake a foreign residence will be encouraged to pursue their studies here . . . The country is full of melody, original, sympathetic and varying in mood, colour and character to suit every phase of composition. It is a rich field. America can have great and noble music of her own, growing out of the very soil and partaking of its nature—the natural voice of a free and vigorous race." (Letter to the editor, *New York Herald*, 28 May 1893)

3. Composers of national music should bury themselves in the music of the nation.

"Every nation has its music . . . but I study certain melodies until I become thoroughly imbued with their characteristics and am enabled to make a musical picture in keeping with and partaking of those characteristics. . . . Opera is by far the best mode of expression for the undertaking, allowing as it does of freedom of treatment. My plan of work in this line is simple, but the attainment is subtle and difficult because of the minute and conscientious study demanded and the necessity to grasp the essence and vitality of the subject." ("For National Music," *Chicago Tribune*, 13 August 1893)

4. American composers should study the music of African- and Native Americans.
   "These are the folk songs of America and your composers must turn to them. All of the great musicians have borrowed from the songs of the common people. Beethoven's most charming scherzo is based upon what might now be considered a skilfully handled negro melody.
   In the negro melodies of America I discover all that is needed for a great and noble school of music. They are pathetic, tender, passionate, melancholy, solemn, religious, bold, merry, gay or what you will. It is music that suits itself to any mood or any purpose. There is nothing in the whole range of composition that cannot be supplied with themes from this source. The American musician understands these tunes and they move sentiment in him. They appeal to his imagination because of their associations." ("On the Real Value of Negro Music," *New York Herald*, 21 May 1893)[10]

5. Dvořák's newest works are somehow American.
   "I have just completed a quintet for string instruments, written lately at Spillville, Ia. . . . In this work I think there will be found the American colour with which I have endeavored to infuse it. My new symphony is also on the same lines—namely: an endeavor to portray characteristics, such as are distinctly American." ("For National Music," *Chicago Tribune*, 13 August 1893)

The upcoming premiere of the symphony on 15 December 1893 seems to have acted as a prism, focusing and concentrating all these viewpoints; certainly it was a busy time for the composer. On Tuesday, 12 December, he received a request for an interview from Henry Krehbiel, and he was probably interviewed by an unknown person from the *New York Herald*, perhaps Alfred Steinberg, on either Tuesday or Wednesday.[11] We know that he met with Krehbiel on Wednesday the

13th, and we assume he was involved in the final preparation for his "New World" Symphony, which was to be performed on Friday and Saturday of that week. On any of those days he may have spoken directly with Arthur Mees, who was compiling the program notes for the performance. We have no record of his activities on Thursday, but on Saturday he attended a performance of the symphony at Carnegie Hall, where he was the object of interest and adulation.[12]

During that week, the usually reticent composer was virtually bubbling over with vital information about his new work. (Interestingly, one of his students made a trip to Vysoká, Dvořák's summer home, several years later for the express purpose of obtaining more information about the symphony—but he learned almost nothing.[13]) Anyone who read the newspapers on 15 December or attended the performance knew at least some of the following: that the work was somehow supposed to be an "American" symphony; that Dvořák believed that the music of African-Americans and Native Americans could and perhaps should be the basis for a purely American style; that Dvořák was fascinated by specific rhythmic and melodic features of American indigenous music (e.g., Scotch snaps and pentatonic scales); that Dvořák felt there were similarities between African-American and Native American music; and finally that the two middle movements of the symphony were inspired by scenes from Longfellow's *The Song of Hiawatha* and were, in some way, sketches for a longer "Hiawatha" project, such as a cantata or even an opera.

There were several reasons for Dvořák's effervescence. One of the most important was the respect that Krehbiel and Dvořák held for each other, which resulted in a long interview in which the composer spoke in some detail about the composition and nature of his symphony. But this sudden barrage of commentary should remind us that we cannot and should not forget the public-relations aspect of nationalism. In other words, "if a nation sounds in the concert hall and no one hears it, can it really be national?" Although Dvořák has the reputation of being a naive country boy, we may consider his revelations during the week before the premiere as an example of the cunning peasant, to appropriate the title of one of the composer's operas.

Though Kovařík complained that the critics erroneously jumped to the conclusion that the symphony had an "American seal" on it, it seems evident that it was the composer who helped to place it there. He altered the title of the work rather enigmatically, employing a common euphemism for the United States of America. He suggested, once again, that the musical materials of the work were also in some inscrutable way related to an American locale—one that his listeners, incidentally, knew no better than he did for the most part. He also suggested, rather vaguely, that there was some kinship between the indigenous American elements, the music of Native Americans and that of the African-Americans. Finally, he forged a link between the symphony and one of the country's most popular poems, *The Song of Hiawatha*.[14]

Perhaps he knew that despite the undeniably expressive dimension of music, specific meaning is elusive unless a figure of great authority (most often the composer) draws attention to an intended connection between a composition and some other aspect of reality. Thus Dvořák could never have been certain, unless he had pointed it out himself, that the supposedly American context of a work would be understood by the audience and become part of the process of assimilation.

It is clear that Dvořák purposely spoke in rather charming generalities and avoided direct statements that might provide his audience with too specific a program. For example, he never said a word about whether he actually used "Swing Low, Sweet Chariot" in the first movement[15] or "Yankee Doodle" in the finale,[16] or precisely which lines in *The Song of Hiawatha* attracted his attention.[17] It was up to the listeners to approach the work, excited by the rather general hints of the composer, and fill in the broad, supposedly American spaces with their own imaginations. The metaphysics of the idea of nation, in all its monumental vagueness, could attach itself to the noncognitive aspect of instrumental music and create massive tension. Although we hesitate to compare Dvořák's American "program" with the lurid autobiographical narrative of Berlioz's great symphony, there does seem to have been a similar electricity in the hall as the cream of New York society listened for and debated the work's national qualities.

The success of the symphony was, of course, phenomenal: Huneker wrote that "the audience, a representative one, threw kid glove conventionalism to the winds and became for a moment as crazily enthusiastic as a continental one."[18] Even Dvořák realized that this work had a truly special reception, as this comment from a letter to Simrock shows: "The success of the Symphony . . . was grandiose, the papers say that no composer ever before had such a triumph. I sat in a box. The hall was filled with the best audience of New York, people applauded so much that I had to take the bow and thank them from my box just as if I were some king!? alla Mascagni in Vienna (do not laugh!). You know that I rather like to avoid similar ovations."[19]

These first performances of the symphony served to heighten further the debate about American music that had been swirling around for the past year. Such luminaries as Philip Hale, Henry Krehbiel, and James Huneker crossed swords on whether or not the work was truly

American. Krehbiel asserted that "all that it is necessary to admit is the one thing for which he has compelled recognition—that there are musical elements in America that lend themselves to beautiful treatment in the higher forms of the art,"[20] whereas the acidic Huneker countered in the following way: "Dvořák's is an American symphony: is it? Themes from negro melodies; composed by a Bohemian; conducted by a Hungarian and played by Germans in a hall built by a Scotchman. About one third of the audience were Americans and so were the critics. All the rest of it was anything but American—and that is just as it can be. . . ."[21]

Several months after the premiere of the "New World" Symphony Dvořák evidently became fed up with the various debates on whether the work should be considered American. Kovařík recorded the following outburst: "So I am an American composer, am I? I was, I am, and I remain a Czech composer. I have only showed them the path they might take—how they should work. But I'm through with that! From this day forward I will write the way I wrote before!"[22]

If we have considered the symphony, in part, as an object lesson in how a composer creates national music, from the use of thematic material to public relations, we might move to a compelling question raised by Dvořák's comment to Kovařík. What does Dvořák mean when he says that he is renouncing this American style and that "from this day forward" he will write in his *real* style? What is his real style, and what does it have to do with being a Czech?

Regarding his Czech style, Dvořák has this to say: "I myself have gone to the simple, half-forgotten tunes of the Bohemian peasants for hints in my most serious work." Many critics have suggested that his music is somehow close to Czech folk music, and the composer's comment reinforces this. But is it true? Before we jump to a conclusion, let us keep in mind that although Dvořák lived outside a large urban center for the first years of his life, there is no evidence that he was in any way part of a folk culture, nor did he even know a great deal about Czech folk music.

To confound the matter further, we must realize, of course, that the expression "Czech folk music" can mean only two things: either songs with Czech texts or songs found within the particular regional boundary of the Czech lands—and this latter definition has never been employed, since it would also include songs in German, Romany, and Hungarian. The notion that there is any stylistic coherence to this music is an absurdity. Not only does the music vary from province to province and from region to region but it may also differ substantially from village to village. Even the idea of "Bohemian peasant music" is vague, encompassing everything from drinking songs of Bavarian origin in the west to bagpipe tunes in the central region to the ancient modal songs of southern Bohemia.

The very notion of national folk music must be understood in relation to the general concept of nineteenth-century romantic nationalism. If we wish to problematize the issue further, we might note as an irony that in an ethnographic sense Dvořák probably ended up knowing far more about Native American and African-American music than about any native music in his own land. We may ask ourselves the potent question: if Dvořák could put on the mask of American national composer so easily, was he putting on a similar mask when he acted as a Czech national composer?

We may remember that Dvořák's approach to the creation of national music required that he "study certain melodies" until he became "thoroughly imbued with their characteristics" so that he could "make a musical picture in keeping with and partaking of those characteristics." I don't think we can ignore the suggestion of late nineteenth-century *realism* in Dvořák's prescription for national music. The notion that an artist filters nature through his or her imagination has the currency of the age. For example, here is Chekhov on his method of writing: "I must let the subject filter through my memory until only what is important and typical in it remains in the filter."[23] Rodin, with his endless modeling, also claimed that the artist has a special way of processing natural images: "The artist . . . sees; that is to say, that his eye, grafted on his heart, reads deeply into the bosom of nature."[24] The author of "On the Real Value of Negro Melodies," probably James Creelman, summarized Dvořák's philosophy in the following realist manifesto: "Take those simple themes and weave them into splendid and harmonious forms. Glorify them: give them breadth. So the Dutch painter talks to his pupils. Do not try to imagine the angel in heaven, but try to paint that wrinkled peasant woman at your side, that the angel in her may be seen by ordinary eyes."[25]

Let us look at two of Dvořák's first big successes, the works that essentially made his reputation in the West, and see the extent to which he applied these theories to the creation of his Czech style. In the fall of 1877 Dvořák sent the first edition of his Moravian Duets as part of his application for a state grant for poor, young artists. The duets immediately caught the attention of Brahms, who thought so highly of them that he sent them to Simrock, who published them.[26]

Although he had been asked to write duets based on songs collected by František Sušil, Dvořák composed his own melodies to the folk texts. A comparison of Dvořák's melodies to the original ones by Sušil is instructive. Sušil's collection was a revelation with regard to the variety and nuance of the folk songs found in the Moravian region.[27] Rich in archaic modal inflection, these songs represented an ideally ancient legacy, the kind of legacy one would have thought a composer would treasure.[28] But Dvořák rejected the original melodies and instead made his own, in every case more "European" (see examples).

Original folk song: *From Slavičíno*

Le - těl no -lú -bek na po -le, le - těl ho - lú - bek na po -le, a - by na - zo - bal své vo -le.

Holub na javoře

Dvořák's version:

Original folk song:

Ve - leť, vtá - čku, ve - leť přes ty ho - re, do - le,

přes ten zá - br - do - vské les! Ach, kýž je mne mo - žná

k to-mu věc po - dǒ - bná svým sy - ne - čkem mlu - vit dnes!

Veleť, vtáčku . . .

Dvořák's version:

· 144 ·

Dvořák's idea of "Moravian" has little to do with any real Moravian music (and of course we must remember that even in Moravia, an area about the size of New Jersey, there are literally dozens of distinctive styles to be found, ranging from northern tunes that employ a dialect similar to Polish, to Hungarian-style tunes in the south). Rather, the Moravian Duets seem to be based on a kind of generic popular village style, with only the merest hint of the kind of modulations found in the more archaic songs collected by Sušil. Although the original Moravian songs contain delicate internal modulations, Dvořák preferred large-scale inflections and the kind of contrast that would later be associated with his "Dumky" style.

In a sense we may consider that Moravia was an exotic place for Dvořák, in many ways as exotic to him as America, a place of mythical peasants, colorful villages, and music of variety and vitality. At the time that he wrote the songs he knew little about the place, and certainly very little about the folk songs of the region. In other words, he may have been telling American composers to immerse themselves in folk music in order to make a convincing "national style," without ever having done it himself.

Simrock was so pleased with the Moravian Duets that, knowing the commercial value of these works (supposedly "national" to Dvořák and his countrymen, and "exotic" to the Germans) he asked the composer to write some more pieces in the folk idiom. The result was the Slavonic Dances. There are a few things we should know about the Slavonic Dances before we comment on their "national" character. Dvořák stated that he was modeling them on the Hungarian Dances of Brahms (in other words, "Slavic" dances, as opposed to "Magyar" ones, rather than "Czech" and "Hungarian" types),[29] and Smetana thought they were so un-Czech that he wrote his own Czech Dances as a moderately angry response. Though we might tend to think that Dvořák's rendering of the Slavic spirit is somewhat more authentic than Brahms's Magyarism, it is difficult to understand how or why this might be. Dvořák was no more familiar with the ethnographic or spiritual source of his materials than was Brahms.

Although we may wish to ask why audiences, particularly German ones, reacted with such unrestrained pleasure to the dances (immediately identifying them somehow as "Czech"[30]) we must also suspect that Dvořák, like Brahms, was fully aware of the effect of the appearance of nationality. Indeed, by keeping the whole idea of what was and was not Czech or Slavic intentionally vague, as he would later do in the United States, he could use the implication of such things to create an aura and mystique in his work while perhaps suggesting at the same time that his Slavonic Dances were a temperamental counterpart to the *magyarische* tone of the Hungarian Dances. He may also have cultivated a persona that reminded the home boys that he was one of them, while appearing like a brilliant and charming Neanderthal to the big-shot Germans.[31]

There was perhaps another reason for the indeterminate Czechness. We find a good deal of evidence that the composer's true patriotism was *Slavic*—at least this comes out strongly in interviews and reminiscences. Here is a passage from Oskar Nedbal's memoirs: "The way Dvořák saw himself in relation to Smetana was interesting. Once he said to me, 'You have all written so much about Smetana and myself and have tried to figure out what is the difference between us, but up until this point, no one has yet arrived at the truth. And it's really simple: Smetana's music is Czech, and mine is Slavic.'"[32] In his public utterances, Dvořák frequently referred to himself as a Slav. Here is an example from an interview in the *Pall Mall Gazette*: "With regard to music it is with the English as it is with the Slavs in politics—they are young, very young, but there is great hope for the future. Twenty years ago we Slavs were nothing; now we feel our national life once more awakening, and who knows but that the glorious times may come back which five centuries ago were ours, when all Europe looked up to the powerful Czechs, the Slavs, the Bohemians, to whom I, too, belong, and to whom I am proud to belong."[33]

As a further example of his pan-Slavonic sympathies, Milan Kuna cites Dvořák's close friendship with Tchaikovsky, whose music he found congenial.[34] Indeed, there was no living composer Dvořák admired more than Tchaikovsky, and his letter to the Russian composer about *Eugene Onegin* is his most glowing tribute to another musician.[35] Although we have suggested a Czech Dvořák, it is also quite easy to configure a pan-Slavonic one as well. The following are works that, by their titles alone, reveal the impact of Slavic nations. I include Moravia as an example of a "foreign" Slavic country, and the Ukranian dumka as a decidedly non-Czech phenomenon:

A Pan-Slavonic Dvořák

String Quartet in D (the third movement quotes "Hej Slovane!")
   (1869)
Moravian Duets, Op. 20; and *Vanda*, Op. 25 (a "Polish" Opera)
   (1875)
Moravian Duets, vol. 2, Op. 29; Moravian Duets, vol. 3, Op. 32;
   Dumka, Op. 35; and *In the National Tone*, Op. 73 (1876)

Moravian Duets, vol. 4, Op. 38 (1877)
A Bouquet of Slavonic Folk Songs, Op. 43 (1877–78)
Slavonic Dances; Three Slavonic Rhapsodies (1878)
Mazurka, Op. 49; Polonaise in A for Piano and Cello (1879)
Mazurkas, Op. 56 (1880)
Dimitrij, Op. 64, first version (a Russian "sequel" to *Boris Godunov*) (1882)
Russian Songs (1883)
Dumka, Op. 12, no. 1 (1884)
Slavonic Dances, vol. 2, Op. 72 (1886)
Slavonic Dances, vol. 2, Op. 72 (orchestral version); Piano Quintet in A, Op. 81 (Dumka movement) (1887)
Dumkas for Piano Trio, Op. 90 ("Dumky" Trio) (1891)
Dimitrij, Op. 6, second version (1895)
Píseň bohatýrská (Hero's Song), Op. 111 (which uses a specifically Slavonic term for "bardic hero") (1897)

In addition to the Slavonic and Czech Dvořáks we could, of course, posit the existence of a rather modest "American" Dvořák and a larger and far more indeterminate "German" or "Habsburg" Dvořák as well. The latter category would include such works as the Trio in F minor and many other chamber works, and symphonic compositions such as the overture *In Nature's Realm* and the Seventh Symphony.

We are mistaken, though, if we think that we are the first to deconstruct the idea of nationality and nationalism in Dvořák's music: the composer himself began the process shortly before leaving the United States. Writing in *Harper's Magazine* in 1895, with assistance from Edwin Emerson, Jr., he stated, "I know that it is still an open question whether the inspiration derived from a few scattered melodies and folk songs can be sufficient to give a national character to higher forms of music, just as it is an open question whether national music, as such, is preferable."[36] He also admitted that American music did not necessarily have to come from the songs of African- or Native Americans: "Just so it matters little whether the inspiration for the coming folk songs of America is derived from the Negro melodies, the songs of the creoles, and red man's chant, or the plaintive ditties of the homesick German or Norwegian. Undoubtedly the germs for the best in music lie hidden among all the races that are commingled in this great country."[37]

But what was Dvořák trying to tell his American audience, or really, find out for himself? Perhaps a clue is provided by another, earlier statement: "I did not come to America to interpret Beethoven or Wagner for the public. This is not my work and I would not waste any time on it. I came to discover what young Americans had in them and to help them to express it."[38]

Dvořák is raising an issue far larger than that of nationality. He appears to be implying that each person, like each nation, has to find his or her own voice. I am reminded of an anonymous outburst at Columbia University: a young composer who had just taken what must have been his tenth seminar in serial techniques threw his hands up in the air and shouted, "I was born in Minnesota in 1949; why do I have to write music that sounds as if it was written in Vienna in 1922?"

It is a commonplace to us that one's individuality is in some way associated with one's surroundings.[39] It cannot have escaped the attention of so-called Czech composers such as Smetana and Dvořák that their idol, Wagner, was writing, in effect, *national* music and that his "universal" status was a result of his writing not "universal" music but German music. Thus, if one wanted to be "mainstream," one could not aim for some watered-down cosmopolitan style—certainly Wagner had much to say on that theme—nor could one really hope to emulate Wagner with any success. One could seek, rather, an essentially *local* quality that, through its raw power, might, in its interaction with the larger historical tradition, *become* universal.

I believe that this is what Dvořák was suggesting for American music and trying to do on his own. Even though he was hardly systematic in his use of local materials in the Czech lands, the ideas of nation and nationality may have saved him at several points in his career from simply aping what was an illusion of mainstream style and technique. In dealing with supposedly "foreign" materials, whether Moravian, Lithuanian, or Kickapoo, he was forced constantly to reexamine his own aesthetic.

For example, in the specific case of the United States, Dvořák's flirtation with "American" sources had substantial consequences as the composer learned some things about sound in his attempts to give musical shape to his experiences in the New World. He expanded his sense of register to reflect the wide stretch of the prairie rather than the more contained pastoral spaces of the village green back home. His sense of rhythmic drive was piqued and enhanced through his contemplation of Native American rhythms, and his sensitivity to melodic shape was profoundly enriched through his study of African-American song. Thus, while Dvořák, in a feisty mood, may have told Kovařík that he was through with the American style, it was not through with him. As can be heard in numerous passages in his later works, the American mask would never quite come off. For example, the overture to *The Devil and Kate* could easily be a prairie portrait, and the dance of the little devils in hell suspiciously recalls Dvořák's Native American style. The exoticism of his last opera, the stupefyingly non-national *Armida*, is filled with the Scotch snaps and pentatonic riffs that characterize the music of the American years.

Music historians are probably the only people left in the world who usually think in a benignly positive and uncritical way about nationalism. The issue has been richly problematized in many other fields, while music history textbooks continue to treat it with a kind of childlike faith, suggesting that "Russian" music, for example, "sounds" the way it does because of "nationalism." If, as Hobshawm states, "nationalism requires too much belief in what patently isn't so," then the same may be said for the idea of national music itself.[40] How are we to grasp the essential tension in the issue?

Let us imagine a folk ensemble from an unknown or even fictional Slavic country, like Slaka in Malcolm Bradbury's *Rates of Exchange*.[41] This gorgeous and talented group is drawn from throughout the country and made up of Slakan villagers and urbanites, "folk" musicians and conservatory-trained performers. French-trained ballerinas cavort with experts in a particularly athletic village dance. Numbering over one hundred, their costumes reflect sixteen regions and forty substyles; their dialects are numerous. Let us imagine further that the troupe performs before an audience consisting of three groups: a typical American concert crowd, a coterie of Slakan intellectuals, and a group of Slakan ethnographers in town for the inevitable conference. Lacking any specific knowledge of local culture, the first group takes the spectacle as a prime example of national spirit and shows their approval in a storm of applause. For them it is primarily an exotic spectacle. The second group feels a surge of national pride, though they may suspect a certain lack of authenticity. No matter; it is about *them*. Our Slakan ethnographers, on the other hand, dissolve into hysterical laughter from the very first number, for it seems to them as if someone is putting on a production of *West Side Story* using everything from Elizabethan garters to flapper outfits, singing "Maria" in an Alabama drawl, and "Tonight" in a Creole patois—in other words, a hopeless, and even comic, combination of unlikely things.

If members of the three groups tried to discuss their experiences afterward there would be a certain stiffness. While acknowledging the points of the ethnographers, more conventional audience members might argue that there was "something" there, a kind of indefinable energy, an *essence* that was quite real and quite specific. The ethnographers, while thinking the whole matter ridiculous, would still have taken those remarks as ethnographic statements, regardless of the fact that they were founded on complete ignorance of local customs.

This quandary might be said to represent our handling of the question of national music. It is not difficult to debunk Dvořák's sense of being a Czech composer. We have already argued that in his case nationality is simply a chimera, a mask that he can put on and take off like an expert actor. We may cast him as the quintessential Habsburg composer, growing up strictly within the canon, falling in love with Mozart, Beethoven, and Schubert and learning the contemporary international style with a heavy dose of Wagner and Brahms. Coming of age literally under the baton of Smetana, we see him absorbing the tricks of Czechness, particularly how to market nationality (both at home and in the United States) through a combination of the specific and the purposely vague, steering a course between the Scylla of chauvinist exclusionism and the Charybdis of cosmopolitanism.

If this were not enough we can insist that, national questions aside, Dvořák was a *composer* first, last, and always, and he seems to have understood things pretty much in terms of how they interacted with his compositional imagination and affected his career. Thus when Dvořák could find stimulation in something "national" he took advantage of it, and he was not above using the idea of nationality as a selling point. When his interests turned away from nation, he found inspiration in anything from *Othello* to the Saracens. We might turn this argument to emphasize further that this, precisely, is the glory of Dvořák's music: the amazing variety, the ability to offer so many different visions. In short, we might find that the notion of any monolithic style, whether Czech, Slavic, American, or Habsburg, is entirely alien to Dvořák.

But still, after all our efforts, we are faced with the reality that Dvořák's sense of identity was bound up with the idea of the Czech nation.[42] We also realize that audiences both within the Czech lands and beyond have listened to his compositions through the scrim of nation. Though we have tried to mock the artifice of national art, like our fictional Slakan ethnographers we may continue to find ourselves subscribing to those very fallacious notions of national ethos in order to draw an increased power from our encounter with the spectacle.

For all our attempts to defang it, to reduce it to a postmodern phenomenon, the question of national music remains a powerful and inscrutable one to this day. We are still confused about the "Master's little joke," perhaps even more confused about the mysterious gravitational pull of national ethos than were our predecessors—which is, one hundred years later, progress of a sort.

NOTES

1. The correspondence includes thirty communications (letters, notes, etc.) containing about 192 written pages from 6 March 1927 until 17 November 1945. Some of the letters are undated. Jarmil Burghauser, who graciously allowed me to see these documents, believes that Kovařík must have kept a detailed diary from which he copied these recollections. The diary has never appeared.

2. See Jarmil Burghauser's commentary to the facsimile edition of the Symphony in E minor (Prague, 1972), p. 11.

3. *New York Daily Tribune*, 22 October 1892. We have reprinted this article here in its entirety on pp. 157–59.

4. The documents reveal that Dvořák was anxious to write a "Hiawatha" opera. Several authors have concluded that the subject was ultimately not congenial to the composer. The truth is somewhat more mundane. For reasons that are not entirely clear—perhaps a commission was involved—the libretto had to be approved by a jury at the conservatory. Two different "Hiawatha" libretti were submitted, and both were rejected. According to Kovařík, Dvořák was devastated by this.

5. It is curious that Dvořák decided to write a symphony to show American composers the way, considering the following remark, which appeared shortly after the completion of the symphony: "The symphony is the least desirable of the vehicles for the display of this work, in that the form will allow only a suggestion of the colour of that nationalism to be given" ("For National Music," *Chicago Tribune*, 13 August 1893). This article is reprinted in *Dvořák in America*, ed. John Tibbetts (Portland, Ore., 1993).

6. In the article by James Creelman (see pp. 177–80 here) we find the following passage, which describes the events leading up to Dvořák's literary activity:

How well I remember the rainy day in New York when the Bohemian composer told me, between whiffs of cigar smoke, that a new school of music might be founded on the so-called negro melodies! His splendid peasant-face was radiant with prophecy as he talked about the American composers of the future weaving the humble folk-songs of southern plantations into glorified forms. Within two weeks I had set forth this picture before the public in a series of articles, and a storm arose. From east and west, from north and south, from France, Germany, Russia and Italy came protests and denunciations. What! Build symphonies, oratorios, and operas upon the songs of a debased and enslaved race? It was madness, sacrilege. Besides, there was no such thing as national music; art could not be localised and a hundred other formulas quite as false and narrow.

7. Cited in "Dvořák as I Knew Him," *Etude* (November 1919): 693–94.

8. This is the article in the *New York Herald* that appeared on 15 December 1893.

9. All the articles I have cited are reprinted in *Dvořák in America*. Dvořák continued to advocate this in his later articles. Here is a passage from "Music in America," published in *Harper's* in 1895: "I myself, as I have always declared, believe firmly that the music that is most characteristic of the nation whence it springs is entitled to the highest consideration. The part of Beethoven's Ninth Symphony that appeals most strongly to all is the melody of the last movement, and that is also the most German."

10. This was the most widely cited passage from a widely cited article. It was reprinted in the *New York Herald* on 17 December 1893 and again by Huneker in *Musical Courier* on 20 January 1894.

11. Important information about Dvořák's activity during this week can be found in two of the letters from Henry Krehbiel to the composer, which appear here on pp. 199–200. The closeness of the two figures is apparent, and the fact that Krehbiel visited Dvořák during the week is beyond dispute.

12. It is a curious fact that Dvořák does not seem to have attended the premiere of the work. Kovařík writes: "Master did not attend the very first performance of his Symphony—on the 15th of December 1893—at the Friday afternoon concert. In contrast to evening concerts these were called public rehearsals at that time, a custom which has since been rejected. I went on my own, the Master and his family heard the Symphony at the Saturday evening concert." Jarmil Burghauser writes: "Kovařík does not give any reason for the composer's absence at the first performance. The *New York Herald* wrote that he had yielded his ticket to someone who was very intent on hearing the work. Šourek expressed his opinion that this person might have been Kovařík. There is also the story of a young girl, perhaps a pupil in the conservatory, whom Dvořák sent in almost by force." See Jarmil Burghauser's commentary on the facsimile edition, p. 30, n.2. It is also possible that the composer was suffering from the nervous tension or agoraphobia that plagued him rather often and about which not much is known.

13. See "A Dvořák Reminiscence: The Man and Musician Recalled in Memories of an American Pupil," by Olin Downes in the *New York Times*, 12 August 1934. The student in question is Henry Patterson Hopkins.

14. For a full discussion of the "Hiawatha" connection see my "Dvořák's 'New World' Largo," *19th-Century Music* (Summer 1992).

15. Harry Burleigh often said that Dvořák had used the spiritual in the symphony and that it was one of Dvořák's favorite spirituals. The chronology of the relationship between Burleigh and Dvořák is not sufficiently clear. We know that Burleigh sang for Dvořák, but we don't know when. Considering that he began the symphony only a few months after his arrival in September 1892, it is possible that his contact with Burleigh occurred after that time. See Jean E. Snyder's "A Great and Noble School of Music: Dvořák, Harry T. Burleigh, and the African-American Spirituals," in *Dvořák in America*.

16. The question of "Yankee Doodle" is a curious one. Krehbiel mentions the possible connection between the song and the main theme of the last movement in his article in the *New York Tribune* on 15 December 1893. Many years later he had this to say about the subject in a letter to H. C. Colles:

I loaned him some of my manuscripts, and he let me see the symphony, quartet and quintet before they were performed. He even went so far as to make a pianoforte arrangement of the symphony which I wanted for lecture purposes before the score had been printed. I recall an amusing incident at the interview which followed my bringing back to him the manuscript. In the last movement there is, you will remember, a recapitulation of the themes of the preceding three movements. Accompanying the Largo melody there is a counterpoint started by the violas which is curiously like "Yankee Doodle." I laughingly called his attention to the resemblance and asked him if it was intentional. He did not say no, but, "Why that's the principal theme in diminution." "So it is," I replied, "but isn't the principal theme 'Yankee Doodle' in augmentation and the minor mode?" He made no answer. (Karel Hoffmeister, *Antonín Dvořák* [London, 1928], p. 78)

17. For speculation on this see my "Dvořák's 'New World' Largo."

18. *Musical Courier*, 20 January 1894. This article is reprinted here in full on pp. 159–65.

19. In *Dvořák in Letters and Reminiscences*, ed. Otakar Šourek (Prague, 1954), p. 174.

20. In the *New York Daily Tribune*, 17 December 1893.

21. James Huneker in *Dvořák in America*.

22. From an undated communication entitled "Poznámky ku vaši stati 'Americká tvorba Antonína Dvořáka'" (Notes for Your Study "The American Works of Antonín Dvořák"), p. 2.

23. Ernest J. Simmons, *Chekhov: A Biography* (Boston, 1962), p. 409.

24. Paul Gsell, *Rodin on Art* (New York, 1971), p. 34.

25. The author of "On the Real Value of Negro Melodies" has never been identified. Some have thought that Krehbiel or even Huneker interviewed the composer, tidied up his prose, and arranged his views. But let us compare the passage cited with the conclusion of James Creelman's article on the Ninth Symphony, given here on p. 180: "The modern painter who expresses the idea of prayer by a haloed woman with folded hands and kneeling attitude, falls far below him who paints a grey-haired woman about to eat a crust of bread raising her reverent, thankful eyes toward Heaven." Creelman claims to have been the one to encourage Dvořák to present his views (see n. 6), and unless we believe he was virtually plagiarizing from the author of "On the Real Value of Negro Melodies," we must cede to him the role of Dvořák's secret helper.

26. See Antonín Dvořák, *Moravské dvojzpěvy* (Moravian Duets), in the complete edition of Dvořák's works, series 6, vol. 3 (Prague, 1962), p. xi.

27. František Sušil, *Moravské národní písně* (Moravian National Songs), 4th ed. (Prague, 1951). This giant collection of more than twenty-three hundred songs is one of the most important sources of nineteenth-century Moravian songs.

28. The most significant analytical modern treatment of Moravian folk songs

can be found in Jan Trojan's *Moravská lidová píseň* (Moravian Folk Song) (Prague, 1980).

29. "Since, however, I did not know how to begin this properly, I have taken the trouble to procure your famous 'Hungarian Dances,' and I shall take the liberty of using these as an exemplary model for the arrangement of the corresponding 'Slavonic.'" See David Beveridge's essay in this volume, p. 65.

30. This is an important problem for future study. It may be said that the sudden and consuming popularity of a new musical work reveals that there is an equivalent of an "environmental niche" that has not previously been exploited. To be cynical, one might call this style "German music with a foreign accent" or "Brahms in peasant clothes."

31. This is made clear in David Beveridge's article on Brahms. We may also observe in Krigar's biography (see pp. 211–13 here) how almost all Dvořák's music was listened to through a scrim of nationality. See also pp. 27–30 of Leon Botstein's essay, in this volume.

32. Oskar Nedbal in "Drobné vzpomínky na Dvořáka," *Hudební revue* 4 (1911): 482. I am grateful to David Beveridge for bringing this passage to my attention.

33. "From Butcher to Baton," in the *Pall Mall Gazette*, 13 October 1886.

34. Milan Kuna, "Dvořák's Slavic Spirit and His Relation to Tchaikovsky and Russia" (an unpublished typescript).

35. *Antonín Dvořák: Korespondence a dokumenty*, vol. 2 (Prague, 1988), pp. 359–60.

36. "On American Music," *Harper's*, 1895.

37. Ibid.

38. "On the Real Value of Negro Melodies."

39. Here is Henry Krehbiel, writing in the *New York Tribune* shortly after the premiere of the symphony: "Your great composer is always a cosmopolite, but if he is truly great, he will inevitably reflect the spirit of his environment—social, intellectual, political, spiritual—even geographical."

40. *Nations and Nationalism since 1780* (Cambridge, 1990), p. 12. This is one of the best new books on the subject and indispensable for anyone wishing to grasp the basic issues.

41. Published in London in 1984. Bradbury creates the fictional capital of Slaka in a rollicking adventure parody of both British academics and Slavic societies.

42. This is particularly obvious in the "Dvořák in the Czech Press" section of this volume, where virtually every writer places Dvořák in an explicitly Czech context.

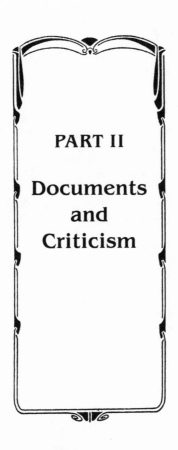

PART II

Documents
and
Criticism

Reviews and Criticism
from Dvořák's American Years:
Articles by Henry Krehbiel,
James Huneker, H. L. Mencken,
and James Creelman

Dr. Dvořák's Reception

HENRY KREHBIEL

During Dvořák's time in the United States, between 1892 and 1895, hundreds of articles about him, large and small, appeared in American newspapers and periodicals. The following represents a tiny but significant selection from these. We begin with Henry Krehbiel's article announcing Dvořák's first public appearance in front of an American orchestra. The next group of pieces, by James Huneker and Krehbiel, offers some insight into the positions staked out by various critics in the ongoing debate about the future of American music—Krehbiel earnest and supportive, Huneker ironic and skeptical. The Krehbiel articles are distinctive for their detail and use of musical examples, which seem to have disappeared from newspaper criticism. The last two articles, by James Creelman and H. L. Mencken, focus on the Symphony in E minor, "From the New World."

We have tried, as much as possible, to let the articles speak for themselves rather than bury them under a hail of notes. Annotations are given only where necessary, since in many cases it is the flow of the articles that marks their success.

This is a description of a concert held in Dvořák's honor shortly after his arrival in the United States. The writer, probably Krehbiel, describes the atmosphere and then dissects Colonel Higginson's oration. Of particular note is the name of the speech, something that might well have inspired the title of Dvořák's symphony. [Ed.]

If Antonín Dvořák, who has lately taken up his residence in New-York under a contract to be for three years director of the National Conservatory of Music, brought with him to this country any of the popular European notions concerning the artistic barbarism of the American people, they must have been pretty effectually dispelled last night. In the Music Hall there took place a concert which had been specially arranged to introduce him to the public of New-York. He appeared in the two-fold capacity of composer and conductor, and while he gave the audience an opportunity to study him, he had in turn an opportunity to learn something about the extent and character of the musical culture of the metropolis. He found ready to greet him an assemblage that crowded the splendid concert room and entered with fervor into the spirit of the unique occasion. It was, moreover, a peculiarly discriminating audience, for nearly all of the musicians of note in the city were present. This fact may have accounted, in part, for the circumstance that the demonstrations of applause which followed the new compositions that were produced under his direction were judiciously temperate, for it might as well be stated at the outset that there were elements of those compositions calculated to make those capable of judgment thoughtful touching the ultimate influence of Dvořák as a model. But of that a word may be spoken later. Nevertheless the eminent musician who has cast his lot temporarily with us had no cause to question the sincerity and heartiness of the welcome which was extended to him and less to be dissatisfied with the manner in which his music was performed. It is a question whether he has ever stood before an orchestra that was quicker in understanding his wishes, or more willing and able to fulfil them than the eighty men in the band last night, the great majority of whom belonged to Mr. Seidl's metropolitan organisation. In respect of ability to read and grasp the contents of new music, the orchestral players of New-York may truthfully be said to be without peer. Mr. Dvořák also found a choir at his disposal which had been gathered together for the occasion by Mr. Richard Henry Warren.[1] Of this the nucleus consisted of the Church Choral Society, that had the honor last spring of singing for the first time on this side of the ocean the Bohemian master's Requiem Mass. It was an effective choir, prompt in attack, fairly well balanced and devoted to its work.

These then, with Mr. Seidl as conductor for a composition not by the hero of the evening, and Colonel Thomas Wentworth Higginson as the orator of the evening, were the factors that took part in the welcoming exercises which opened with "America" sung by the choir, while the listeners stood in their places and Mr. Warren wielded the baton.[2] Afterward came the oration of Colonel Higginson, in which he discussed a subject announced as "Two New Worlds: The New World of Columbus and the New World of Music." It was an effort calculated to make use of the patriotic feeling stirred up by the celebration of the last week, but it made sad havoc of musical history. It is perhaps too much to ask that one who is thrown on popular writings for his information about music shall know the exact status of the art 400 years ago, but, in the interest of the verities of history, the stamp of public condemnation ought to be put upon every effort to make the public believe that music began with Palestrina. The Palestrina myth belongs to the childish things of a past age, notwithstanding that it still haunts the books. There were masters in the fifteenth century, contemporary with Columbus, entirely worthy of being placed by the side of Palestrina. The familiar story of the reformation of music by the supreme master of the sixteenth century is a grave exaggeration as even Baini, Palestrina's devout eulogist, confesses. As for Colonel Higginson's rebuke of the Puritans, we can only wish that he may some day take the trouble to read the many tracts and sermons written by the clergymen of New-England two centuries ago on the subject of church music, and learn how much they helped to introduce music into this country. Between some of the members of the Council of Trent, supposed to have been converted to artistic music by Palestrina's mass, and some of the Puritan fathers, there was little choice in respect of liberality and taste when it came to the matter of a proper church service.

After a performance of Liszt's "Tasso," conducted by Mr. Seidl, who was received and rewarded with several rounds of applause, Dr. Dvořák appeared and conducted the first performances of three new pieces for orchestra, which he calls collectively a "Triple Overture" and a new "Te Deum." In the latter work the solo parts were sung by Mme De Vere and Mr. Emil Fischer. Concerning these compositions we have to say something on another occasion.

[Source: *New York Daily Tribune*, October 1892]

Dvořák's New Symphony: The Second Philharmonic Concert

JAMES HUNEKER

After the premiere of the Symphony in E minor, "From the New World," virtually every newspaper published detailed critical commentary. One of the most substantial essays appeared in the *Musical Courier*. Though unsigned, it was clearly the work of James Gibbons Huneker, who was Professor of Piano at the National Conservatory and a prominent critical voice in the United States.[3] The coverage in the *Musical Courier* is quite impressive. First, the journal reprinted, in its entirety, Henry Krehbiel's long analytical article about the symphony, which had appeared in the *New York Daily Tribune* on 15 December 1893. Krehbiel's article, with numerous musical examples, was written after a lengthy interview with the composer.[4] In addition to his discussion of the music, Krehbiel took a strong position regarding the American character of the work. This is Huneker's response. [Ed.]

This was the program presented at the second public rehearsal last Friday afternoon and repeated at the second concert, last Saturday evening, of the Philharmonic Society:

Overture, scherzo, nocturno, from
   "A Midsummer Night's Dream"...................Mendelssohn
Concerto for violin in D major, Op. 77....................Brahms
   Allegro non troppo (cadenza by Henri Marteau)
   Adagio
   Allegro giocoso, ma non troppo vivace
Mr. Henri Marteau
Symphony "From the New World," no. 5, E minor ....Dvořák
   (new: first time in America; manuscript)
   I. Adagio, allegro molto
  II. Larghetto
 III. Scherzo. Molto vivace
 IV. Allegro con fuoco

When the smoke of criticism has cleared away it will be noticed, first, that Dr. Dvořák has written an exceedingly beautiful symphony; secondly, that it is not necessarily American, unless to be American you must be composite. The new work, thematically considered, is composite, sounding Irish, Slavic, Scandinavian, Scotch, negro and German. The latter nationality enters into its construction, for the form is purely symphonic in the conventional style, as exemplified by Beethoven, while the coloring and treatment is modern and altogether Dvořák's— which means Czech.

The New York "Herald" printed on Sunday Dr. Dvořák's remarks as to the value of national musical themes. Here is what he said:

I am now satisfied that the future music of this country must be founded upon what are called the negro melodies. This can be the foundation of a serious and original school of composition to be developed in the United States. When I first came here I was impressed with this idea, and it has developed into a settled conviction. These beautiful and varied themes are the product of the soil. They are American. They are the songs of America and your composers must turn to them. All of the great musicians have borrowed from the songs of the common people. Beethoven's most charming scherzo is based upon what might now be considered a skillfully handled negro melody. I have myself gone to the simple, half forgotten tunes of the Bohemian peasants for hints in my most serious work. Only in this way can a musician express the true sentiment of the people. He gets into touch with the common humanity of the country. In the negro melodies of America I discover all that is needed for a great and noble school of music. They are pathetic, tender, passionate, melancholy, solemn, religious, bold, merry, gay, gracious or what you will. It is music that suits itself to any mood or any purpose. There is nothing in the whole range of composition that cannot find a thematic [sic] source here.

The "Herald" then goes on very ungraciously to speak of the so called critics who ventured to disagree with the great Bohemian, and furthermore harped on "the conspiracy of silence" which the newspapers waged against Mrs. Thurber and the National Conservatory.

The "Herald" seems to forget that Mr. H. E. Krehbiel, the music critic of the "Tribune," was one of the "so called critics" that did not entirely agree with Dr. Dvořák. Mr. Krehbiel has modified his opinion on the subject—witness his scholarly exposition of the new symphony in last Friday's "Tribune," which we reprint elsewhere in full. Dr. Dvořák has been accorded a full meed of justice in this city, and Henderson, of the "Times"; De Koven, of the "World"; Finck, of the "Post"; Spanuth, of the "Staats-Zeitung"; Steinberg, of the "Herald"; Mrs. Bowman, of the "Sun"; the "Advertiser" and the "Recorder" have all borne testimony time and time again to his worth as a composer, and it seems a little arrogant, not to say in bad taste, for the "Herald" to accuse the press of trying to subvert or silence Mrs. Thurber's manifold efforts for the cause of music.

THE MUSICAL COURIER has often dwelt on this woman's pluck and zeal, and certainly she must have felt that her efforts were not altogether fruitless when she saw Dr. Dvořák accorded such a magnificent reception last Saturday night in Music Hall. Her selection of the wonderful man as Director of the National Conservatory was certainly vindicated then and there. THE MUSICAL COURIER believes in justice and embraces this opportunity to take up the gauntlet for the critical confraternity which has been thrown down in such a bad tempered manner in last

Sunday's "Herald." Mrs. Thurber may well exclaim, "Deliver me from my friends." In justice to Mr. Steinberg and his assistants, it should be stated that these absurd charges were not written in the critical but in the news department of the paper. Mr. Van Cleef should carefully read and edit such "rot," for it does harm in all directions.[5]

Antonín Dvořák is a genius—no question about that. His new symphony does not, however, prove it, as much as the two earlier ones in D and D minor (although it comes perilously near being a great work), and some of his other music. He was called "the Schubert of Bohemia" last Sunday, and in the same journal Robert Schumann's remark about Chopin also was quoted. "Hats off, gentlemen; a genius!" We say the same. Dr. Dvořák has much of the naive, sunny and fertile qualities of Franz Schubert, and he is to be praised for not giving us huge doses of the pessimism we find in the spirit of Brahms and Tschaikowsky's music. He is still a child at heart, and he takes you into his forest, where there are also many-colored flowers, and bids you pluck and be gay. The sun is bathing naked in the azure and God is yet with the world.

Little matter if the flowers he offers be those of the north, south, east or west. They are beautiful and are richly scented, and the indescribable bloom of early life hovers about them. Onto no hot Horsel, with its heavy, dangerously seductive atmosphere, does Dvořák lead us. He lives in the open air, he is the great landscape painter of music of the century's end, as Tschaikowsky dealt in characteristic dramatic figure subjects, and Brahms in subjective introspective, psychological in his musical musings. It is this quality of youthfulness, natural, unfeigned gaiety, cheerful, strong, manly life that Dvořák puts into his music, and after such a performance as last week's we are spiritually braced and exhilarated, and the soul, as Walt Whitman said, "loafes and invites itself."

The most abiding impression of the new work is its extreme musical character and the utter absence of striving after local flavor, either in the character of the themes or their treatment. Dr. Dvořák has thoroughly assimilated his material, and nowhere do we find his motifs obtruding themselves impertinently on our notice. All are blended dexterously and all are well digested, and the themes are his own. He has evidently saturated himself with the so-called negro music of the South, and has evolved thematic material which preserves some of the spirit and color of the original, while lending itself readily to symphonic treatment. But these themes are all greatly metamorphosed. They are musicianly and fit for the composers' crucible.

Dr. Dvořák is primarily a symphonist. This symphony embodies his impressions of the New World. Dr. Dvořák is a Bohemian. His new symphony in E minor is not American. The writer was the first to suggest to the composer the employment of characteristic negro melodies for symphony or suite, citing John Brockhoven's charmingly conceived "Suite Creole."[6] This was a year ago. Dr. Dvořák listened attentively and evidently was predisposed to favor the idea. Who knows but that the Bohemian came to America to boldly rifle us of our native ore! At all events he accepted some specimen themes and also a book on the characteristic songs of the American birds. How he has utilized all this and other "disjecta membra," dug up for his benefit, we were able to judge of in this fifth symphony. But why American? Is there such a thing yet as native American music, music racy of the soil? The most marked theme of the first movement is Celtic in quality, and it reappears in every movement of the work. Dr. Dvořák evidently believes in organic unity being preserved. It is excellently adapted for treatment and is handled superbly by the composer. The second subject is negro or oriental, just as you choose. The slow movement is poetically conceived, and there is a sense of loneliness, of enormous perspective, suggested by the English horn and its melancholy background of divided strings. This movement is certainly not American.

The scherzo, with its curiously harmonized and macabre suspension, before the entrance of the flute solo, is Slavic and eminently Dvořákian. The last movement contains as a leading subject a suggestion of the theme of Grieg's A minor piano concerto. It may be American but it sounds very Celtic or very Scandinavian. It also contains a curious touch of the "Venusberg music." This movement is as ingeniously constructed as the last movement of Tschaikowsky's Fifth Sympathy [sic]. It abounds with vigor and passionate rush. The slight hint at "Yankee Doodle" announced by the violas must be accepted as a jest.[7] The sympathy [sic] works up into a singularly powerful coda, and ends in an unexpected manner in the major.

Of the cunning workmanship, the multitudinous rhythms, the wealth of orchestral coloring, the clever employment of the pentatonic scale, the giant intellectuality in the development it is unnecessary to dwell upon at length. The composer is a past master in his art, and his reverence for older forms prevents his out-Heroding Herod in the mad chase after musical ugliness which seems to have bitten the younger generation of composers. Dr. Dvořák believes in euphony; his orchestra always sounds well, and there is no turgidity in his polyphonic writing, no crabbed, abstruse scholasticism in his handling and developing of his themes. All is spontaneous, clear, airy, healthy, sane and logical. The so-called "American Symphony" will be an enormous favorite with the public, and will doubtless be played all over the world.

The reason is not afar to seek. The themes are simple and understandable, their exposition enjoyable, and the lustre and brilliancy of the instrumentation, the many delightful rhythms, all conspire toward making the symphony a popular work. And it has that unmistakable ring of the folk song which will endear it to all nationalities.

Yet the American symphony, like the American novel, has yet to be written. And when it is, it will have been composed by an American. This is said with all due deference to the commanding genius of Dr. Dvořák.

Henri Marteau has added several inches to his artistic stature since he was here last. He is as graceful in his playing as ever, and if the Brahms concerto was a little too deep water for him, yet he nevertheless played it brilliantly and clearly. When the young man's beard hath grown, he will realize the grave import of Brahms' musical utterance, which he dashes off so ripplingly and unconvincingly. His cadenza was as much like Brahms as is Vieuxtemps'. It was boyish and good fiddling, but revealed nought of the Hamburg composer. For encore Marteau gave the G minor fugue from the first violin sonata of Bach, which he roughly treated. But he has a positive genius for his instrument, and above all has the gift of delivery. His elocution, as the actors would say, is perfect. As he ripens, he will doubtless develop other necessary qualifications. At present he is a fascinating young virtuoso. He received an ovation.

Mr. Seidl deserves warm words for the manner in which he conducted the Dvořák symphony. It was given with great swing and breadth, and every individual member of the orchestra put forth his best effort.

Mendelssohn's music was duly played, and in the accompaniment to the Brahms concerto Mr. Seidl was apathetic, even unsympathetic. When, however, the last movement was reached, Mr. Seidl became another conductor, and it was given with fire and freedom. The first theme sounds a bit like a Hungarian version of the last movement of Bruch's G minor violin concerto. Mr. Seidl is a Hungarian.

After the larghetto of the symphony had been played the audience, a representative one, threw kid glove conventionalism to the winds and became for a moment as crazily enthusiastic as a continental one. Dvořák was yelled for then he finally did appear in one of the upper boxes and bowed to the sea of faces upturned to him and then pointed to Mr. Seidl. It was a graceful act and was instantly appreciated. Many comments were made on the new work and they were all of a complementary sort. Its extremely Celtic character was patent to numerous people and the general opinion seemed to be that Dvořák had not been long in discovering what a paramount factor the Irish were in the political life of this country. Said one: "Why not call it the 'Tammany Hall' symphony![8] That is Indian and Irish, and are not Indian and Irish American?" It will probably be many years before a Philharmonic Society concert will be talked and written about as was this second one December 16, 1893.

Dvořák's is an American symphony: is it? Themes from negro melodies; composed by a Bohemian; conducted by a Hungarian and played by Germans in a hall built by a Scotchman. About one third of the audience were Americans and so were the critics. All the rest of it was anything but American—and that is just as it can be.

[Source: *Musical Courier*, 20 December 1893]

Dvořák's American Compositions in Boston

HENRY KREHBIEL

The following three articles were written by Henry Krehbiel between 1 and 13 January 1894. Krehbiel (1854–1923) was among the most prominent music critics of his time (see Joseph Horowitz's essay in this volume, pp. 94–95). A man of wide-ranging interests, he lectured on such diverse topics as Greek music theory, Wagner, and the folk music of African-Americans. He had a special relationship to Dvořák and, between 1892 and 1896, wrote thousands of words about the composer, including two major journal studies and dozens of newspaper articles. Although their avowed purpose is to review Dvořák's compositions in Boston, these three articles offer measured and detailed discussion of the composer's "American" style. It may come as a revelation to us, one hundred years later, to see such detailed treatment of music in a daily newspaper, including musical examples. This may remind us that Dvořák's United States was a place brimming over with musical activity and ambition, where a musically literate audience could choose from among six or seven major daily newspapers, each with its own prominent critic. In these pieces Krehbiel is particularly eloquent in his defense of the idea of American music. [Ed.]

Dr. Dvořák's symphony, "From the New World," was performed in Boston on Saturday night at a concert by the Symphony Orchestra. Its success with the public, while pronounced, was not so emphatic as it was in New-York, for which fact an explanation might be found in the circumstance that it was not so well played. Mr. Paur[9] had evidently

· 165 ·

taken ample pains in studying it with his band, but he misconceived the tempo of every movement so completely that the work was robbed of half its charm. It reminded one of the dinner at which everything was cold except the ice-cream. Every movement was played with great moderation, except the larghetto, which was played much too fast. The temptation is strong to say that Mr. Paur, a newcomer in America, unconsciously gave a certificate of national character to the work in showing so convincingly his inability to grasp its spirit. The newspaper critics in their reviews are unanimous in praising the beauty of the music and denying its right to be called American. The sarcastic and scintillant Mr. Philip Hale of "The Boston Journal," in particular makes merry of the term and thinks it wondrously amusing that anything should be called American which has attributes or elements that are also found among the peoples of the Old World. Much of this kind of talk is mere quibbling.[10] Mr. Hale does not deny that Dr. Dvořák's melodies reflect the characteristics of the songs of the negroes in the South, and that the symphony is beautifully and consistently made. If so, why should it not be called American? Those songs, though they contain intervallic and rhythmic peculiarities of African origin, are the product of American institutions: of the social, political and geographical environment within which the black slave was placed here; of the influences to which he was subjected here; of the joys and sorrows which fell to his lot here. The crude material may be foreign; the product is native. In the sense which seems to be playing hide and seek in the minds of the critics and musicians who object to the label, there is no American music and can be none. Every element of our population must have its own characteristic musical expression, and not one element can set up to be more American than another. But suppose the time come when the work of amalgamation should be complete and the fully evolved American people have developed a fondness for certain peculiarities of melody and rhythm, which fondness in turn shall disclose itself in a decided predilection for compositions in which those peculiarities have been utilized; will that music be American? Will it be racy of the soil? Will such compositions be better entitled to be called American than the music of to-day, which employs the same elements but confesses that it borrows them from the songs of the Southern negroes? Those songs are folk-songs in the truest sense; that is, they are the songs of a folk, created by a folk, not by an individual, giving voice to the emotional life of a folk, for which life America is responsible. They are beautiful songs, and Dr. Dvořák has showed that they can furnish symphonic material to the composer who knows how to employ it. To use this material most effectively it is necessary to catch something of the spirit of the people to whom it is, or at least it seems, idiomatic. A native-born American ought to be able to do this quicker and better than a foreigner, but he will not be able to do it at all unless he have the gift of transmuting whatever he sees or feels into music. If he have the magic talisman, genius, he may write American music; if he have it not he will not write music at all; he might as well be a Hottentot as an American.

It has not occurred to The Tribune to claim that with his symphony Dr. Dvořák has founded a national school of composition. The only thing that has been urged in the matter is that he has showed that there are the same possibilities latent in the folk-songs which have grown up in America as in the folk-songs of other peoples. Those folk-songs are accomplished facts. They will not be added to for the reason that their creators have outgrown the conditions which alone made them possible. Modern civilization is as great an obstacle to the creation of true folk-song as it is to the creation of legends and mythologies. It has atrophied the faculty which brings them forth. Only once in a long while do we see it stirred into activity, and then only among people who are living far from the destructive influences of modern life. The introduction of railways in Germany has given rise to a locomotive myth, but it was among the naive and ignorant peasantry of Bavaria; the same people accounted for the triumph of the Prussian arms in 1866 by inventing a legend to the effect that Bismarck had got the needle-gun from the devil in exchange for his soul. But such exercises of the faculties which create myths and folk-songs are growing scarcer daily. It is inconceivable that America shall add to her store of folk-songs. Whatever characteristics of tonality or rhythm the possible future American school of composition is to have must, therefore, be derived from the songs which are now existent. Only a small fraction of these songs have been written down, and to those which have been preserved the scientific method has not yet been applied. It ought to be looked upon as a privilege, if not a duty, to save them, and the best-equipped man in the world to do this, and afterward to utilize the material in the manner suggested by Dr. Dvořák, ought to be the American composer. Musicians have never been so conscious as now of the value of folk-song elements. Music is seeking new vehicles of expression, and is seeking them where they are most sure to be found—in the field of the folk-song. We have such a field and it is rich. Why not cultivate it? Why these sneers at the only material which lies to our hand? What matters it if the man who points out the way be a Bohemian scarcely two years in the country? The peripatetic gypsy is the universal musician, and he makes Hungarian music in Hungary, Spanish music in Spain, Russian music in Russia, and English music in England. In each country we recognize the individuality of the musician in his music, but also the fact that however unsophisticated, it still belongs to the soil. It is characteristic of the vagueness which haunts the musical mind, let us say of Boston, in this matter that the fact that the stamp of Dvořák's individuality is upon this score is cited as proof that it is not American. It would be a pity if so pronounced a personality as Dvořák should conceal himself in a composition, but it would be a greater pity if the idea should prevail that in order to be American a composer must forswear himself, and follow a model which is, as yet, non-existent. There are in music schools of materials, schools of manner and schools of models. The new symphony is a highly successful experiment in the first of these.

The symphony was the first composition which Dr. Dvořák wrote in America. It was written in New-York last spring. In June and July, while living in Spillville, Iowa, he composed two other works in the classical forms—a quartet and quintet for strings. The former will be played by the Kneisel Quartet this evening in Boston.[11] The performance will not be embarrassed by misconceptions of the composer's purpose, and no doubt the reviewers and musicians of the city will embrace the opportunity to continue their studies in musical nationalism. It will make for good that the quartet is to be heard before the impressions made by the symphony are effaced. It was composed while Dr. Dvořák's mind was yet warm with the glow created by his work on the symphony. That is obvious to the first glance at the score. Not only the mood but the formal material, also, of the first movement of the symphony has been carried over into the first movement of the quartet. Its principal subject

No. 1

has a close kinship with the principal subject of the symphony—the melody that the composer chose for the purpose of stamping structural unity upon his work by means of quotation in the slow movement, the scherzo and the finale. The kinship is none the less obvious because the symphonic theme is in the minor mode and this in the major. It has both the characteristics that Dr. Dvořák has chosen to exploit most persistently in order to give local color to his American compositions— that is, it is pentatonic and it employs the effect of syncopation which is called the "Scotch snap," and has carried so much comfort for that reason to the souls of the doubting Thomases of Boston. The effect of this little melody is that of cheerful and not too aggressive energy. It is

as frank and lighthearted as the melody of the scherzo of Mendelssohn's Scotch symphony. Its emotional contents lie on the surface.
Not so with the second subject of the movement no. 2 in which

No. 2

ppp

there is a fine exposition of the romantic feeling of which the five-note
scale is capable. Here is a melody that is as beautiful and expressive as it
is simple. It illustrates a little oddity of form which once would have
called for discussion, but does not now. It is nominally in the key of A
major which stands in the relationship of a third to the key of the
quartet, which is F major. The orthodox dominant relationship is thus
ignored, but the device is not new (Beethoven resorted to it in his
"Waldstein" sonata) and the pentatonic coloring of the melody mod-
ifies the key effect very materially. Dr. Dvořák has no desire to be
heterodox in any respect, and his slow movement, of which the principal melody is here given

No. 3

Molto esforco

(No. 3), moves along decorously enough in D minor, the relative minor
of the key of this quartet. It is absolutely void of all straining after
effect, and in manner is as ingenuous and honest as a movement of
Haydn's. It is positively refreshing in these days of infinite yearnings
and strivings after capacious expression to hear a piece of chamber
music in which the four instruments are willing to be just what they are
and do not try to become a whole Janizary orchestra. So, too, there is no
confusion in the form. Dr. Dvořák is content to cultivate the old laws of
symmetry. It is easy for the tyro to follow him in the exposition, illustration and repetition of his themes, and instead of filling his vessel with
dramatic contents, he puts in only those qualities which seemed to
Galuppi to compass all true music: "Beauty, clearness and good
modulation."[12]

The third movement is a scherzo of exceedingly simple structure with this principal subject (No. 4):

The movement is vivacious and full of humor, but wholly unpretentious. Its second part is a quasi trio, but instead of a new subject it makes use of the scherzo melody turned into the minor mode and treated in augmentation, as follows:

An accompaniment melody which goes with this has significance enough to entitle it to separate mention, but we are not attempting an analysis of the quartet, but only trying to convey an idea of its melodic contents and style. The finale is a merry movement as is amply attested by the beginning of its principal subject:

As a whole, the quartet in F major, which is Dvořák's ninety-sixth numbered work, is a cheery, sunshiny, outdoorsy piece of music, which will not cause any brain-racking to the listener, but will make its appeal directly and compellingly. It was composed (so notes on the autograph score indicate) between June 12 and 23, 1893. It will be played at Mr. Charles Dudley Warner's house, in Hartford, soon, and also in Washington. On January 12 it will be given here at a concert by the Kneisel Quartet at which the new quintet and also a sextet of the composer's will be brought forward.

[Source: *New York Daily Tribune*, 1 January 1894]

Dvořák's American Compositions

HENRY KREHBIEL

The critical mind of Boston is troubled because of Dr. Dvořák's new compositions, or rather because of the fact that The Tribune has recognized American characteristics in the music of the symphony in E minor and the quartet in F major. It has fermented variously and vigorously, and seems as yet unable to get itself into a clarified state. It would be agreeable to come to its relief with a few suggestions touching rudimentary principles and analogies, but such intellectual disturbances are so beneficial as a rule that it would be unwise to check the fermentation violently. Besides, there is a better argument than words, in this case, and that is having its influence. It lies in the music itself. The symphony and quartet have been performed in Boston, and no doubt Mr. Kneisel and his associates will take an early opportunity to give a hearing also to the quintet. As for New-York, having been privileged to hear the symphony on the 15th and 16th of last month, it is to enjoy the two chamber compositions next Friday evening at the third concert of the Kneisel Quartet.

It was the sapient observation of the Hon. Bardwell Slote, we believe, that though potatoes might sound better in French than in English, they tasted the same in all languages; wherein the statesman perceived that the humble tuber possessed a most admirable virtue. Something of the same nature might be said without disrespect of the new compositions by Dr. Dvořák. It has pleased the composer to characterize them as his first, second and third compositions "in America." He has further taken the liberty of giving a sort of programmatic title to the symphony, in which The Tribune has ventured to see a manifestation of an intention to identify the work with an avowed belief that there are available musical elements in the songs of the negroes of America. We have therefore urged that these compositions be listened to as American music; but it really doesn't matter what they are called so their contents be appreciated. We believe that in addition to the evidence of their Americanism which we have enumerated they contain spiritual proclamations that fall with peculiar agreeableness into the American mind and heart. They do say something which sounds native in a style which is pleasant and natural in the ears of the people, the vast, vague, varied people of America. Down in Louisiana, knowing what the conventional meaning of the term is, they do not scruple to speak of Creole eggs and Creole chickens, meaning eggs that were laid and chickens that were hatched in the State. In the North the term Creole has a very misty meaning, and is most often wholly misunderstood. That fact, however, should not prevent a New-York gentleman enjoying to the full the flavor of the egg or chicken provided for his breakfast by a New-Orleans host. There has been much consternation created by the reference to the possibility of a school of composition. Needlessly. The matter is extremely simple. We must not juggle with sounding phrases. Schools are the products of imitation. They are begotten by creative artists of strong individuality and developed by the desire to achieve success through emulation of the methods of the strongly individual creative artist who has hit the likings of a people. In other words, schools come into existence because younger composers who have something to say strive to say it in a way in which somebody who succeeded gave expression to his ideas. The success of the somebody came from the fact that his ideas, or his mode of expressing them, were or was for some reason or other "racy" of the people for whom he wrote. Your great composer is always a cosmopolite, but if he is truly great, he will inevitably reflect the spirit of his environment—social, intellectual, political, spiritual—even geographical. That is the reason why Handel, a German, trained in Italy, is, after all, an English composer. Rhythms and melodic intervals, which stamp national character upon musical compositions, are generally derived from the characteristic music, the folk-tunes of a people; but characteristic rhythms and melodic intervals are not the only factors or elements in national schools of music. The Neapolitan school of opera writers was once addicted to the use of the "Scotch snap," which is common in the folk-songs of the American negroes and may have been derived from any one of three sources—English, African or Aboriginal American; but the essence of the Neapolitan school did not consist in the use of the "Scotch snap," surely. Go to! The problem is too simple.

There is one of the three American compositions of Dr. Dvořák remaining for review by The Tribune; it is the quintet to which reference has been made and which is to have its first public performance next Friday evening. This quintet in three of its movements may be said to show the influence of American life and American music upon the composer. The other, the slow movement, is in no sense national, being an example of music pure and simple—a set of variations of extreme loveliness permeated with the spirit of Dvořák and his admired models, Beethoven and Schubert.[13] The composition was written last July. The first date on the autograph score is the 11th of the month and is appended to the first movement. The second movement was begun on

July 12 and finished on July 20; the third begun on July 22 and finished on July 27; the fourth begun on July 29 and completed on August 1. It is obvious that the composer was in no hurry, for he is an extremely rapid writer, it being in evidence that he composed and scored his "Stabat Mater" inside of six weeks. The key of the quintet is E flat major, and its opus number 97. Like the symphony and quartet, it is still in manuscript, but has been purchased by Simrock, the Berlin publisher. It is scored for two violins, two violas and a violoncello. As in the symphony in G major, the composer attains the effect of an introduction without prefacing the first movement proper with a short, slow movement. He begins at once, Allegro non tanto, in the fundamental key with a phrase which is soon discovered to be the kernel of the principal subject of the movement (Ia):

This melody is an augmentation of the first phrase of the principal subject, extended from two measures to four, as will be seen from the following quotation of the subject in full:

Here we have again the intervallic characteristic of the first movements of both symphony and quartet; the melody is pentatonic—i.e., built on the diatonic major scale with the fourth and seventh tones rejected. In the second subject, which we avoid quoting because of contingencies of space, there appears also the rhythmical element of which the negroes are so fond that they deliberately distort their song texts to attain it, as when they sing "Go down Moses" with the temporal and accentual stress on "down" and "ses." The third melody, moreover, which is as follows (Ic):

Ic.

provides so useful a rhythmical figure to the texture of the composition in the eighth and sixteenth notes separated by a sixteenth rest, that it must be set forth. From this little figure comes a great deal of the sprightliness of the music, as will be observed not only while listening to the first movement, but the last also.

Attention has already been called in The Tribune to the fact that as yet Dr. Dvořák has not borrowed forms from the music which he has studied here. He has given us the spirit of the tunes, and even suggested the hilarity of some of our old-fashioned country dances, but he has not set himself to work to idealize a breakdown. The spirit of his jocose movements remains the spirit of the Symphonic Scherzo as perfected by Beethoven. He does not adhere to the Scherzo form, however, in all its details, and in this quintet goes so far as to abandon the orthodox triple rhythm. As in the two other American compositions, his Scherzo is a sort of merry intermezzo with a second part corresponding to the old Trio. He introduces the principal melody with the rhythmical phrase (IIa)

IIa.   Viola

like the rattle of a snare drum, which publishes at once a promise of the hilarious humor of the movement derived from the following madcap melody (IIb):

IIb.

The genial effect of contrast is provided by this suave melody in D major (IIc):

The slow movement, to the character of which reference has already been made, consists of a set of five variations on a dual theme, the first half in A-flat minor (IIIa)

(in which the curious may trace a resemblance to one of the melodies in the "Feramors" ballet music of Rubinstein), and the second, in A-flat major (IIIb),

which speaks from the tongue and from the heart of Beethoven himself.

In the last movement Dvořák permits his innocently playful mood to run riot. Here he is, even to the ears of the least discerning, the naive musician to whom the simplest themes are factors to be multiplied into a product of beauty and the seemingly vulgar is aristocratic. The spirit of Haydn breathes through the movement, the chief of whose melodies is this (IV):

What American suggestions lie in this merry tune we scarcely dare suggest, as not wishing to mar innocent and pure enjoyment with hints of the ignoble; but that it reflects some of the pleasures of the lowly is obvious enough. And it is delightful music.

[Source: *New York Daily Tribune*, 7 January 1894]

Dr. Dvořák's American Music

HENRY KREHBIEL

The third concert of chamber music by the Kneisel Quartet, which took place last night in the cosey room in the Music Hall set apart for such occasions, was devoted wholly to compositions by Antonín Dvořák. A quartet, quintet and sextet, all for strings, were played, the first two being the compositions, already described in this journal, which were written last summer in Iowa, and under the influence of American surroundings. The popular interest in these works was attested by the largely increased attendance at the concert. For the first time at a chamber concert the room was filled and the gallery called into requisition. A most amiable spirit of anticipation was observable, too, in the conduct of the auditors, and the obvious desire to enjoy the new music was amply gratified. After every movement of the quartet and quintet the applause was loud, long, and enthusiastic, and the composer, who sat among the listeners, was several times called to his feet and compelled to bow his acknowledgment of the hearty tribute paid to his genius. The whole concert was a season of keen delight, and the lovers of the highest form of absolute music were gratified beyond measure at the evidences of its pleasure-giving potency.

Mr. Kneisel's plan of consorting the new compositions with an earlier one (the sextet is Dr. Dvořák's, Opus 48) served an excellent purpose, especially for those who were anxious to discover wherein the characteristic elements of the American music lay. In the sextet Dr. Dvořák is a Bohemian. Two of its movements are cast in national forms. The slow movement is a Dumka, that is, a Bohemian elegy; the jocose number is a Furiant, a wild Czechish dance. Moreover, the majority of the melodies bear the Bohemian character. The quartet and quintet have nothing in common with the sextet, save some peculiarities of Dr. Dvořák's style. Most of their melodies, as we have tried to show, smack of the tunes which appeal to the popular feeling of this country. Not only do they show rhythmic and intervallic peculiarities which are native to the folk-tunes of the South, but there is that in their spirit which differentiates them broadly from the melodies of the sextet. It was interesting and instructive to note these things, and also to discover that with his resort to new material Dr. Dvořák has adopted a different manner. The new compositions are compacter and simpler in form than the older one, and their expression is more direct. If some of their melodies are less distinguished in character than those of the sextet, they are at least more spontaneous, more ingenuous, and their treatment is less la-bored. Dr. Dvořák's habit of excessive elaboration, a trait which he shares with his admired model, Schubert, does not obtrude itself in these new works. One is even tempted, while listening to his Haydn-like frankness and simplicity, to believe that he has purposely reverted to the style of the father of the string quartet in order that the composers who may undertake to work on the lines which he has marked out may have the clearest model before them. The music is not profound nor heavily weighted with emotion, but it is full of ingenuity, replete with gracious fancy, clear as crystal and inspiriting in its unalloyed happiness. Mr. Kneisel and his associates (Mr. Zach, viola, and Mr. Schulz, violoncello, assisting in the quintet and sextet) played as if the music was a pleasure to them, and enjoyed the finest triumph that has yet fallen to their lot in New-York. The quartet had previously been played in Boston, Hartford, and Washington; the quintet had its first public appearance on this occasion.

[Source: *New York Daily Tribune*, 13 January 1894]

Dvořák's Negro Symphony

JAMES CREELMAN

James Creelman (1859–1915) was an American journalist and author. Beginning in 1878 he worked for the *New York Herald* as an editor and correspondent. During Dvořák's New York years he was the editor of the *New York Evening*

Telegram. His work often took him to Europe, and he became manager of the British edition of *Cosmopolitan Magazine.* This no doubt explains the presence of his article in the *Pall Mall Budget.*

This article is an intimate account of Dvořák's thinking at the time. Undoubtedly shrouded in a haze of romantic imagery and possible self serving, the article nonetheless speaks eloquently about the issues involved; and, as I have argued, Creelman is probably the invisible voice behind Dvořák's articles. Although we may find Creelman's racism ignorant and unacceptable today we cannot say that the deeper beliefs of Americans have changed significantly since his time, only the reluctance among the educated classes to express them in this manner. [Ed.]

To vindicate a remark made in a moment of artistic enthusiasm, Dr. Antonín Dvořák wrote his greatest symphony, and London will hear it for the first time to-night (Thursday). How well I remember the rainy day in New York when the Bohemian composer told me, between whiffs of cigar smoke, that a new school of music might be founded on the so-called negro melodies! His splendid peasant-face was radiant with prophecy as he talked about the American composers of the future weaving the humble folk-songs of southern plantations into glorified forms. Within two weeks I had set forth this picture before the public in a series of articles, and a storm arose.[14] From east and west, from north and south, from France, Germany, Russia and Italy came protests and denunciations. What! Build symphonies, oratorios, and operas upon the songs of a debased and enslaved race? It was madness, sacrilege. Besides, there was no such thing as national music; art could not be localised and a hundred other formulas quite as false and narrow.

Well, when Dvořák realised what he had done, he locked himself in a room and turned the lights out. For an hour he remained alone. No one knows what he did, but I strongly suspect that he folded his arms, set his teeth and stared at the darkness. It is a way he has when the world is too much for him. The next day Dvořák wrote an article reiterating his theory. He declared that the negro melodies expressed every shade of feeling or thought—merry, frolicsome, tender, passionate, bold, solemn, majestic. They were the utterances of the lowly, born of the very soil. Even Beethoven had gone to the old folk-songs for themes. Upon such a foundation composers might rear the stateliest structures. Once more the critics raved over the composer's depravity. Rubinstein sneered, Brahms wagged his head, Saint-Saëns scoffed. But Dvořák stood his ground. He had gone to America in search of new territory, and having found it, he was not to be frightened away. It was so with Wagner, and it must be so with every discoverer. The summit of the mountain is always lonely.

At last the strain of the controversy became too great, and in sheer desperation the great Bohemian announced that he would write a symphony suggested from beginning to end by negro melodies.[15] He dashed off a few bars in his note-book—which through the courtesy of the composer, we reproduce, and started out on a long summer vacation at Spillville, Iowa. Here, among a few Bohemian emigrants, surrounded by the mighty plains and filled with a sense of the vastness and solitude of the West, he poured out his soul in harmony. Day after day he sat at his table, working with his memories of plantation songs. On Sundays he would go to the village church and play the half-forgotten peasant-hymns of his native country until the simple old Bohemian farmers would cry with emotion. Before the frost came he had written one of the noblest works since the death of Wagner.

A great audience gathered to hear the first performance of the symphony in New York last winter, and I had the satisfaction of sitting beside Dvořák in his box, and hearing the roar of applause that swept through the hall at the close of the concert. The whole audience stood up and shouted. The members of the orchestra waved their instruments in the air. Billows of hands and faces seemed to surge below us. The critics mobbed the composer's box, each struggling to be the first to congratulate him. Then when it was all over and he reached the street, Dvořák took his hat off and mopped the perspiration from his brow.

"It is well," he said in his simple way. "He who will can, he who can must."

It must be supposed that Dvořák's "Fifth Symphony"—for that is the regular title—is made up of negro melodies. The composer has not taken the external forms of plantation music, but has here and there reflected their internal nature. Instead of adapting old slave-tunes he has used his own themes suggested by the southern music. Now and then the motifs and the rhythms strongly suggest the origin of the symphony. There is one little thread of melody that lilts itself in and out, strangely reminiscent of the negro, and yet in no way approaching negro melody. The symphony is marvelously free from affectation, and it is quite evident that Dvořák at no time allowed his theory to bind him, but wrote spontaneously, giving free rein to his imagination. It is a masterpiece of tone-painting, rich, generous, suave.

But that is not all. The National Conservatory of Music, of which Dvořák is director, has been thrown open to negroes of both sexes, so the white and black composers are now working out their destinies together under his watchful and affectionate care. This result is due to the president of the National Conservatory, Mrs. Jeanette M. Thurber, who has devoted her life and fortune to the cause of music in America.

The story of her life and of the sacrifices she has made would read strangely in these mercenary days. There is a Bill now pending before Congress providing for a grant of land in the national capital upon which a new conservatory is to be built for the co-education of black and white musicians. Dvořák's enthusiasm is almost pathetic. I fear that he does not yet appreciate the limitations of the negro race. In all that relates to melody and to temperament they are natural musicians, but it will take many generations of culture to develop their intellects to the point of appreciating the higher and larger forms of music. Meanwhile they may serve as hewers of wood and carriers of water to the white race, originating melodies which can be transformed in other hands. Surely if the warblings of birds, the murmuring of streams, and the sound of the wind among the trees speak to the souls of the great composers, the songs of a people living close to the soil are not without inspiration.

The quarrel between the dramatic and lyric schools of music— Dvořák representing one side and Rubinstein the other—hinges on the idea that controlled Dvořák in writing this symphony. The lyricists contend that the power of inventing melody is the supreme factor in music, that melody stands above and beyond all other things. The dramatists insist that the power of translating melody into the grander forms of harmony is the main thing. An ignorant slave may originate a tune, but only a poet can write a symphony. It is not too much to say that Dvořák is the foremost living composer, and that his word carries more authority than that of any contemporary. And for that reason his work among the negroes of America will be watched with profound interest. Had he chosen to content himself with the mere utterance of theories on the subject he might have failed to arrest the attention of the world, for musicians are commonly dreamers; but his symphony is an enduring monument on the shore of a new land.

Dvořák believes that great suffering is indispensable to great music. With a few exceptions, the world's composers have all endured poverty and contumely. Their music is full of the sorrows and triumphs of their loves. He believes that music conceived in the throes of bitterness and distress will suggest the surroundings from which it emerged, and in that sense it may be considered local. It is better to go to the common people for themes, for only that can survive which expresses their natures. The modern painter who expresses the idea of prayer by a haloed woman with folded hands and kneeling attitude, falls far below him who paints a grey-haired woman about to eat a crust of bread raising her reverent, thankful eyes toward Heaven.

[Source: *Pall Mall Budget*, 21 June 1894]

Antonín Dvořák

JAMES HUNEKER

James Gibbons Huneker was a prominent music critic and pianist. He became friendly with Dvořák shortly after the latter's arrival in New York. In addition to including descriptions and listings of the instructors active at the National Conservatory, this passage from Huneker's autobiography includes a delightful, and quite plausible, apocryphal description of a pub crawl through New York City. Some Dvořák scholars find this passage scandalous, and others see it as charming and refreshing. According to Kovařík's memoirs Huneker was deeply disappointed that Dvořák would not grant him an interview and took revenge directly after the premiere of the symphony by initiating a rumor that Dvořák's symphony was not written in America at all but rather in Europe. I have been unable to confirm Huneker's role in this story, nor has it been possible to confirm Kovařík's story about the interview. Some readers may find themselves disturbed by the characterization of the composer and the somewhat dismissive tone he takes toward his music, or, more likely, by the racist undertone to the discussion of American music. The Czech novelist Josef Škvorecký used this passage as a model when he put together a similar scene in his novel *Dvořák in Love*. [Ed.]

It was Rafael Joseffy who introduced me to Mrs. Jeannette M. Thurber. This energetic and public-spirited lady, who accomplished more by her failures than other people's successes, met with an enormous amount of critical opposition when she started the American opera movement. Some of her opponents would have liked to mount the "band wagon," and, failing, abused her audacity. But she had the right idea which was the French one. She first founded a National Conservatory in 1881, where musical talent was welcomed and tuition free. There was a "théâtre d'application," with Emy Fursch-Madi, Victor Capoul, Emil Fischer, M. Dufriche, Jacques Bouhy, and other famous opera singers and teachers, wherein the rudiments of acting and vocal delivery could be mastered. What a list of artists the faculty comprised! Antonín Dvořák, the great Bohemian composer, in his prime, was musical director; Rafael Joseffy and Adele Margulies—a fine pianist and founder of the Margulies Trio—headed the piano department; Camilla Urso, greatest of women violinists, Victor Herbert, then a leading solo violoncellist, Leopold Lichtenberg, formerly of the Boston Symphony Orchestra, and one of the most brilliant American talents I recall—although John F. Rhodes, of Philadelphia, had an immense technical gift, Anton Seidl, Otto Oesterle, the flutist of the Thomas Orchestra and the Philharmonic Society, conductor Frank Van der Stucken, Emil

Paur, C. P. Warren, organist, Bruno Oscar Klein, Horatio Parker, Wassili Safanoff, Gustav Hinrichs, John Cheshire, the harpist, Sapio, Fritz Geise, great Dutch cellist of the Kneisel Quartet, Leo Schulz, first cellist of the Philharmonic, Julia Wyman, all these and others were teachers at this institution, which was then located on Seventeenth Street, east of Irving Place. Well I remember the day that I begged Harry Rowe Shelley, the Brooklyn organist, to submit his compositions to Dvořák; later he became one of the pupils of that master; some of the others were Rubin Goldmark, nephew of the famous composer, himself one of the most gifted among our younger Americans. Harvey W. Loomis, Henry Waller, Harry T. Burleigh, the popular coloured barytone, now a composer of repute, and William Arms Fisher. Henry T. Finck, the faithful, still lectures in the National Conservatory at its new building on the West Side. I taught piano classes twice weekly for ten years, and in addition was the press representative of the Conservatory and secretary to the Secretary, Mr. Stanton, and after he died, I was a secretary to Mrs. Thurber, my chief duty being a daily visit at her residence, where I sat for an hour and admired her good looks. She was a picturesque woman, Gallic in her "allures," but more Spanish than French in features. She spoke French like a Parisian, and after thirty years I confess that her fine, dark, eloquent eyes troubled my peace more than once. But I only took it out in staring. Curiously to relate, Mrs. Thurber has changed but little, a grey lock or two, which only makes her more picturesque than ever.

Old Borax, as Dvořák was affectionately called, was handed over to me by Madame Thurber when he arrived. He was a fervent Roman Catholic, and I hunted a Bohemian church for him as he began his day with an early Mass. Rather too jauntily I invited him to taste the American drink called a whisky cocktail. He nodded his head, that of an angry-looking bulldog with a beard. He scared one at first with his fierce Slavonic eyes, but was as mild a mannered man as ever scuttled a pupil's counterpoint. I always spoke of him as a boned pirate. But I made a mistake in believing that American strong waters would upset his Czech nerves. We began at Goerwirz, then described a huge circle, through the great thirst belt of central New York. At each place Doc Borax took a cocktail. Now, alcohol I abhor, so I stuck to my guns, the usual three-voiced invention, hops, malt, and spring water. We spoke in German and I was happy to meet a man whose accent and grammar were worse than my own. Yet we got along swimmingly—an appropriate enough image, for the weather was wet, though not squally. He told me of Brahms and that composer's admiration for Dvořák. I agreed with Brahms. Dvořák had a fresh, vigorous talent, was a born Impressionist, and possessed a happy colour sense in his orchestration. His early music was the best; he was an imitator of Schubert and Wagner, and never used quotation marks. But the American theory of native music never appealed to me. He did, and dexterously, use some negro, or alleged negro, tunes in his "New World Symphony," and in one of his string quartets; but if we are to have true American music it will not stem from "darky" roots, especially as the most original music of that kind thus far written is by Stephen Foster, a white man. The influence of Dvořák's American music has been evil; ragtime is the popular pabulum now. I need hardly add that the negro is not the original race of our country. And ragtime is only rhythmic motion, not music. The Indian has more pretensions musically as E. A. MacDowell has shown in his Suite for Orchestra. This statement does not impeach the charm of the African music made by Harry Burleigh; I only wish to emphasise my disbelief in the fine-spun theories of certain folk-lorists. MacDowell is our most truly native composer, an Alsatian born is now our most potent American composer. His name is Charles Martin Loeffler, and he shared the first desk of the violins in the Boston Symphony Orchestra with Franz Kneisel, a noble artist. I mention Loeffler lest we forget.

But Borax! I left him swallowing his nineteenth cocktail. "Master," I said, rather thickly, "don't you think it's time we ate something?" He gazed at me through those awful whiskers which met his tumbled hair half-way: "Eat. No. I no eat. We go to a Houston Street restaurant. You go, hein? We drink the Slivavitch. It warms you after so much beer." I didn't go that evening to the East Houston Street Bohemian café with Dr. Antonín Dvořák. I never went with him. Such a man is as dangerous to a moderate drinker as a false beacon is to a shipwrecked sailor. And he could drink as much spirits as I could the amber brew. No, I assured Mrs. Thurber that I was through with piloting him. When I met Old Borax again at Sokel Hall, the Bohemian resort on the East Side, I deliberately dodged him. I taught one class which was nicknamed "in darkest Africa" because all the pupils were coloured. I confess a liking for negroes, possibly because of my childhood days spent in Maryland. They are very human, very musical, their rhythmic sense remarkable. I had a talented pupil named Paul Bolin, who also studied organ with Heinroth; and another, Henry Guy, whose piano talent was not to be denied. I had the pleasure of hearing this pupil play Mendelssohn's "Capriccio Brillante" in B minor with an orchestra conducted by Gustav Hinrichs, well known to Philadelphians for his pioneer work there in opera. Both these young men are now professionals, and like the many hundreds educated at the National Conservatory, are earning their living in a dignified manner. What Mrs. Thurber has done for the negro alone will, I hope, be credited to her account in any history of the coloured race. Her musical activities are still unabated. In 1891, Congress granted her school a charter, and the privilege of conferring the degree of musical doctorship.[16] With the war over, the National Conservatory should by right of precedent, and by reason of the vast good accomplished in the musical world since 1881, be made a national institution. So mote [*sic*] it be.

[Source: James Gibbons Huneker, *Steeplejack*, 2 vols. (New York, 1920), vol. 2, pp. 65–69]

Dvořák (1841–1904):
An American Symphony

H. L. MENCKEN

We offer this article about Dvořák's "New World" Symphony for several reasons. First, Mencken was one of the most influential writers in this country for many years and had strong and well-developed views on a number of subjects. In addition, although this article appears in a collection of writings called *Mencken on Music* I have decided to reprint it here because it is hardly known among Dvořák scholars. Like Creelman's article, Mencken's has a racist tinge to it that some may consider distasteful, but collecting a sanitized version of the past is not the task of the historian or of this project. [Ed.]

Antonín Dvořák's symphony, "Z nového světa" (From the New World) which Mr. Strube and his estimable tone artists are to unroll at the Lyric on Friday evening, was written in 1894 or thereabouts, while old Antonín was undergoing three years' penal servitude in New York.[17] He had come to America in 1892 to become director of a conservatory, and, like many other visiting musicians (for example, Paderewski) he had been greatly intrigued by the lively niggerish swing of American popular music. The result was that he gave a lot of hard study to American folk-song, and particularly to the folk-song of the Negroes, and the second result was a group of three very excellent compositions—his string quartet in F, his string quintet in D flat [*sic*] and the aforesaid "From the New World."

The latter made an immediate success and has since remained one of the most popular works in the classical repertoire. A fashion of sniffing at it has grown up among the musical pundits, but the fact is not of much significance, for exactly the same sniffs are directed at a number of indubitable masterpieces, including Beethoven's incomparable Eighth Symphony, which Mr. Strube presented last season. The truth is that "From the New World" is a first-rate work of art, honestly constructed and superbly written. It is clear; it is ingenious; it is sound; it is beautiful. If, made mellow by its luscious phrases, you find yourself rolling your eyes at the performance, then please, I prithee, do not blush. It is well worth an oscillation or two of even the most cultured eye. You will search a long while, indeed, among the symphonies of these later years before you find better writing and better music.

The question as to how much of the work is Bohemian and how much American has long engaged those who delight in musical anatomizing, and the weight of opinion seems to be that the composer's nationality over-balanced his purpose, which was to introduce Americans to their own music. The verdict is both platitudinous and unsound. It is platitudinous because all art is revealed in terms of the artist's temperament, and in Dvořák's case temperament was indistinguishable from nationality. He was, indeed, a Bohemian of the Bohemians, and he could no more conceal the fact when he sat down to write music than he could change the contours of his peculiarly baroque and dog-like visage. And it is unsound because even the most cursory examination shows enough genuine niggerishness in his symphony to outfit a Kerry Mills.[18] He was not trying to write a symphony— a thing rigid in its design and even in its details. The form he worked in was German and the temperament he brought to the business was Bohemian, but the materials he made use of were at least two-thirds American, and so he was quite right in calling the product an American symphony.

If you don't believe it get a good edition of the Jubilee Songs and the score of the symphony and go through them at the piano on some quiet Sunday afternoon. In the very first subject of the first movement you will find a plain reminiscence of "Roll, Jordan, Roll," and in the characteristic jumpy figure which immediately follows (and which holds together the whole first movement) you will encounter an old friend. This figure, perhaps, cannot be traced to any definite Negro song or dance, but it is nevertheless as indubitably niggerish as hog and hominy. And out of it (first tooted by the woodwind, and then taken up by the strings) there grows a subject which strangely suggests "Didn't My Lord Deliver Daniel?" and on top of it there comes a palpable borrowing from "Oh, Redeemed," unchanged even in key. These three subjects, beautifully worked out, supply the materials of the whole first movement. Nothing else is in it. And all three come straight from the Jubilee Songs.[19]

The other movements show fewer direct borrowings. They are, indeed, rather paraphrases of American music than direct imitations of it. Dvořák, one fancies, was inspired to undertake the work by the powerful appeal of one or two tunes, especially "Roll, Jordan, Roll"— and exhausted them in his first movement. But in the second movement—the succulent and famous largo—there is still a clear echo from the plantation. The curve of the melody is his own, but the rhythm owes much to such songs as "Nobody Knows the Trouble I See," and "Rise, Mourners," and the plaintive, wailing spirit of Negro music is in every measure of it. Turn to "Many Thousands Gone," so beautifully realized in later years by S. Coleridge-Taylor, and you will note the kinship at once. Even in the wild episode which breaks into the lament there is true Negro color. No Negro, it may be admitted, ever danced to this precise tune, but many a Negro has shaken his legs to tunes curiously like it.

The Scherzo goes further afield. One discerns in it many characteristic fragments of Negro rhythm, but melodically it is sophisticated and European. Its two surpassingly beautiful episodes are wholly beyond the range of Negro song; they suggest Schubert, not Booker Washington. Moreover, the very time signature is exotic, for the blackamoor almost invariably hoofs his fandangos and sets up his caterwauling in four-four time; the triple measure belongs to the late stage of musical evolution. But in the last movement—a very fine piece of writing— Dvořák returns to his muttons. Here, as in the largo, it is difficult to track down definite sources, but here again the swing and color are unmistakably niggerish. The thing starts off with a loud braying and stamping of feet; it proceeds to a wild hoedown; it ends in whoops and snorts that die down to whispers. For all its prodigality of melody, a Negro-like monotony is in it; the violas drone a fierce and savage figure while woodwind and fiddles sport with fragments from the second and third movements above them. And toward the end, against a musical fabric made up of these figures and others, all the choirs in their turn fling a barbarous syncopated phrase that infallibly suggests the loud cries of a Negro dance.

The last movement, it is true, contains some of the best writing that Dvořák ever did. It is, for him, extremely complex in structure; there is scarcely a moment of pure homophony, the polyphonic web is elaborately woven. And yet, for all that intricacy of design, there is perfect clarity in it, and even a sort of naked simplicity. One feels that he has gone beyond the plantation songs to the rude and violent chants of the jungle; the atmosphere is one of frank savagery; it is difficult to listen to the rush of sound without being stirred.

But the first movement is the most remarkable of the four, for in it Dvořák accomplishes something that he seldom accomplished elsewhere. That is to say, he sticks to the strict sonata form, without episodes, and is almost as austere in his use of materials as Brahms. The old fellow was not at ease in this sort of writing. His natural bent was toward a gigantic and somewhat disorderly piling up of ideas, as in his Dumky trio, his string quartets and the scherzo of the present symphony. So many melodies buzzed in his head that it was hard for him to settle down to the laborious development of two or three; new ones were always pressing to be heard. But here, as I say, he retained his Bohemian exuberance with German *Zucht*, and the result is a very fine piece of writing, indeed.

On the side of instrumentation the whole symphony is extremely lovely. Dvořák's long years of service in the orchestra pit gave him a firm grip upon all the tricks, and so his score glows with gorgeous colors. Give your ear to the largo if you would hear a perfect concord of sounds. From the incomparable opening chords to the last arpeggio of the muted violins there is one long procession of beauties. And in the last movement, again, he shows himself a genuine master of the orchestra. The thing often sounds barbarously harsh and naif, but there is deft and thoughtful workmanship in every measure of it.

Dvořák was the son of a Bohemian tavern keeper and butcher, and his father designated him for the latter art. But he took to playing the fiddle in his nonage and soon became so proficient that he decided to study music. This, however, was easier planned than done, for the elder Dvořák was poor and there were few competent teachers in the neighborhood. When he was 12 years old he was sent to a town called Zlonitz, where an uncle lived, and there he had some lessons from an organist named Liehmann. Regarding this Liehmann the chronicle is otherwise silent, but he seems to have taught young Antonín the rudiments of organ-playing and enough harmony to keep him going. His first composition belongs to this period. It was a polka for the village band at home. The polka itself seems to have been very creditable, but in scoring it the boy forgot to transpose the trumpet part, and so the first performance ended with yells for the police.

Late in his teens Dvořák went to Prague, and there, for a good many years, he played the fiddle in theater orchestras and made a scanty living teaching. All the while he was piling up compositions on his shelf—songs, string quartets, operettas, even a symphony or two. Most of these things were unperformed: there seemed little likelihood that he would ever be heard of beyond the town. He was 32 years old before he got his chance. It came when he was commissioned to write music for a cantata by Hálek, a favorite Bohemian poet. The result was "Die Erben des Weissen Berges" ("The Heirs of the White Mountains"). It made a considerable success, and some of Antonín's cobwebbed compositions were exhumed and performed, including a symphony in E flat never published. But this success led to little, and Dvořák remained unknown in the great world until he was discovered by Brahms in 1877. Brahms then did for him what Schumann, years before, had done for Brahms himself; that is, he advised him, encouraged him, and, more important still, talked about him. A year later Dvořák published his "Slavische Tänze" and was a made man. These dances swept through Germany as Brahms' Hungarian dances had swept through it a few years before. The musical publishers, once so coy, now besieged the composer with offers, and he answered them with a flood of manuscripts. By 1880 he was securely on his legs.

Hans von Bülow, a sincere admirer of Dvořák, almost cooked his goose for him by calling him "Der Bauer im Frack" (the peasant in a dress coat). This apt and yet unfortunate label has stuck to him ever since, and most criticism of his work has taken color from it. The result is that he is commonly regarded as a sort of inspired clodhopper, with a fine musical gift but with little genuine musical skill. Nothing could be further from the truth. The fact is that Dvořák, though almost self-taught, acquired a sure command of the methods of composition, and that his best work is highly discreet and sophisticated. He had a better command of polyphony, indeed, than Schubert, but like Schubert he was often carried away by the exuberance of his own verbosity. Melodies gurgled from him like cider from a jug; he could scarcely get one to paper before another came bubbling out. The consequence, particularly in his early compositions, is a confusing oversupply of materials. They seem, at times, to be no more than disorderly strings of unrelated episodes.

But in his later years he made a deliberate effort to bring his genius into better discipline, and the effects of that effort are plainly to be seen in the New World symphony. The first movement, in particular, is full of evidence of a restraining intent. The three subjects, for all their barbaric color, are still somewhat terse and austere—that is, for Dvořák—and their working out is carried on with a relentlessness that he seldom shows anywhere else. No episodes creep in to relieve and corrupt the business; what other material is used (putting aside the monotonous, juggling figure which runs from end to end) is manifestly derived from them; the whole thing hangs together; there is unbroken clarity in it.

In the largo the composer returns to easier devices. The form is that of a simple lyric, with a sharp and characteristic change of mood in the middle section. This is the sort of writing that came most gracefully to

Dvořák's hand; one finds it again in the most familiar of all his compositions, the celebrated "Humoresque." And in the scherzo, as has been
said, two episodes of extraordinary beauty are dragged in, almost by
the heels. But in the gaudy and turbulent last movement, for all the
piling up of tunes, there is a return to letter form, and toward the end
of it the composer rises to brilliant heights. Here the whole symphony is
rehearsed. Bits of the first and second movements are borrowed to
adorn the fabric; there are violent contrasts in tempo, rhythm and
dynamics; the thing goes with a rush that conceals its ingenuity of
design and execution.

Dvořák had a hard time of it as a young man. His salary at Prague,
where he was organist for a while, was $80 a year. But after success
overtook him, toward middle life, he prospered financially as well as
artistically, and during his three years in New York he received $15,000
a year, besides what he could make playing at weddings. A portrait of
the period, printed in Grove's Dictionary of Music, shows him elegantly
accoutered, with no less than three diamond horseshoes in his cravat.
In 1891 he was given the degree of doctor of music by Cambridge
University. He died on May 1, 1904.

NOTES

1. Richard Henry Warren (1859–1933) was an organist, a composer, and the
founding conductor of the Church Choral Society, which gave the first American performances of works by Dvořák and others. [Ed.]

2. Thomas Wentworth Higginson (1823–1911) was a reformer, soldier, and
author. He was a noted supporter of women's suffrage and a fierce opponent of
slavery. After serving as a Unitarian minister he became colonel of the first
African-American regiment in the Civil War. His books include *Army Life of a
Black Regiment* (1870), *History of the United States* (1875), and books on Long-
fellow and Whittier. He is also credited with discovering and heralding the
American poet Emily Dickinson. He is not to be confused with Henry Lee
Higginson (1834–1918), who founded the Boston Symphony Orchestra. [Ed.]

3. James Gibbons Huneker (1860–1921), a gifted pianist and critic who
wrote for the *Musical Courier* when Dvořák was in New York. About him his
colleague, William James Henderson, said: "In his early days in New York,
Huneker was fonder of a witty saying than of serious thought and this feeling
never left him." But he was acknowledged by Henderson and others as a
brilliant figure who was deeply interested in both new and older music. [Ed.]

4. An annotated version of this article appears in *Notes* 49, no.2 (December
1992): 447–73. [Ed.]

5. These comments are a response to an article that appeared in the *New York
Herald* on 17 December 1893. Perhaps the tone of the article can best be

understood by noting that the piece has a title and four subtitles that read: "Dvořák's Symphony: A Historic Event / First Rude Draft of the Original Thought Appeared in the Herald / Eve of a New Musical Epoch / Much Credit Is Due to the Persistent Labors of Mrs. Jeannette Thurber / Critics Suffer a Defeat." It is also curious that the writer of this article believed that Dvořák had written his symphony in response to a negative evaluation of his "On the Real Value of Negro Melodies." Actually, the opposite is true; the writings first appeared immediately after the conclusion of the symphony. [Ed.]

6. According to Huneker's memoirs, part of which are reproduced in this volume, Jeannette Thurber asked him to look after the Czech composer shortly after his arrival in New York. We do not know precisely what "specimen themes" Huneker claims to have given Dvořák. [Ed.]

7. This reference to "Yankee Doodle" is found in Krehbiel's article: "It is (whether intentional or not it is not for us to say) a paraphrase of 'Yankee Doodle,' a fact which would be more strongly forced upon the attention were it not that it seems to have been introduced only as an accompaniment to the subject of the slow movement, which soon makes its appearance in another part of the score. We strongly suspect that Dr. Dvořák is a wag, and that the little phrase, instead of being the innocent offspring of the finale's subject, is really its progenitor." [Ed.]

8. Following Boss Tweed's thievery and insider contracting in the 1860s and 1870s, and the later efforts of Bosses Croaker and Kelly, Tammany Hall was well known as a corrupt Irish and German political organization. The readership of the *Musical Courier* would have certainly been amused by the reference. [Ed.]

9. Emil Paur (1855–1932) was born in Bukovina in Sub-Carpathian Ruthenia. He was a conductor and violinist. Before coming to the United States he conducted in Kassel, Königsberg, Mannheim, and Leipzig. He was the conductor of the Boston Symphony Orchestra from 1893 to 1899, succeeding Nikisch, and succeeded Seidl at the New York Philharmonic Society from 1898 to 1902. He was conductor of the Pittsburgh Symphony from 1904 to 1910. He was also director of the National Conservatory after Dvořák's tenure there, from 1899 to 1902. He died in Mistek, Czechoslovakia. [Ed.]

10. Philip Hale (1854–1934) was music critic for the *Boston Journal* (1891–1903) and music and drama critic for the *Boston Herald* (1903–33). He was also a highly successful program annotator for the Boston Symphony Orchestra between 1901 and 1934. [Ed.]

11. The Kneisel Quartet was founded in 1885 and is the earliest American quartet to achieve international prominence. The founding members were the principal string players of the Boston Symphony Orchestra. In its thirty-two years of existence the quartet introduced the works of Brahms (who was on close personal terms with the members of the group) and Dvořák to the United States and premiered the compositions of many American composers. (The editor is grateful to Daniel Swartz for his help in assembling this material.) [Ed.]

12. Baldassare Galuppi (1706–1785), an enormously successful Italian composer especially significant in the development of opera buffa. This phrase

comes from Charles Burney's *Music, Men, and Manners in France and Italy, 1770*, ed. H. Edmund Poole (London, 1974), p. 82. [Ed.]

13. The tune of these variations, though, was suggested by Dvořák as a replacement for the American national anthem. See Jarmil Burghauser's article "My Country 'Tis of Thee," in *Dvořák in America*, ed. John Tibbets (Portland, Ore., 1993). [Ed.]

14. This indicates that Creelman may well be inspiration for "On the Real Value of Negro Melodies," published in the *New York Herald* on 21 May 1893. [Ed.]

15. Creelman must have his chronology wrong here. By the time Dvořák's articles on national music appeared, the symphony was finished, apart from some minor details of tempo and scoring. The notion that the symphony was written in Spillville had quite a bit of currency. It is, of course, entirely false. [Ed.]

16. For a good history of the National Conservatory see "Dvořák at the National Conservatory" by Emanuel Rubin, in *Dvořák in America*. [Ed.]

17. Of course, the symphony was written from the end of 1892 to the autumn of 1893, with the vast bulk of the work completed by the spring of 1893. [Ed.]

18. Kerry Mills (1869–1948) was a publisher and a popular song composer. He wrote "At a Georgia Camp Meeting" and "Meet Me in St. Louis, Louis." [Ed.]

19. These Jubilee Songs were arrangements of Negro spirituals presented by the Fisk Jubilee Singers. This group was organized in 1871 to raise money for Fisk University in Nashville. This group was the first to introduce this repertoire to white audiences. Of course, Mencken is wrong here. [Ed.]

Letters from Dvořák's American Period: A Selection of Unpublished Correspondence Received by Dvořák in the United States

The following letters were all received by Dvořák during his years in the United States and, unless otherwise indicated, have never before appeared in print. They range from professional greetings and salutations to the cries of amateur instrumentalists from the musical wilderness. Here are letters from the critic Henry Krehbiel, which include African-American songs from Kentucky, and a letter from an unknown student, Michael Banner, which begins in a desultory manner and evolves into a passionate tribute. These letters reveal that the composer served as a kind of magnet for a wide range of individuals, particularly those with a serious interest in American musical phenomena. Finally, we include some letters from a Czech friend in Spillville, Iowa, which reveal the charm of Dvořák's less exalted relationships.

We are indebted to Milan Kuna, general editor of *Antonín Dvořák: Korespondence a dokumenty* (Prague, 1987–89), for allowing us to use this material. Economic conditions in the Czech Republic have made it impossible to continue publishing further volumes at this time. Should it be possible to continue with the series, the material offered here will appear in vol. 4.

.

At the end of November 1892 Dvořák traveled to Boston to conduct his *Requiem*. The following two letters document that visit and the response to his work. [Ed.]

November 26, 1892

Esteemed Sir,

Permit me to add to the many greetings, you may receive at your first visit of Boston, a few hearty words of welcome from the Administration and Faculty of the Conservatory of Music, of which I am the Director. We are all happy to have an opportunity of hearing one of your master works under your own direction and you have our sincere wishes for a great success.

I asked Mr. Lang,[1] whether you might not be interested to look over our Institution and he thinks, you would be able to arrange for it and would probably be quite interested in doing it.

I shall be at the Conservatory all day any day next week and if you should decide to favor us with a visit, I should be very thankful, to receive a few lines in advance, stating day and hour when you intend to come. I will make your visit just as formal or informal as you desire.

Hoping to receive a favorable reply I remain very respectfully yours

Carl Faelton[2]

Pemberton Sq., Boston
December 15, 1892

My dear Doctor,

I am directed by the government and members of the Cecelia to extend to you their cordial thanks for the honor which you conferred upon them in conducting their first performance of your glorious "Requiem."[3] The opportunity thus given them of making your personal acquaintance, of listening to your instruction, of singing under your baton and of paying you their sincere homage, is something which will not be easily forgotten by them.

Of the beauty of your noble composition it would be impertinent to speak. When the musical world has already spoken, any small body of music lovers can find nothing to add. Boston is fortunate in receiving its first impression of the great work at the hand of its great composer.

In the earnest hope that your stay in America may be as pleasant to yourself as it will surely be profitable to the country, and that Boston may have many more occasions of renewing an acquaintance so delightfully begun, I am my dear Doctor, most gratefully and respectfully yours.

S. Lothrop Thorndike

Many people wrote spontaneous letters to Dvořák from the "wilder" parts of the country. We do not have a full record of his responses, nor can most of these people be identified as anything but amateur musicians, but these letters reveal how important his arrival was to many Americans who were pursuing art and culture in more provincial areas. [Ed.]

San Diego, California

October 26 [1893?]

Dear Sir,

On this remote California shore close to the Mexican line so remote and isolated that perhaps the place has never been brought to your notice, we have a prosperous musical society and are faithfully studying the works of Dr. Dvořák. We encounter almost insurmountable problems since it is difficult to obtain even a catalogue of your music but have great enthusiasm and reverence for the Master who is doing so much for the development of music in America. Would it be too presumptuous to ask Dr. Dvořák to send us a few words of encouragement and advice?

Yours with sincere devotion,

Flora B. Arndt

104 Sixth St., San Diego, California

·

San Francisco

November 14, 1894

Dear Sir,

I take great pleasure in sending you the enclosed programme, which you will see contains one of your master-works, the Quartet in E♭. It was received with the greatest enthusiasm. Our organisation, which has been giving chamber concerts for the last four years, has already produced some of your Piano Trios, the Piano Quintet and has been especially successful with the beautiful Terzetto for strings. I have been enquiring for your latest String Quartet, but have not been able to get it.

Pray accept the expression of my sincere admiration, and believe me to be yours very truly

Sigmund Beel

1925 California Street

San Francisco, Cal.

·

January 28, 1895

Dear Sir!

Some time ago I took the liberty of sending you a programme containing your E flat Piano Quartet, which was successfully performed here for the first time. I hope you receive the same. And I now enclose you a programme containing another of your works, which created a sensation in the musical world here. I have no doubt the enclosed cuttings will have some interest for you. I cannot resist telling you how much my colleagues and myself have enjoyed the F major Quartet. The slow movement being wonderfully, beautiful. I am very proud, indeed, to have produced your works in California for the first time.

With heartiest esteem and admiration, I beg to remain yours very sincerely

Sigmund Beel

.

From William Smythe Babcock Matthews[4]
Chicago, April 18, 1893

Dear Sir,

I have been hearing your works such as "The Spectre's Bride," the "Requiem," symphonies, a violin concerto, and in New York a quartet of yours by the Kneisel Quartet (where I attended in company with Dr. William Mason[5]) and it was not lost upon me the honor which your coming to America conferred upon our country. It was my desire to print a sketch of you, and a picture, in the magazine I edit, a copy of which I have directed to be sent you. But I found myself treated with what I regarded as unnecessary rudeness at the Conservatory, and therefore decided to give myself no further trouble in the matter. This was wrong in me, for I believe you to be either the very first of living composers, or at least one of the two or three very first. Mr. Schoenfeld[6] has today been telling me how nice you were to him. The object of this is to say that I am going to make a little sketch of you in connection with the "Requiem," which pleased here very much last week, and to print your picture. I would also like to mention anything of yours which you would prefer—in case of compositions not yet performed. In case you should feel free to say anything of America, or music, that I could print, I would be glad to put it in.

But my immediate object is to say to you that if you feel free to say anything encouraging concerning Mr. Schoenfeld's work, anything that I could publish, it would do him good, and I should be very glad to get it.

In regard to your "Requiem," I will say that it appears to me one of the purest musical works the Apollo Club has done for years. That you are not everywhere in it governed by the same principles, is a fact due to the transitional state in which music just now is. For instance I find what the painters call "impressionist" methods in the general treatment of the text (but a very deep and poetic impressionism) and in other places the long rhythmic swing of the classic method (as in the "Quam olim Abrahae" and another movement that I cannot at the moment recall); and yet again a trace of realism, as when the congregation mutters its prayers, as the "requiem aeternam" in 16th notes.

In short it is a great work. Your orchestration pleased us all very much, and I was particularly gratified with the moderation of it, considering the temptation to let loose after the manner of Berlioz on the "Dies irae." All this, however, you will care but little for. And so allow me once more to introduce myself as a real admirer of the composer, and a would-be friend to the man.

I hope you will remain in America a long time.

Very respectfully

W.S.B. Matthews

·

Boston, May 23, 1893

My dear Sir,

I have just read the *New York Herald* statements of your views upon the future school of music in America, and want to thank you most heartily for the good such opinion so forcibly expressed will do.

I am desirous of your knowing of the peculiar song building, to coin an expression of the negroes employed in the great tobacco shop at Richmond in the state of Virginia. So few people interested in music visit these places that you can hardly have become acquainted with this subject through your studies since your arrival.

These shops are filled with negroes from all parts of the old slave states. They bring their old time "tunes" with them and from day to day new "tunes" are built up in this way.

A man or woman at one bench breaks out with a theme, fitting words of any sort to it, his neighbor catches it up and adds to it and so it is passed on until a song is the result. Some of these shops had regular programmes which the people sung for visitors; when I had visited Richmond and I assure you they get surprisingly pleasing results. It may offer a suggestive field for some of your students.

Pardon the liberty thus taken with your time and believe me to be your sincere admirer.

Fred R. Bacon

·

Louisville, Kentucky
March 2, 1895

Honored Sir!

May I address you upon a subject in which you seem to be much interested: viz—street cries. After reading your article in the February

Harper[7] I looked up a collection of street cries I have been gathering for several years and am writing an article for the Women's edition of the *Courier Journal* to be illustrated with these cries I send you.

I collected them just for the interest I took in them never expecting to make any use of them but since I began the study of composition I have found them very useful. The negro always uses the syllable "quo" instead of "coal" as you see in the illustration. After reading your article and because I am such a lover of your music I made a trip of nearly three hundred miles to hear Mr. Seidl direct your New World Symphony in Cincinnati. I was so carried away by it that I determined to send you the enclosed examples. It takes a real southern person to really understand your work in that Symphony, in my humble opinion. I also have a number of unpublished negro hymns which are fine specimens. Harper Brothers have them now for examination. Hoping you will find these street cries of interest I am very respectfully

Mildred J. Hill

1109 2nd Street

Louisville Kentucky

.

In 1894 Dvořák collaborated with the critic Henry Finck on an article on Schubert for the *Century Illustrated Monthly Magazine*. The following letters are related to that project and offer a glimpse of the inner workings of Dvořák's collaboration with Finck. [Ed.]

May 24, 1893

My dear Dr. Dvořák,

The *Century* appreciates very sincerely your courtesy in the matter of the article on Schubert and reluctantly acquiesces in your wish in the matter.[8]

I should explain that there is no haste in the matter of the corrections, as the article will not appear for some months, being part of our series by living composers of the Great Composers of the Past. In this series Mr. Reyes has written of Berlioz and Mr. Paderewski will write of Chopin and Mr. Grieg of Schumann and the series on a similar scale will include, we hope, Messrs. Brahms, Rubinstein, Verdi, Boito, Tschaikowsky, Sullivan and others. The *Century* appears once a month.

Pray accept these copies of the magazine containing Mr. Krehbiel's article on yourself,[9] and believe me (again with thanks) very respectfully yours,

R. U. Johnson

November 2, 1893

Dear Mr. Dvořák:

I do this hesitantly, for I know you are very busy, but I am coming to trouble you once more with the essay on Schubert. Namely, it pleased the editors of the *Century* very much but it is *too short*. The essays by Grieg on Schumann and Saint-Saëns on Liszt, etc., are significantly longer and now the editorial staff would like me to have another meeting with you in order to collect still more of your opinions.

In order to make the matter as convenient as possible for you, I have put together the attached outline. I ask you to read it through a couple of times and to give me a chance to see you at your home or in the Conservatory sometime within the next 8–10 days. The whole thing will be done very honestly. In a footnote it will be stated that you are responsible only for the *opinions* in the essay, not for the exact wording—in other words more like an interview.

I have taken *great* pains to come up with interesting points of view, because I love Schubert very much. I know that you love him too, and believe that for *this* reason you will be willing to be disturbed once more, for this article in a monthly like the *Century* will contribute a great deal to the popularity of Schubert in America.

With friendly greetings,
H. T. Finck

This is a letter from Henry Thacker Burleigh, Dvořák's friend and sometimes inspiration, introducing Will Marion Cook. Cook ultimately did become a student of Dvořák and played a significant role, like Burleigh, in the development of African-American music. [Ed.]

August 13, 1893

Dear Doctor,

I want to introduce to your consideration Mr. Will M. Cook,[10] a former pupil of the great Joachim. Mr. Cook has marked ability in the line of composition and desires very greatly to meet you and speak with you about his work. He has composed an opera, the principal role of which I will sing. You remember I sang Mr. Ainney's two songs at your last concert at the Conservatory last May.

I am going away from Chicago today but will leave this note for you and Mr. Cook will call and see you.

I sincerely trust you will listen to his work and give him your opinion. Hoping you will be blessed with continued good health and success and that I will meet you in the Conservatory next September, I have the privilege to remain yours very truly

Harry T. Burleigh[11]

These two letters were written to Dvořák by the important critic and writer Henry Krehbiel (for more on Krehbiel see Joseph Horowitz's essay and the reviews and criticism from Dvořák's American years, in this volume). These two letters are of particular importance because they prove that Krehbiel's article on the symphony, which appeared on 15 December 1893 in the *New York Tribune*, was based on a lengthy interview with the composer. That article has been reprinted, with annotations, in the December 1992 issue of *Notes*. [Ed.]

152 W. 105th St.
New York, December 12, 1893

My dear Dr. Dvořák!

I have heard your symphony at a rehearsal and read the score. I am delighted with it and intend to print an article to help people to understand and enjoy it on Friday.[12] May I call on you on Wednesday to show you the excerpts I have made from the score?[13]

On Saturday afternoon I will lecture on "Folk-Song in America" at a reception of the Women's University Club. Will you do me the honor to attend and hear the songs which I have for illustration? I am sure you will be interested in the music if not in the lecture and the ladies of the Club would be glad to see you. Please drop me a note and let me know when to call on Friday and where, if you are willing to see me.

With much admiration and respect.

H. E. Krehbiel

"Castle Hotel"

Saturday

My dear Dr. Dvořák,

I am overwhelmed with your kindness in making the notes on your symphony.[14] It not only relieved me of embarrassment but enabled me also to enlist in a peculiar degree the interest of about 40 young ladies to whom I talked about the work Thursday night and who heard it yesterday afternoon. I have no greater happiness from 20 years of labor on behalf of good music than has come to me from the consciousness that I may have been to some degree instrumental in helping the public to appreciate your compositions and especially this beautiful symphony. I wish that there were some way in which I could show my gratitude for this last act of kindness but till I find out I must content myself by thanking you most cordially and sincerely.

Faithfully your friend and admirer

H. E. Krehbiel

·

Little more than a week after the premiere of the Ninth Symphony, Krehbiel sent Dvořák some samples of African-American songs, shown here in facsimile. [Ed.]

152 W. 105th St., N.Y.
December 26, 1893

Dear Dr. Dvořák,

Will you kindly let me know when I may have an hour of your time to look on the quartet and quintet again. Say next Friday or Saturday. I have just received three more singular negro songs from Kentucky. I send the melodies for you to examine and would be more than delighted if you care to suggest a harmonization.

Sincerely yours
H. E. Krehbiel

·

Dvořák's association with the New York Philharmonic Society was extremely warm, forming one of the most successful chapters in the composer's life. The following four letters document both the preliminary request for the Symphony "From the New World" and Dvořák's honorary membership in the Society. [Ed.]

New York, February 22, 1893

Dear Doctor Dvořák:

On behalf of the members of the Philharmonic Society of New York, the undersigned has the pleasant duty of expressing the profound gratitude of the directors and members of the above-mentioned Society for personally directing your First Symphony on the occasion of the second concert of the current season.—To be able to appreciate this composition, at once so successful and characteristic, under the baton of the genius who created it was to enjoy an artistic pleasure that will

/52 W 105ᵗʰ st. N.Y.
Dec. 26, 1893.

Dear Dr. Dvořák.

Will you kindly let me know
when I may have an hour of your time
to look on the quartet & quintet again.
Say next Friday or Saturday. I have
just received two three more singular
negro songs from Kentucky. I send
the melodies for you to examine and
would be more than delighted if you
care to suggest a harmonization.
Sincerely yours
H. E. Krehbiel

Henry Krehbiel's letter to Dvořák of 26 December 1893

remain vivid in the memory of the public and of your collaborators.

In the hope of having the honor of working together again often in equally rewarding circumstances, I remain, in the name of the Philharmonic Society, respectfully

Aug. Roebbelen[15]
Secretary

Negro melodies that Krehbiel sent to Dvořák on 26 December 1892

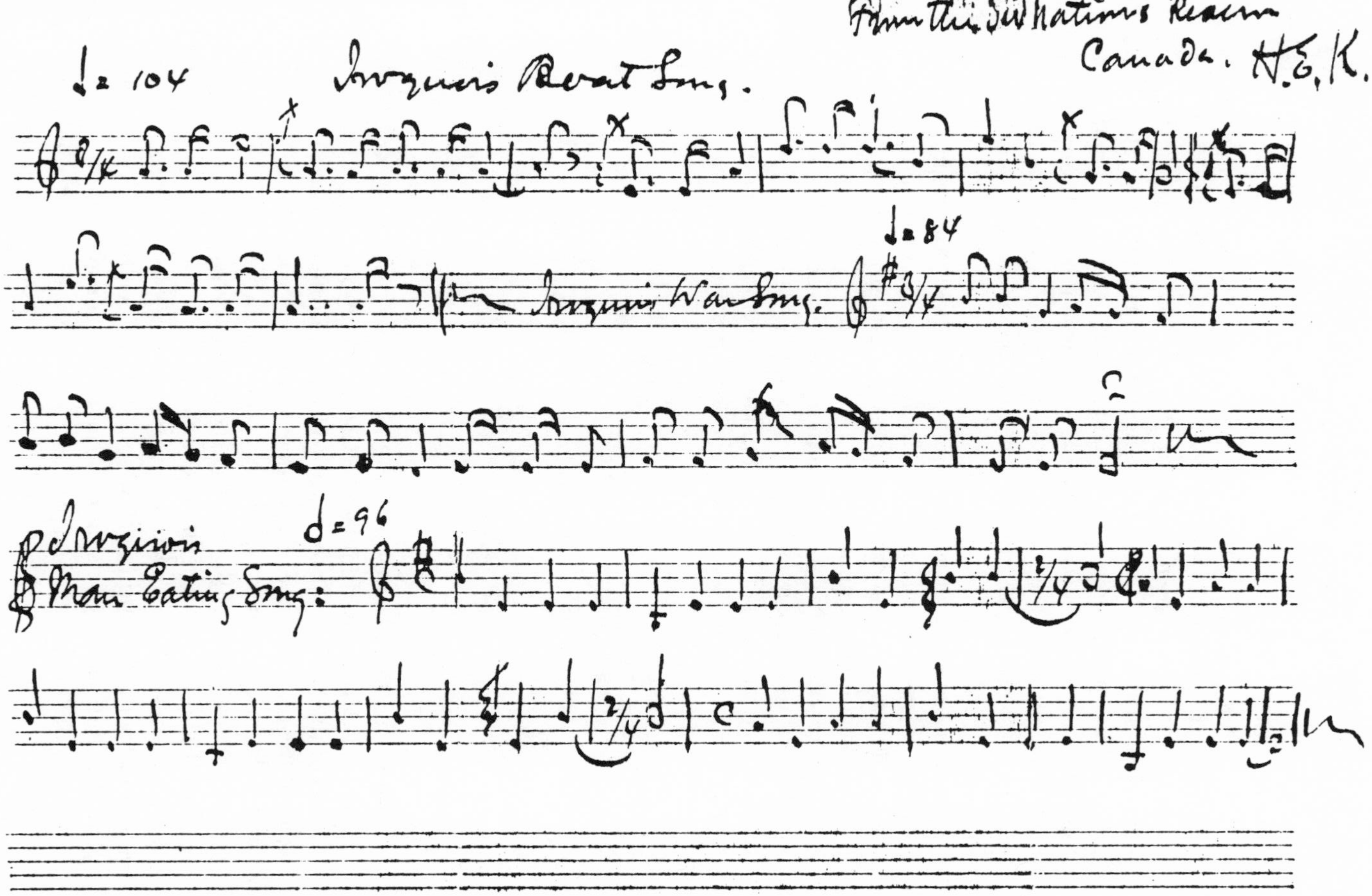

From the Six Nations Reserve
Canada. H. E. K.
♩= 104
Iroquois Burial Song.
♩= 84
Iroquois War Song.
Iroquois
Man Eating Song:
𝅗𝅥= 96

September 12, 1893
Dear Doctor Dvořák:
The directors of the Philharmonic Society of New York herewith ask you respectfully whether you would be inclined to be so good as to give your newest Symphony no. 5 to the Philharmonic Society for its premiere performance. The performance could probably best take place in the second public rehearsal and concert on December 15 and 16 of this year, and the greatest conceivable effort would be made on the part of our Society to try to assure that your newest creation in the realm of musical art would be presented in a rendition that would be worthy of it in every regard.

If you are so inclined, it would in any case be of mutual interest to make the numerous admirers of your art aware of the coming performance of this eagerly anticipated novelty in the forthcoming prospectus announcing the coming season.

In consideration of the imminent publication of the above-mentioned prospectus, you are respectfully requested to inform the undersigned promptly when the Philharmonic Society may expect to receive your kind response in the above-mentioned matter.
Respectfully,

Aug. Roebbelen
Secretary of the N[ew] Y[ork]
Phil[harmonic] Soc[iety]
429 Park Avenue

January 1, 1894
Dear Sir,
The Board of Directors of the Philharmonic Society of New York unanimously requested me at the last meeting to express to you the thanks of the Society for the favor so kindly granted by you to the Society of the performance of your new Symphony no. 5 "From the New World" from the manuscript before publication.

The performance of this work at the Society's concerts of December 15th and 16th was epochal in its character, for it was the first production of a new work, by one of the greatest composers, written in America, embodying the sentiment and romance derived from a residence in America and a study of its native tone-expressions.

The immediate and immense success of the work (of which you yourself were a witness) was a sincere gratification to the Society and testified not only to the greatness of the work, but also to the recognition by the audience of the Society of the justness of the title of your new tone-poem.

With the sincere thanks of the Society for the privilege of its first performance, I remain respectfully yours,

E. Francis Hyde[16]
President

April 18, 1894

Dear Doctor Dvořák:

In the meeting that was held today of the Philharmonic Society of New York, in recognition of your outstanding service to the art of music in general, and the Philharmonic Society in particular, you were elected as an Honorary Member of the latter by unanimous decision.

Article II, Section 3, of the enclosed constitution of the Philharmonic Society contains information about the rights of Honorary Members, while the list of the previously elected Honorary Members is given on pages 6 and 7 of the enclosed annual report 1892–93.

Kindly inform the undersigned of the favor of your acceptance of the election, so that the diploma that is meant for you can be made out and sent to you.

Respectfully
Aug. Roebblen
Secretary of N[ew] Y[ork]
Philharmonic Society
429 Park Ave.

The following two letters, from Rubin Goldmark and Michael Banner, respectively, are testimony to the close relations that existed between Dvořák and his American students. [Ed.]

December 10, 1893

Most honored Doctor Dvořák:

As you see, I am already taking advantage of your friendly invitation to write to you on occasion. The thing that gives me a particular reason, even urges me to do so at this time is to congratulate you on the colossal success of your new symphony. It must have been a real triumph and every American will reflect with pride on the fact that this epoch-making work was written here in this country. How much prouder must someone feel who has the good fortune to call himself your student, and who, moreover, has the great advantage of having learned from you. I cannot begin to tell you how much I regret that I had to be away from home this year, of all years, when I am missing so much as a result of my absence. But it was very necessary that I leave New York in haste, even more necessary than I originally thought. My life here is very secluded and quiet, in a very beautiful but icy cold area. I am out of doors almost the whole day and do everything possible to regain my health as quickly as possible. I already feel somewhat better, but gaining strength is always a slow process.

Music is something I can only read about in the newspapers, for the moment; at present I do not even have a piano at my disposal, but I hope to have one soon. And then one sees so many suffering and sick people here that one almost loses one's desire for the aesthetic, for art, at least until one has gotten used to it.

I therefore follow what is happening in N[ew] Y[ork], especially at the Conservatory, with all the greater interest. I have read about the planned concert in Mad[ison] Sq[uare] Garden, and the one that was recently given by the student orchestra, and I would be only too pleased to know how things are in the composition class, in the orchestra, in the chorus, etc.

I would like to wish you and your worthy family very pleasant holidays, "Merry Christmas and Happy New Year," with the wish that you may long continue in your illustrious work.

With my most cordial regards to your wife and the dear children, I sign myself respectfully your always grateful student

Rubin Goldmark[17]
Saranac Lake, N.Y.

Please give my greetings to Mr. Kovařík.

.

Brooklyn
July 29, 1894

My illustrious Teacher!

Instead of writing to you from the country, as I at first anticipated, I am writing to you from Brooklyn. It is very warm here, though it was sometimes very warm in the Conservatory in midwinter, but that was study, and the present heat arises from summer. Circumstances have prevented me from going to the Adirondack Mountains, and I am spending the summer with my parents. I correspond with my friends who are in the mountains, and employ my time in an easy manner, that is I go bathing about twice a week, and I go to New York quite often to visit some people that I have not the time to see during the winter. Last week I played for a blind man, an old friend of mine, and it made him feel very happy. I am really anxious to see you again, my good and strict teacher. I read in the papers that your American Symphony had a great success in England. Whenever I feel sad or unhappy I write counterpoint, and it helps me very much. I often think how kind you were to accept me as a pupil. My progress in music allows me to see more of the inner essence of Music, and my lack of real musical knowledge and inability to express my thought in a worthy manner, is becoming more and more apparent. I read lately that Gladstone speaking about human progress said that constant progress was at the same time constant humiliation. You have opened my eyes to a higher conception of Art, you have showed me the path, the Way and the Truth in Music and I write you this, my dear Master, in order that you may know I think of you and that my gratitude to you is unceasing.

I send you my tribute over the ocean, my homage and my love. If you have a few minutes' time to spare, I would be very happy to hear from you, but I will (anyway) write to you again before very long.

Wishing you and Mrs. Dvořák a very happy stay and looking forward to meeting you again, with the greatest of happiness I am, Dr. Antonín Dvořák, your obedient and ever grateful pupil.

Michael Banner

Please address: United States of America
239 Rockaway Avenue, Brooklyn, N.Y.

·

It is well known that Dvořák spent the summer months of 1893 at the Czech-speaking settlement of Spillville, Iowa. He did so because the parents of Josef Kovařík, Dvořák's secretary, lived in Spillville. These two letters are from Jan Josef Kovařík. The first was written before Dvořák's visit, and the second afterward. The letters capture both the rhythm of village life and Dvořák's relationship to it—certainly the older Kovařík addresses Dvořák not as a great master but rather as an old drinking buddy. [Ed.]

Spillville, Iowa
May 8, 1893

Dear Sir,

As per your instructions I have found you a six-room apartment on the second floor.

Of course I would much prefer to be your host and have you stay in the same house with us, but I know that you would have to give up many comforts and therefore I have in this way reserved the above mentioned apartment for you. The owner of the house and his old wife live on the first floor and there are just the two of them. Thus you will not be disturbed by anything.

Josef knows the family; at least I think he remembers them; just tell him it is the Plechars or, as we say here, the Tin-smiths. I think it would be best if during the time of your stay you keep your own house, that is what concerns cooking.

I would find you a cook; furnishings such as beds, pillows and blankets and bed sheets, all that we would have ready for you.

Please, let me know whether you agree with my suggestion and if you do, let me know when approximately you would be arriving.

With regards to your family I remain respectfully,

J. J. Kovařík

Spillville, Iowa
December 21, 1894

Dear Doctor Dvořák,

In vain I have been waiting to hear from you. Of course, in your case I am not surprised, undoubtedly you have again a symphony up your sleeve and won't rest until you have transferred it onto some 30 sheets of music paper; but I am surprised that neither dear Madame nor any of your children write to me. Now I know nothing whatsoever about you apart from what I find from time to time in magazines.

Even Josef does not send me a single word. I received the last letter from him 6 weeks ago. You have all virtually conspired against me.

Here there is nothing much new. Your old friends Kumpal, Bily, Krnecek, Grandfather are all still alive—every day they trek to the little church to worship and then to gossip a little on the way back. Grandfather Bily is now happy at the priest's house. The Reverend is supposed to be paying him well for his work, occasionally treats him to a glass of wine or a cigar and Grandfather likes that very much.

Old Mr. Kaug had an accident. He was on his way home from Calmar; as he was coming to the railroad tracks, the horses got scared by a train which was just then approaching and went wild. He fell out of the buggy and dislocated his shoulder. The doctors managed to set it right but his arm will certainly go lame. Beside that he got hurt internally—the doctor came to see him every day. Now he is getting better.

Think of us on Christmas Eve. We still celebrate Christmas Eve after the golden Czech custom; for us the day is still full of poetry—for the Americans not a bit—we fast in order to see the golden piggy at night, but we do take a drink of cumin liquor in the morning, it sharpens the imagination and it is then easier to spot the piggy. "Ah, Christmas Eve, oh wondrous night!" Indeed it is a wondrous night. Oh, if only you could be here with us that day and on Christmas day and sing with us the old Czech carols after Holy Mass.

During the Holy Mass we sing Gregor's Czech Pastoral Mass and Gregor's Gradual, also in Czech. We put Latin aside for that day.

Happy and Merry Christmas Holidays and a Happy New Year from me and also from my family.

J. J. Kovařík

NOTES

1. Benjamin Lang (1837–1909), a pianist, composer, and the first-rate choral conductor of the Apollo Club and the Cecelia Society. He was a gifted teacher; his students included Arthur Foote and his daughter, Margaret Ruthven Lang. [Ed.]

2. Carl Faelton (1846–1925) was born in Germany (which may explain the faulty English in this letter). He was a pianist and teacher who taught at the Hoch Conservatorium in Frankfurt and at the Peabody Institute in Baltimore. He was director of the New England Conservatory from 1890 to 1897 and founded Faelton Pianoforte School in Boston in 1897. [Ed.]

3. The Cecelia was a Boston Choral society that participated in the opening of the new Boston Symphony Hall. [Ed.]

4. William Smythe Babcock Matthews (1837–1912) was an organist and a writer on music. He was a music critic for the *Chicago Tribune* from 1878 to 1886 and founded and edited the *Musical Monthly* in Chicago in 1891. [Ed.]

5. William Mason (1829–1908) was a pianist, composer, and educator and the son of Lowell Mason. He studied in Boston, Leipzig, Prague, and with Liszt in Weimar. [Ed.]

6. Probably Henry Schoenfeld (1857–1936), a pianist and composer. He studied at the Leipzig Conservatory and settled in Chicago where he conducted a German male chorus from 1891 to 1902. Some of his later compositions used Native American materials. [Ed.]

7. This is a reference to "Music in America," which was published by *Harper's Magazine* in 1895. [Ed.]

8. I have no idea about what is going on in the first paragraph of this letter. Perhaps Dvořák insisted that it be co-authored, as is mentioned in the second letter. [Ed.]

9. This is a reference to an article published in *Century Illustrated Monthly Magazine* 44 (September 1892): 657–60, and timed to coincide with the composer's arrival in the United States. [Ed.]

10. Will Marion Cook was a conductor and composer. He attended Oberlin Conservatory at the age of thirteen in 1882 and studied violin there, in Germany, and at the National Conservatory in New York. He concertized briefly and then devoted the remainder of his life to compositions for the musical theater. [Ed.]

11. Henry Thacker Burleigh (1866–1949) was a singer and composer-arranger. He was trained at the National Conservatory in New York and became an intimate friend of Dvořák's while the composer was in New York. Burleigh apparently sang African-American songs for Dvořák over an extended period. Burleigh later became popular as a songwriter and arranger of Negro spirituals for voice and piano. [Ed.]

12. Krehbiel is referring here to the first performance of the symphony on 15 December 1893. [Ed.]

13. The second letter in this set indicated that Krehbiel did indeed call on Dvořák on Wednesday, 13 December. [Ed.]

14. It is not clear how extensive the notes were that Dvořák made on the symphony, since they have not been found; but of special interest is the fact that Dvořák seems to have told Krehbiel that the Largo of the symphony was based on Hiawatha's wooing from Longfellow's *The Song of Hiawatha*. [Ed.]

15. August Roebbelen was a violinist as well as both secretary of the New York Philharmonic Society and a member of its committee. [Ed.]

16. Francis Hyde was a lawyer and philanthropist who served as president of the New York Philharmonic from 1888 to 1901. [Ed.]

17. Rubin Goldmark (1872–1936), a nephew of Karl Goldmark, was a composer and teacher. He studied with Dvořák and Rafael Joseffy at the National Conservatory and became head of the composition department at Juilliard in 1924. His works include the *Hiawatha* Overture, the *Negro Rhapsody* (1923), and *The Call of the Plains* (1925). [Ed.]

Antonín Dvořák:
A Biographical Sketch

HERMANN KRIGAR

TRANSLATED BY SUSAN GILLESPIE

WITH CRITICAL COMMENTARY BY
JARMIL BURGHAUSER

In 1992 Clipeus Press in Leiden published a commemorative volume containing the earliest biographical sketch of Dvořák, by Hermann Krigar. Containing
extensive commentary by the noted Dvořák scholar Jarmil Burghauser, this
book was published in a special limited edition of only 110 copies. After reading the material I thought it appropriate to offer the material to a larger
audience, and I obtained permission from Dr. Burghauser to reprint it here.
We find the opening remarks on national characteristics to be particularly
interesting: they tie in very neatly with certain points made in the essays in Part
I, and the critical stance taken toward some aspects of Dvořák's creative output
is still a part of the reaction to the composer's work. All the notes are Burghauser's work. On a few occasions we have freely adapted the material. [Ed.]

[Source: *Musikalisches Wochenblatt*, Leipzig (December 1879–February 1880]

The traveler from Northern Germany, when he crosses the Erzgebirge
mountains into Bohemia, will remark upon the sudden change in the
physiognomy of the inhabitants. This difference is one not merely of
facial expression or language but of the whole manner of being—a
difference that should not be studied and explained in the columns of a
journal on music but should rather be the subject of an ethnographic
study, as indeed it has been on numerous occasions. Let me say only
that the striving for general knowledge, and consequently the cultural
level of the population, has advanced much further here than on the
other side of the border. It is possible that the reason lies in the deep

valley, ringed about by great mountains, which is more inhibiting to the flights of higher culture than the lowland plain of Northern Germany. Needless to say, I am speaking of the level of education in general, not in particular.

The differences that have arisen between the population here and there are most clearly evident in the nature of musical sensibility, which is acquired here, while there it is inborn. When it comes to learning a musical instrument, the native of Bohemia hardly needs the nurturing guidance or supervision of a teacher to discover and perfect his musical talents. He does not ask himself whether he has talent; he knows he does, and at the most tender age he is already so skilled in the use of a hand-carved willow flute, violin, or zither, such as may be found in almost every household, that he is able to reproduce the captivating songs and melodies of the national dances with a remarkably fine ear and peculiarly exaggerated technique, to his great joy and that of his fellows. One learns from the other, and without ever having had the benefit of systematic instruction, the student, with no urging, easily reaches a certain degree of mastery and attains the level where dilettantism and artistry coincide. One oddity I must mention is that both in the countryside and in the smaller cities I came across entire bands of musicians playing without scores, like gypsies, who could only tell me in the rarest instances who had composed the piece they had just performed so nimbly.

This is the natural bent of the German-Bohemians. Penetrating deeper inside the country, we come upon the Slavic tribe, the Czechs. They are by no means inferior, in their talent for and practice of music, to the German-Bohemian populace; indeed, they demonstrate an even greater and bolder individuality in their musical practice, which perfectly reflects the essential Czech nature. This mirroring of [national] character is a notable feature of all the Slavic peoples. The Russians, who among all the Slavic tribes betray the greatest tenderheartedness and an unmistakably childlike quality, maintain these qualities in their folk music. The Poles are different. Their emotional character is stamped with a certain elegant regret—one, however, that does not exclude courtliness. Their music is coquettish in a way that is not completely free of ostentation, and, sensing its lesser quality, it does not refrain from decking itself out in foreign feathers. The Bohemians, fundamentally different from both these others, display a reserved, melancholy, but not infrequently crafty turn of mind. They are superior to the others not only in profundity and inner depth of feeling but also in tenaciousness of will. The distinct stamp of these character traits shines forth in their national music, as well. They are the most artistically gifted among the Slavic tribes.

A population so richly endowed could hardly fail to bring forth performing artists of significance. But it must seem odd that no force emerged from this lively musical mixture to combine the Slavic individuality and the higher art forms in its compositions. There may have been isolated attempts of this sort, but they did not penetrate beyond the national borders, and as lesser lights they soon faded from view even within their own circle. However, one may now conclude with certainty, and without undue deference, that the dam has broken, the old spell has been lifted at one stroke. Approximately a year ago, the news flashed across the German music world of a miraculous talent residing in Prague, who is holding forth in spirited creation with astonishing productivity and a striking wealth of melodies, and who for years has been laying up treasures, sprung from his muse, that are as mysterious as they are appealing.

This newly awakened talent is Anton Dvořák, who has aroused widespread excitement in Germany with his Slavic Dances.

Great thanks are due to Mr. Louis Ehlert, who was the first to publish, in warmly acknowledging words, his admiration for the Bohemian artist's very original style of composition. It requires no small amount of courage to express an opinion to the critically knowledgeable German public, which does not like to be told what to think and for which distrust of everything original and disinclination to trust in any new phenomenon are as inborn as the world's capacity not to miss what it knows nothing about, and always to have time to wait.

Anton Dvořák was born on 8 September 1841, in the town of Mühlhausen on the Moldau, near Kralup, not far from Prague. It was here that his father, Franz Dvořák, had his presumably not very profitable butcher business, with which, as is often the case in Bohemia, a modest inn was associated. The son helped his father in the shop from his earliest years, and it was quite clear that he would someday learn his trade.[1] An inn means dances, and the high spirits of the young people who streamed in from all the surrounding villages reached their climax at the country fairs that were held several times each year. The band that Franz Dvořák brought in played no small part in the joy that was felt on such days, for a Bohemian does not attain the degree of cheerfulness that makes him really comfortable until he hears music. Here, one could see the young Anton receiving his first musical impressions—as if spellbound, he stood in front of the fiddlers and trumpeters and followed the movements of the instruments with glowing cheeks and shining eyes. What these musicians produced was certainly not "high music," but the genuine Bohemian polkas and marches were nonetheless capable of making Anton's young musician's blood race. Youth craves the enjoyment of sound; it does not possess the seriousness and critical faculty to lift itself higher.

The attentive father, who himself felt great pleasure in the enjoyment of music and who played the zither with more than ordinary skill, did not fail to notice the sensitivity and the constantly growing delight and love of music that inspired the boy.[2] He did not want to leave whatever talent the boy possessed—which he could make use of, together with him, at the inn—to uncultivated growth or an unduly unplanned, random development, and so he arranged for the local schoolteacher to instruct him in the rudiments of violin and singing.[3] Whether that instruction, in the long run, would have been beneficial is not something I was able to discern; but within two years, thanks to his dedication and talent, the student displayed such progress that he was permitted to play a violin solo at a country fair, which resulted in an acknowledged success for him.[4] He was less fortunate at singing. During a solo of only a few bars, with which he was entrusted during Easter week, he was seized with such panic that he could not produce a single tone and thoroughly ruined the passage. This unfortunate event made a lasting impression—he never sang again.[5] But as time went on, the father may have experienced some doubts about the method of instruction he had been employing. He made a change and chose a stricter pedagogy for his son, entrusting him to a relative in Zlonitz[6] who arranged for him to study harmony and organ with the organist Liehmann.[7] The latter, an adroit and very strict gentleman, was not one to scorn secular music, despite his churchly position, and allowed his exuberant fantasy free reign in marches and polkas for which he himself created the arrangements. The student, who in this way experienced his first introduction to the mysterious world of orchestration, sat full of admiration before the many line-systems of his master, and— had to copy the parts. It is quite easy to imagine that the ambitious student, faced with the monotony of the copying work, had the idea of making his own attempt at an orchestrated polka. He had brought the composition, about which his teacher knew nothing, and which he kept well hidden, along with him on a visit to Mühlhausen, to surprise his father during the next country fair. The scores were distributed, the polka began, but the sound of the orchestra was terrible. The musicians were beside themselves, the father upset, the son at a loss. After a while, the trumpeters discovered that the ambitious youngster had written the parts for the F trumpets as if they were really in F major, so they naturally came out in B♭ major. The damage was soon undone and the polka restored, to the joy of all present. An odd circumstance is the fact that he correctly understood the much more difficult transposition of the clarinets.[8]

Anton Dvořák remained in Zlonitz to pursue his studies until 1856, when he was sent for a year to Böhmisch-Kamnitz, near Bodenbach, to learn the German language and perfect his knowledge of harmony and organ.[9]

I have now come to a turning point in the life of the young Dvořák. The years of childhood, which seem to have slipped by in carefree high spirits among sensory impressions that were scarcely ever raised to the level of consciousness, were drawing to a close. The seriousness of life was knocking at the door. The father and some of his friends, considering what future fate might await him, decided that the boy should become a butcher, since as the oldest of eight siblings he could be a substantial support to the household and the business. But eventually he gave in to the urgent pleas of his son, who begged his father in tears not to make him learn the butcher's trade but to let him become a musician. The honest master butcher, who took the decision very seriously, may well have fought a hard battle with himself, driven by worries about the survival of his family but responding, at the same time, to his duty toward his talented son; in the end, thanks to his selflessness and a clever calculation, the outcome of his struggle was such as to be productive and unexpectedly influential for the artistic world. The world may have one less sausage-maker, but in the process it has gained a high master of art.

It was not without considerable sacrifices on the part of his parents that Anton Dvořák, at the age of fifteen, was sent off to Prague for the most serious studies. Professor Carl Pitsch, who was the director of the organists' school, and Krejčí, the director of the conservatory, offered him the opportunity to lay a foundation for his knowledge and energetic will, so that in 1859, thanks to his diligence and lively susceptibility, he was able to cease his lessons, which he had attended steadily and with the greatest success.[10] It was probably also during this period that he taught himself to play the piano and perfected his violin technique.[11] But I have not been able to learn anything certain about this. The support of his parental household had continued up until this period. It could not continue any longer. Thus the young artist found himself alone in the big city, left to fend for himself. There followed years of the most bitter disappointments, of need and privations of the sort that have caused many a strong nature to succumb. But, trusting in himself and keeping his head up, he did not lose heart and bore his hard lot with equanimity—hardly the lot he is likely to have dreamed of during his carefree youth. To earn the barest necessities of life, he was compelled to become a violist in one of the many pick-up orchestras that played for a pittance in the inns and coffee houses, and to remain in this kind of employment until the year 1862. His prospects improved somewhat as a result of the opening of the Bohemian National Theater in that year; he would play in its orchestra until the year 1871.[12] But even during this period, his income fell short of the most modest expectations.

In the midst of these material pressures, which weighed heavily on him and could not help but have a paralyzing effect on an untroubled sensibility and on his artistic activity, the creative urge awakened within him, with a powerful summons. He felt himself called to mine the richly laden treasure within himself, but he was aware, at the same time, of his inability to bring it up into the light of day, vivid, concise, polished, and purged of impurities. He sensed that the knowledge of harmony, the merely mathematical fine points of a scholarly counterpoint, even in combination with virtuosic technique on several instruments, would not suffice. His formal ability was not well rounded, and in general he lacked skillfulness and transparency of form. In this matter he had only himself to rely on, since no one ever taught him or helped him with the finer points. This whole important branch of compositional instruction seems, in his case, to have been neglected. Then there was the impossibility of gaining entry into the better concerts, in which chamber music and symphonies could be heard. He was not even permitted—this would have answered a burning wish on his part—a glance at the scores of such works, let alone their possession. Under such unfavorable circumstances, it would not have been surprising if even a richly endowed talent, in a place otherwise as musically rich as Prague, had been destroyed, had it been accompanied by a less energetic will and relentless drive.

What feelings, and perhaps doubts as well, may have gone through the composer's mind as he put his first string quintet (1862) on paper is impossible to know.[13] The work remained unknown, like much else that was composed in this period.

A ray of light suddenly lit up his dark path and allowed him, at last, to find what he so keenly lacked and fervently desired. He met Carl Bendl, a very talented musician, loyal friend, and advisor, who is now a *Kapellmeister* in Nice.[14] The latter put his sizable musical library, which contained the scores of symphonies and quartets by Beethoven and Mendelssohn, at his disposal. The ravenous hunger with which the young composer fell upon these offerings can be imagined in a general way by anyone at all versed in the psychology of moods, but only those who were close to him at the time will really know. Day and night, these splendid treasures, from which he drew knowledge and growing confidence, ordered along the lines of his own soaring ideas, left him no peace. He studied with as much diligence in the bright sunlight as by the guttering light of his lamp, staving off sleep in the attempt to impress the creative forms upon his mind. Schumann's songs, which he got to know during this period, also exercised an irresistible magic through the charm of their melodies and the quite unique character of the text.

In this way, learning with tireless diligence and sparing no pains, he felt himself aroused by the study of these masters to even greater creativity—like any strong spirit that is goaded on to action by its own inner strength. This period of ferment saw the creation of a symphony in B♭ major (1864) and one in E minor (1865), which, as experiments, he shut away in his desk, where they have remained to this day.[15] The same fate befell many comprehensive works for full or chamber orchestra, or chamber ensemble, that he composed before 1872, the year in which he gave notice of his departure from the burdensome theater group in order to devote himself exclusively to composition. Life began to take on more favorable contours for him. In order to gain a measure of security, however, he began giving piano lessons, and in addition to the more carefree support of his household that this income made possible, he made the acquaintance of all the older and more recent masters of that art, with whom he gradually became so familiar that he could copy the style of each of them with ease. Like any ambitious artist, he had his favorites, to whom he was all-powerfully attracted and whom he worships to this day with awe and enthusiasm—Beethoven and Franz Schubert.

If we consider the life of Anton Dvořák before 1872—a period of tireless activity and unceasing struggle under the most oppressive conditions—we might be struck by the fact that at the end of this period he had reached a rather considerable age without having to his credit any significant number of works that have become familiar. In spite of his energy, his undeniable gifts, in spite of ambitious attempts at composition, he had not succeeded in drawing attention to his unusual efforts. Whether the reason lay in excessively severe self-criticism or in a lack of responsiveness is something we must set aside for the moment; I have not been able to find out. The following year, 1873, brought his first recognition as one of the local talents. A hymn, *Die Erben des weissen Berges* [The Heirs of the White Mountain], a large choral work with orchestra—most likely a tendentiously patriotic piece—was given a performance in Prague.[16] The performance rescued his name from obscurity with a single stroke. Encouraged by this fortunate success, and despite the fact that his material circumstances had not improved in any way, he now commenced his real creative period, in which those works were created that would later also have an impact on musical life beyond Prague. The period of experimentation was finally over, and now, thanks to his untiring industriousness, he could look forward to reaping the fruits of a rich harvest.

It was also during this period that he had the happy thought of requesting a state scholarship from the Ministry of Culture, which, after he appended several compositions to his application, and upon the recommendation of Herbeck and Hanslick, he received. This recognition by the government, which must finally be regarded as a not insignificant source of support, was repeated for five years. In 1877, following Herbeck's death, a change occurred in the commission that met to distribute the scholarships. Brahms took the place of the deceased, and it was he who, after examining the compositions Dvořák had submitted—among them the songs for two voices "Klänge aus Mähren" [literally "Sounds of Moravia," usually translated as Moravian Duets]—was immediately inspired with such a lively interest in the as yet unknown native of Bohemia that he promptly arranged to have a look at his earlier products.[17] They captivated his perceptive artist's eye. But Brahms did not only respond as an enthusiast; he realized that the artist could not live on high-sounding words or recognition alone, and he knew that practical intervention means much, indeed often everything in life. Thus, he communicated his rich discovery to Herr Simrock in Berlin. This gentleman, a highly sensitive music connoisseur and the possessor of an artistically trained virtuosity on the piano, noticed very quickly what hidden treasures waited to be brought to the surface here, and he did not pass them over, but rather became Dvořák's publisher by dint of purchasing a select number of larger and smaller works. The enterprising and perceptive head of the firm of Bote and Bock also saw himself, before long, as the owner of a group of outstanding compositions.

Thus, in the thirty-sixth year of his life, Dvořák, after disappointments of all kinds, after suffering bitter privations, which, however, completely failed to destroy his strength of character or his mission, finally found the recognition he had so fervently desired and sought. He suddenly saw himself relieved of worry about the next day and could look to the future, for the first time, with an untroubled heart. Nothing was more natural than for his creative urge to awaken again, more intensely than ever.

In order to provide a complete picture of his diligence, creative spirit, and versatility, I will give, in the following pages, as comprehensive as possible a listing of all the compositions that he wrote in the years 1873–79. One cannot fail to be amazed at his productivity. Many of these works have already survived the trial by fire of public reaction with the best of success, although regrettably many a work that is surely worthy of notice still slumbers in obscurity.[18]

I. Dramatic compositions

König und Köhler [The King and the Charcoal-Burner], a comic opera (performed in Prague); *Vanda*, a large-scale tragic opera in five acts; *Der Bauer ein Schelm* [The Cunning Peasant], a comic opera; and an overture published as Op. 37 by Simrock[19]

II. Choral works with orchestral accompaniment

Hymn *Die Erben des weissen Berges* [The Heirs of the White Mountain], Op. 4;[20] and *Stabat Mater*, Op. 28[21]

III. Symphonic works, chamber music, etc.

Symphony in D minor; Symphony in F major; Symphonic Variations for Full Orchestra, Op. 40;[22] Serenade in E major for String Orchestra, Op. 22 (Bote and Bock); Serenade in D minor for Wind Instruments, Op. 44 (Simrock); Three Rhapsodies for Full Orchestra, Op. 45 (Simrock); Piano Concerto with Orchestra, Op. 33; Concerto for Violin and Orchestra; Two Nocturn[e]s for Orchestra, Op. 8;[23] Romance for Violin and Orchestra, Op. 11 (Simrock); Mazurka for Violin and Orchestra, Op. 49 (Simrock);[24] Trio in B♭ major, Op. 21; Trio in G minor, Op. 26 (Bote and Bock); Quartet in A minor, Op. 16; Quartet in E major, Op. 27; Quartet in D minor, Op. 34; Quartet in E♭ major, Op. 51 (Simrock); Quartet in C major; Sextet in A major, Op. 48 (Simrock); and Piano Quartet in D major, Op. 23

IV. Piano Music

Dumka, Op. 35 (Bote and Bock); Variations, Op. 36 (Bote and Bock); Two Furiants, Op. 42 (Bote and Bock); Slavonic Dances for Four Hands, Op. 46 (Simrock); Bagatelles for Four Hands, Op. 47 (Simrock); and Waltzes

V. Vocal Music

Lieder with Pianoforte Accompaniment, Opp. 6 and 7 (Simrock); Duets with Pianoforte Accompaniment, Opp. 20 and 38 (Simrock);

Thirteen Duets "Klänge aus Mähren" [Moravian Duets] with Pianoforte Accompaniment, Op. 32 (Simrock);[25] and many songs for solo voice with pianoforte accompaniment, and choral songs

There would have been a more comprehensive evaluation of the composer's unusual and pronounced talent and compositional versatility if all compositions listed above had become more widely known. But there has been, until now, no insight into two important genres that he pursued with evident favor: opera and the symphony. Based on familiarity with those works with which he has made such a rich contribution to the musical world, we may assume, and can affirm based on second- and thirdhand reports, that he took up these branches of the musical art with the seriousness that is native to him. It is to be hoped that, given the continually increasing attention that is paid to this composer, the time is not far off when these products of his pen will be made available, either in performance or in print, to a world that is hungry to experience them.[26] But even without the knowledge of these works, there remains enough that is accessible to the sensitive music-lover, and it is of sufficiently significant a nature to assure that making a judgment at this point will not be premature. Without delving into actual criticism, which is beyond the scope of a biographical sketch, I may be permitted to characterize with a few brief explanatory words the position that the composer occupies.

The most eminent proof of Anton Dvořák's skill in handling the larger musical forms is given by his three Slavonic Rhapsodies, Op. 45, for full orchestra and, secondarily, by his two Serenades, Opp. 22, for strings, and 44, for wind instruments. In the rhapsodies he created a form that was serviceable and well suited for him and that may distantly recall the inner or outer form of a symphonic movement or concert overture, although it is fundamentally different from these in its thematic construction and development. The thing that most clearly characterizes the basic difference between this form and the other is a certain conceptual simplification, by means of which a principal idea, to which the most effective formal secrets of counterpoint have been added, reappears in almost unrecognizably reformulated but always new and interesting physiognomy. These artistic tonal creations, rich in canonical melodic developments that ascend to near-perilous levels, are borne along by the colorful brilliance of a strangely appealing instrumentation. No instrument is demeaned by having to play the role of filler; each speaks, in its own way, an eloquent language, and even the harp, which has gained more and more ground in the modern orchestra, has an important word to say. Defenders of cleanliness in musical movements will shake their heads and lay the score aside over many a rule that seems to have been broken with relish, and will turn instead to some old codex that offers more correctness and boredom for their heart and soul. I find the Third Rhapsody (A♭ major) to be the most national, the Second (G minor) the most significant, and the First (D major) the most beautiful. With their lighter construction and more transparent fabric—consequently more easily accessible to the opponents of novelty—the two Serenades show themselves to be two thoroughly graceful mood paintings, of several movements each, which never for a moment deny the character of what they are intended to portray: an untroubled, flowing night music. What fine artistic expression, what compelling melodies and touching harmonic progressions the composer has at his disposal is as evident in these Serenades as in his Slavonic Dances, Op. 46, for piano–four hands, which have gained such quick acceptance, and the Bagatelles, Op. 47, whose rhythmic boldness and effervescent invention first elicited the lively interest of open-minded listeners.

Obeying an urgent inner call, he turned to the most difficult and sublime musical genre, the combination of solo string instruments. Thus, in quick succession, he created quartets, quintets, and his sextet, which, to the extent that they have become known, have not escaped the notice of the musical public. When one considers how early one must begin with this kind of composition in order to attain even a certain degree of mastery, and when, on the other hand, one observes, in this particular case, with what difficulties and at what an advanced age Dvořák yielded to the powerful urge to test his powers in this genre as well, then his accomplishment must simply be termed truly miraculous. Although he still struggles with the polishing of the form and the individualized melodic line of the various instrumental voices, although many a link is not quite well rounded and sure, nonetheless the strength of will of the entire construction, which approaches boldness, and the compelling character of its coloristic richness make up for many an uneven patch. Thus I would like to characterize the Sextet in A major, Op. 48, and the Quartet in E♭ major, Op. 51, in spite of their minor shortcomings, as highly significant works that have been dictated by a magnificent and authentic mentality. There is nothing smallminded about them; they are not patched or pasted together, nor is he worried about making concessions or pretty phrases. With his soul always full of the whole, large in form, he shows himself a poet through and through. How many eel-smooth contemporary compositions in this genre, by contrast, collapse back into the nothingness from which they have emerged.

He moves with great agility in the territory of the vocal song. It is as if his Slavic nature were leading him in this direction. The edited compositions, the Lieder, Opp. 6 and 7, the Duets, Opp. 20 and 22, and the "Klänge aus Mähren" (Thirteen Duets), Op. 32, have spread quickly and found a home in the best music rooms. It is the last-named duets, in particular, that have won the hearts of singers thanks to their attractive popular (in the best sense of the word) tone and witty brevity, with its unusual language in the text. Not on the same level, although it contains enough that is original and beautiful, is the piano music. It gives an impression as if the performing technique, which is more orchestrally than pianistically conceived, were somehow standing in its way. Today's piano-player demands a technique that is adapted to the instrument. Apparent translations from orchestral scores do not provide the requisite thrill for the ears and fingers. While admitting that those piano-players are not entirely mistaken, one must, at the same time, remember that such an orchestrally conceived piano piece, executed in a manner that is not in itself unskillful, deserves, in the end, only very modest criticism, and the person who does not find the composition Theme with Variations, Op. 36, with its many moods, to be a brilliant performance piece would be well advised to choose instead one of the berceuses or rêveries that are all too popular in our country.

What particularly heightens the charm of Dvořák's compositions is the sharply etched nationality that accompanies them like a letter of safe conduct. This Slavic dowry is so much part of the composer's blood that its characteristic quality is mixed in with almost every theme and every motive, and as a result the erroneous but widely accepted notion that the composer made use of national [folk] melodies could easily be mistaken for the truth.[27] I am in a position to assume that Dvořák wrote melodies that indeed embody the innermost essence of the Slavic character so well that they will one day be adopted by the people as their own; and also to declare, with certainty and with particular pleasure, that the composer, in all his works, be they for orchestra, chamber music, voice, or piano, *never made use of a single national [folk] melody* but, on the contrary, presented nothing but his own creations. One may only wish that this nationality will not one day push him over the precipice into one-sidedness and, finally, mannerism. Let us hope that his creative powers, his artistic seriousness, and his sound good sense will protect him from any such premature decline.

Here ends my report, which I have written down to the best of my knowledge and with the purest of intentions. The talented man should know that with his entrance onto the public stage he set foot on a path that is thorny enough to make him suffer the bitter blows of life more acutely, and he will unfortunately have to experience petty jealousies and ill will lurking in ambush even from the side of his colleagues. Then he may remind himself, as consolation, of the friends he rapidly made, who approached him in the most unselfish manner and introduced him to the world: Brahms and Joachim, two names that are as resounding as any in the world of art.

Commentary

The earliest biographical sketch that we possess for the greater part of the life of Antonín Dvořák (1841–1904), which until now has unfortunately gone practically unnoticed by biographers, is also— remarkably—the most authoritative. In the composer's estate, namely, three letters were found (now preserved in the Museum of Czech Music) that were written to Dvořák by the editor of the *Musikalisches Wochenblatt* (Leipzig), E. W. Fritzsch (letter of 27 November 1879, inv. no. 708), and his colleague Hermann Krigar (letters of 7 December 1879, inv. no. 789, and 17 February 1880, inv. no. 799). These letters confirm that the editor and author of the "biographical sketch," to which they refer, had requested the necessary information from Dvořák himself and later thanked him for it.

E. W. Fritzsch asks Dvořák to send the information for a biographical sketch to H. Krigar in Berlin, who is to write something based on it for the next volume of the *Musikalisches Wochenblatt*. Dvořák's letter, which evidently followed, has not been preserved; however, its contents may be gleaned from Krigar's letter to Dvořák of 7 December 1879:

Dear Sir,

With reference to your friendly letter of the 29th of this month I am sending you herewith a biographical sketch of Stockhausen written by me, which I offer, by the way, not as a model of a German essay, since it was edited and cut by the publisher in an incomprehensible fashion without my knowledge, but rather to give you an approximate guideline as to what belongs in an essay of this kind.

Particularly interesting and necessary, to the degree permitted by discretion, would be extensive data concerning year, date, and place of birth, parents, youth, first musical impressions, schooling, composition, etc. I would also like to be informed whether in your Rhapsodies,

Serenades, in the Sextet and String Quartet actual folk melodies have been included, and if this is the case, which ones? Perhaps you would be so kind as to acquaint me with the same by means of musical examples.

Regarding the references to your works that have appeared in print and are in my possession, I am confident, since all of them give me particular pleasure and are very interesting to me, that you will be satisfied with my judgment of the same.

I feel quite conscious of my difficult task and hope, however, to resolve it in the interest of an educated reading public and with my very best intentions, which fill me with enthusiasm for the project.

My request now is to find myself, as a result of your friendly assistance, in possession of these facts *as soon as possible*.

You will forgive me if I send you these few words in the handwriting of another, since I am momentarily unable to write because of an illness that affects my right arm.

Your very devoted

H. Krigar

West Berlin, Sigismundstr. 3

The information sent by Dvořák, which must evidently have been quite comprehensive and included a photograph, from which a xylograph was then prepared for the *Musikalisches Wochenblatt* (the frontispiece of our publication [see facsimile, facing page]), is unfortunately not preserved in the original. Krigar's confirmation of its receipt is clearly reflected in the—somewhat belated—letter from Krigar to Dvořák of 17 February 1880:

Dear Sir,

The expression of my warmest thanks for the extensive information about your life comes somewhat late; I hope to be excused by the fact that I wanted to provide you simultaneously with a complete copy of the biography. Whether you will be satisfied with my work I do not know, but I hope so, for I have not undertaken it without considerable pains, although gladly. In case indiscretions should have crept in, it occurred for one reason only, in order to better motivate your profession and the firmness of your will, and to make them appear in a more brilliant light. You have allowed me to select and use whatever I deemed appropriate from the picture that you painted of your life and candidly shared with me, and in this case I believe I have done so in a way that will not give offense, since I have aimed for moderation in my

Antonín Dvořák as shown on the frontispiece of Hermann Krigar, *Antonín Dvořák: Eine biographische Skizze* (Leiden, 1992)

expression. If, later, through more extensive information, whether verbal or written, I should be in a position to add anything essential or perhaps to make corrections, I am very willing to send a postscript.

Permit me, honored sir, to assure you of my very particular respect, with which I sign myself,
    Your devoted

H. Krigar

This sketch, in other words, is expressly more authorized—and also in fact more reliable—than the analogous sketch that was written five years later by Josef Zubatý (Leipzig, 1885 and 1886), which in all probability was also based on information that Dvořák himself provided (unfortunately we have no direct proof of this); however, the greater length of time that had passed since the events that are described had further reduced the sharpness of Dvořák's memory. Thus, for example, the year in which Dvořák was sent to Böhmisch-Kamnitz (Česká Kamenice) is given correctly in Krigar (the school report card that has been preserved bears witness to this); in Zubatý, by contrast, it is given incorrectly as 1855. A single circumstance that is omitted in Krigar but mentioned in Zubatý is the fact that in Zlonitz Dvořák "had to absolve the third school class." Some of the earlier biographers did not understand this; they supposed, incorrectly, that Antonín attended school in Mühlhausen (in Czech: *Nelahozeves*) for only two years. In fact, he completed the full required five years, as is proven by the book he received as a "reward for diligence" from Prince Lobkowits, which is dated 1853 (now in the Dvořák Museum in Prague). The "third school class" was actually a private parallel class in German that was taught in addition to the two regular classes of the Zlonitz school and that could serve as a two-year continuing education course for those students who had completed the first level of their required primary schooling. Had the young Dvořák entered a butcher's apprenticeship, he would have had to attend the so-called Sunday School, whose registers, which have been preserved, do not contain the name Dvořák, as the "Books of the Butcher Apprentices" from Zlonitz likewise do not. Compulsory education, according to the legal requirements of that time, lasted seven years.

NOTES [BY JARMIL BURGHAUSER]

1. As the latest research confirms, there were two periods in the life of the young Dvořák during which his parents had the serious intention of forcing their son to learn the butcher's trade. The first was the beginning of his life, before he revealed his extraordinary attraction to music, and then from the summer of 1855 until the summer of 1856, after Antonín had already completed both levels of compulsory schooling and his father was having a harder and harder time in his shop. As several passages in this document make clear, Dvořák never officially began to learn the butcher's trade. The decision to permit the boy to follow the path of a musician may also have been encouraged by the fact that he was rather late to develop physically; he described himself in a memoir as having still been a "skinny child [Czech: *vyzle*] at the age of fifteen."

The "Butcher's Certificate of Apprenticeship," which is frequently mentioned in the literature after its "discovery" in 1937, is a naive fabrication, as I have proven in a study published in *Časopis Národního muzea* (Prague, 1987).

2. After the father's failure in his original line of work, he devoted himself to professional zither playing in public places, for which he acquired a license (a new discovery from the Kladno district archive).

3. The teacher was Josef Spitz (Špic, 1809–66).

4. Here the information is not quite accurate. According to a recollection from the year 1884 (reported by V. J. Novotný in *Hudební revue* [1911]: 445), Dvořák played his first violin solo in the year 1854, on a visit (already from Zlonitz) to his home town. It was probably the offertory "Ave Maria" by Liehmann (preserved in the Zlonitz Dvořák Memorial), which actually contains an extensive violin solo concertante.

5. The failure of his debut as a singer did not have such lasting negative consequences. Antonín appeared as a singer while still in Zlonitz, usually in duet with Liehmann's daughter Terinka.

6. The relative was Antonín Zdeněk (1823–?), the composer's maternal uncle, a steward at the manor house of Prince Kinský in Zlonitz.

7. Antonín Liehmann (1808–79).

8. The story of this first compositional attempt for orchestra is repeated in the literature in several variants. [See, e.g., H. L. Mencken's account in this volume, on p. 187.]

9. As noted, required school attendance ended for Antonín with the conclusion of the school year 1854–55. The following period, up until his move to Böhmisch-Kamnitz, was evidently devoted to helping out in his father's shop as well as participating frequently in various musical activities—church choirs, dance bands, and chamber music with the officials of the manor. Whereas the village of Nelahozeves and the market town of Zlonice were purely Czech, the city of Böhmisch-Kamnitz was populated almost exclusively by Germans. Dvořák's other music teacher there was a graduate of the Prague Organ School, named Franz Hanke (Hancke? b. 1807? 1823?).

10. At that time, the course of study at the Organ School regularly lasted two years. Dvořák entered in September 1857. Carl (Karel) Franz (František) Pitsch (1786–1858) was also the editor of the most significant collection of old Bohemian organ music, *Museum für Orgelspieler* [Museum for Organists], Prague 1832–34. Josef Krejčí (1821–81) assumed the post of director of the Organ School in December 1858. In 1865 he was named director of the Prague Conservatory (definitively by 1866).

11. Dvořák completed his studies at the end of the school year 1858–59 as the second-best student in the class. His compositions for the final examination have been preserved and were published in 1980 in the context of the complete critical edition. He played a selection from these pieces himself at the closing concert on 30 July 1859.

12. The director of the orchestra, which was probably the best one in Prague at that time, was Karel Komzák (1823–93). The first opera director of the Czech National Theater (which was then located in the building of the Interim

Theater), Jan Nepomucký Maýr (1818–88), hired the whole orchestra for his opera performances, which began in November 1862. In 1866, Bedřich Smetana (1824–84) took over the position of opera director. Dvořák left the post of violist at the end of the 1870–71 season (the end of July).

13. The first string quintet, in the key of A minor and identified as Op. 1, was composed in June 1861. In 1862, immediately after his first exemption from military service, Dvořák composed his first string quartet (in A major, Op. 2).

14. Karel Bendl (1839–97) got to know Dvořák while he was still a student at the Organ School, which he completed in 1858.

15. Dvořák's first symphony, in the key of C minor (evidently misread by Krigar in the information provided by Dvořák), was written, in the clean copy that has been preserved, in February and March of 1865. The date of origin of a possible and quite probable draft (the clean copy shows almost no erasures or changes) is unknown. The Second Symphony, in B♭ major, was written in the period between August and October 1865. The composer, according to his own report, sent the First Symphony to a competition in West Germany and never saw it again.

16. Dvořák revised the cantata *Die Erben des Weissen Berges*, to words by Vatězslav Hálek (1835–74), twice and published it in the later version in 1885 with Novello (London) as his Op. 30.

17. It is inexplicable why the statement that Brahms was not a member of the commission for the state scholarships in 1874 but joined later—which is also confirmed by Hanslick's first report about Dvořák (*Neue freie Presse*, 12 November 1879, reprinted in the book *Concerte, Componisten und Virtuosen* [Concerts, Composers, and Virtuosos], 3d ed. [Berlin, 1896])—has not been taken seriously by any of the subsequent biographers, from Kalenský to Šourek to Clapham. The latest research in Viennese archives has identified the members of the first commission, which signed the decision in November 1874, beyond any doubt: it consisted of Johann von Herbeck (1831–77), Felix Otto Dessoff (1835–92), and Eduard Hanslick (1825–1904). The fact, mentioned by Krigar, that Dvořák received the government subvention for an unbroken period of five successive years—which is also confirmed by the new research—was questioned by his biographers. An inadequate excuse may be found in imprecise statements that were later made by Dvořák himself, for example, to the reporter from the London *Pall Mall Gazette* ("From Butcher to Baton," 13 October 1886), in which Dvořák claims that in the year in which he included the score of the *Stabat Mater* with his application he did not receive a scholarship.

18. Dvořák occasionally, and even repeatedly, changed the opus numbers of his compositions, especially following the self-critical reevaluation of his previous creations in December 1873. Further confusion in the opus numbers was caused—against Dvořák's express will—by his publisher Fritz Simrock, who continued to give new opus numbers to older works that he subsequently included in his publications.

19. Dvořák's first opera, *Alfred*, to a German text by K. Th[eodor] Körner, is not mentioned. Dvořák composed the opera *Der König und der Köhler* twice, to the same text, with completely different music.

20. The *Hymnus* originally bore the opus number 14. After the second revision, in the Novello edition, it was given the number 30.

21. In the printed edition, the *Stabat Mater* was given the opus number 58.

22. In Krigar's article the Third Symphony, in E♭ major, is never mentioned. It was completed in 1873 and premiered under the direction of Bedřich Smetana in Prague on 29 March 1874. It originally bore the opus number 20; then 14, and finally 10. However, it was first printed by the publisher Simrock in 1911 "from the estate" without opus number, like the [Fourth] Symphony in D minor, which is mentioned, and which bore the opus numbers 24, 13, 18, and 19, in that order. It was composed in the first three months of the year 1874; the Scherzo may already have been written toward the end of 1873 under the name *Capriccio.* The F-major [Fifth] Symphony, composed in the summer of 1875, originally bore the opus number 24 but was published by Simrock in 1888 as the "Third" under the opus number 76. The *Symphonische Variationen* [Symphonic Variations], composed in the months of August and September 1877, originally bore the opus number 28 but were published by Simrock in the year 1888 as "Op. 78."

23. There were in fact three Nocturnes for Orchestra, originally Op. 18. Except for the string parts of the second, which is called *Mainacht* [May Night] and was premiered in Prague on 30 March 1873 under the baton of Ludvík Slánský, they have completely disappeared, unless we assume that the Nocturne for Strings in B major, Op. 40, might be one of them.

24. It is not clear why the later orchestral version of the Slavonic Dances, which was already printed in 1878 by Simrock, is not mentioned. The "waltzes" are evidently the Waltzes, Op. 54.

25. All of Dvořák's original duets—with the exception of "O Sanctissima" for alto baritone with organ accompaniment—actually belong to the *Klänge aus Mähren;* they are Opp. 20, 29, 32, and 38, and two independent numbers that were published elsewhere. The no. 22 that is cited here must be a [typographical?] error.

26. It is unnecessary for me to add here that all three of the above-named operas have been performed at the Bohemian National Theater in Prague and have continued to be part of the repertory, with enduring popular success.

27. The same false conclusion is drawn, naturally in a much different geographic version, in regard to the compositions of Edv[ard] Grieg. [This note stems from the publisher of the *Musikalisches Wochenblatt* and is attributed to "The Editor."]

Dvořák in the Czech Press:

Unpublished Reviews

and Criticism

TRANSLATED BY TATIANA FIRKUŠNÝ

Very little of the writing about Dvořák in the Czech press has appeared outside of Czechoslovakia. There are a variety of reasons for this, the most obvious being problems with accessibility and comprehension. In the past several decades it was not always easy to find nineteenth-century Czech newspapers, and even if one could, they seemed archaic, opaque, and even ephemeral. The change, however, that might revive interest in such works has nothing to do with newly opened archives but rather with a new curiosity about the nooks and crannies of history. Twenty years ago, much late nineteenth-century writing might have seemed hopelessly unscientific and riddled with linguistic idiosyncrasies. Those very characteristics are what attract us to them today. We are convinced that they offer us an important insight into their time and that, since Dvořák is part of that time, a significant insight into his world as well. It is instructive to note how pervasive were the generalized claims about Dvořák's Czech character and, consequently, about his value to the Czech nation. His identity as a purely Czech composer was a given, and almost all aspects of his music were seen exclusively through a scrim of romantic nationalism.

Dvořák's sixtieth birthday was marked by many celebrations and tributes. One of the most beautiful was the following article by Karel Hoffmeister, which appeared in the periodical *Zlatá Praha* (Golden Prague) in 1901.[1] Hoffmeister (1868–1952) was a pianist, writer, and educator who became one of Dvořák's great champions. We also include a photograph of the first page of the periodical with its Jugendstil drawings of the muses and its charming silhouette of Prague. [Ed.]

Antonín Dvořák: On the Occasion
of the Maestro's Sixtieth Birthday

KAREL HOFFMEISTER

Salgon alto, cantando senza le antiche lire
questi liberi e forti re de la giovinezza;
e i popoli adorando guardan alto salire
i nove semidii flugenti di bellezza.
—Gabriele d'Annunzio

There are artists whose works depend upon circumstances and are brought forth by certain events in their lives, dictated by their individual fates, which lead the hands forming them. Artists whose oeuvres are but diaries of their own lives, artistic autobiographies.—And there are, on the other hand, those in whom the soul of art is so vigorously alive that no outside event ever becomes tinged with the blood of their personal sufferings, nor does the wide, powerful stream, by which the soul pulsates within them and the work surges out of them, ever become gilded with the rosy glow of their joys. Artists whose creative processes bear no relation to their life stories and to their fates; whose works reflect but the slightest touch of the outside world; whose bosoms, turned into deep wells of tones or into vast worlds of colors and shapes, suffice as their source of everything.

Antonín Dvořák represents the latter strain.

For that reason the Maestro's biography, no matter how detailed, will be of no special importance in understanding his works. In this case, on the contrary, the works determined the course of his life.

A poor country boy who was driven to Prague to study elementary composition at the Organ School by a strange yearning, whose love for art enabled him to endure courageously a number of rather unpleasant years in the subordinate position and modest circumstances of an organist and subsequently of a violist in a civil band, later in the orchestra of the Interim Theater, who worked his way up to become a world-famous composer holding title to one of the foremost positions in the arena of European art, which even those not most amicably disposed toward our nation unanimously grant him; to whom, despite the fact that he never even attempted to open the rusty clasps of ancient scholarly volumes, two universities, those of Prague and Cambridge, did not hesitate to award the Doctor's cap; whom America, unable to call him her own, at least borrowed for a number of years; of whom the Prague Conservatory is so proud—of its teacher of composition and its direc-

First page of *Zlatá Praha* 18, no. 45 (1901)

tor of such renown that, its famous past notwithstanding, it has never had at its head one like him before.

This represents all the requirements for a universal victory.

As I have indicated earlier, his is not an oeuvre of a subjective nature that, in forming the musical feeling of an individual, mirroring his totally subjective moods prompted perhaps by certain events and circumstances of his life, would reverberate only in souls equally attuned, perhaps equally destined. Dvořák's works, just like Smetana's, in their best and most significant parts, are no less than the musical feeling of our nation captured in a definite artistic form. The entire musical soul of the Czechs, the soul of our entire nation is incarnated here in the oeuvre created by one individual. All that Czech musicians ever sang about, rejoiced in, cheered, wailed, and cried about—all those notes resound in Dvořák's compositions so beautifully and expressively as they have never done for anyone else.

So beautifully and expressively, so powerfully! And in all their universality!

This fulfills an additional requirement for the inevitable victory of Dvořák's art.

The rhythms that pulsate so energetically and vigorously in the artery of his music seem so familiar to us, as though for a very long time their distinct beats had been throbbing in our souls. But no one before Dvořák used them so markedly and with such abundance in creating a work of art. At the most, they were but hinted at. And the melodies, the songs so sweet and ardent, the variations of cantilenas and the subsequent harmonic and modulatory changes dictated by them—all that seems familiar to us, as if our national songs have resounded with it since time immemorial, as if all the beauty of the lavish melodies has been lying dormant in our hearts since time immemorial.

Perhaps many of those elements can really be found in the works of the minor, forgotten prophets who, with a modest song or a choral work, were preparing the time of maturity.

But to condense them, all dispersed and only felt and sensed, and to give them form, to make them into works of the widest range and of the highest style—only Smetana was able to do so in the field of dramatic and program music; in the same field, partially complementing Smetana, and in absolute music it was Dvořák.

These two were the first to speak the great, magic, liberating language of Czech music. And Dvořák's language sounded in a natural way because he spoke primarily in the idiom of symphonic and chamber music, of absolute music, thus in a dialect far more accessible than that of opera or program music, to the widest circles of the music world. And the music world wondered at his singular innovations. The whole treasure of new musical elements, the naive, unpremeditated straightforwardness of his work, the boundless wealth, so freely disbursed, of his amazingly natural musical fund of Schubertian force, all that had the effect of a current of fresh outside air entering a hall permeated with the heavy scent of the dying old Germanic culture. One of the foremost representatives of that culture, of its melancholy and of its statuesque art always arranged in classically predetermined poses, Johannes Brahms, was the first to welcome this new spirit of Slavic nature. He welcomed this wholesome, life-loving art of Dvořák even more readily because he saw in it something that he, a lonely recluse, and even his sadly magnificent oeuvre were denied: the happily singing joy of bubbling life.

He longed for it, searched for it and, not having found it himself, appreciated it in another. He fell in love with the lively whirl of the Slavonic Dances and with the exuberantly jubilant joy and happiness resounding throughout the wide landscape of the symphonies and chamber music, a landscape in full springtime bloom hardly ever touched even by a puff of fleeting sadness—he who, even in his scherzos, was scarcely able to offer a kind, quiet smile . . .

In cold England it was another aspect of Dvořák's work that brought him the famous wonderful reception and gained him a permanent place on English soil otherwise so unfavorable to anything foreign. It seemed that after Mendelssohn's oratorios the form was left exhausted. No newcomer capable of reviving it, of breathing new life into it, of infusing new blood into the old body was within sight.[2] Dvořák was able to fill the old symphonic forms with new, uncommon contents. He could do the same for the oratorio. There is a trait in his soul with which no other modern artist, albeit the greatest, could do it. He believes, simply and strongly. In every respect he is akin to the great original masters of the oratorio—both in the naiveté and straightforwardness of his creative process and in the profound and genuine nature of his religious feeling.

It is precisely through the innovative and singular character of his musical ideas and through his modern approach to the creative process that he brings all old forms close to us, modern men. For his work—incidentally, not only in oratorios but in everything else as well—has very little in common with scholarly themes, with the counterpoint of voices that intertwine, pile up on top of each other, grow out of another like stone traceries of medieval Gothic. It is closer to nature and free of sweat—he intertwines melodies with countermelodies and one theme with another like garlands of flowers: softly, freely, at times very freely, and fluently. Even in this polyphony every voice sings in an unaffected manner. The instrumentation supplies the new and singular phraseology, stylized in a new and singular manner, the appropriate coloring. Dvořák, a full-blooded musician with a universally developed musical instinct, recognizes and values the importance of color as equal to that of idea and form. And the color, as all his work, is usually jubilant, radiant, sparkling. Even in those places where it was inevitable to mix colors into muted, softer tones, the sparkle of life does not disappear from his palette—at least a pale, silvery moonshine illuminates Dvořák's darkened nocturnal moods. His last operas and, above all, his symphonic poems are perhaps the best examples of his developing into a great colorist of Rubenesque boldness.

Since I am touching upon the later works of the Maestro: Dvořák's turn from absolute music to program music is usually considered progress. Does, then, the cultivation of program music constitute in itself a progress in comparison to the creation of music whose purely musical content is sufficient in itself? Is there not an abundance of symphonic poems by German bandmasters that contain nothing new, that simply perpetuate old familiar phrases and color combinations of the neo-German school, which thus do not contribute anything whatsoever to musical progress?

Dvořák is undoubtedly a progressive artist even in his symphonic poems. But not simply because he follows the course of program music. Here he is the same progressive artist as in his other works written in, for instance, traditional symphonic form. An artist who contributed to the European art a whole range of new musical elements, of new rhythms, of new melodic, harmonic and modulatory variations, of new orchestral colors. An artist not so much of new forms but of new musical contents. That is why he strides through the world as a colossus, "the free and strong king of vigorous youth." That is why the world "watching his stride, worships him, the new magnificent hero of beauty . . ."

And that is why, since all the beauty and all the innovation he has brought are ours, are from our Czech, Slavic blood—that's why he is so especially dear to us. . . . That's why we rejoice so much in what he has given us and look forward to what he, God willing, will yet keep offering us for many years to come and in generous measure from his precious treasures.

·

This genuinely bad poem is offered not for its artistic value but as a document that illustrates the way in which the sentiments of the time were often structured. It appeared in the periodical *Našinec*[3] on 1 May 1892 and clearly refers to the composer's impending journey to America. [Ed.]

King of Music:
To Dr. Antonín Dvořák

Dead is the nation that once was the terror and threat to all its
neighbors;
O, it is dead—its descendants turned to rabble, its language dead—
its house deserted;—
Yet it is not; God's almighty hand did not wish it to sink into
nothingness;
It beckoned, solemnly saying: "Rise again, and be resurrected to a
new life!"

And the nation rose; it was the Czech nation, and it manifests its life
through sciences and arts!
And in vain were all the enemies' screams—and it marches on—
diligent, not idle.
O, a new institute of sciences has been established there, which the
vivacious nation founded by itself;
Science there is cultivated solely in Czech words; that is a source
from which it draws new strength.

And the arts? O, who of the new era does know the world-famous
Czech names?
Which are harmoniously ordered and which have made the Czechs
famous in the eyes of the world?
O, who doesn't know the creations of the Czech poets? Hynais's
beautiful formations?
Ondricek's, Brozik's Czech clans, which to us are gifts from Heaven
itself?

Yet, behold, you excelled above all others, your fame has spread
throughout the world;
Like a visitor coming to us from a higher realm, you are the most
beautiful blossom of Czech ingenuity.
In the constellation you are the star brighter than any other, you
have attained the zenith of your brilliance;
You seized the palm of sonic beauty;—you appeared abruptly—you
came out of hiding.

O, king of sounds, your eyes are turned upon other regions, and
your spirit dwells in other spheres;
For perhaps in your soul Heaven itself is making music, and an angel
dictates your compositions to you.—
Who knew you before?—Nobody in your entire native land guessed
the greatness of your spirit
But as soon as it began to harmonize sounds, the whole world
paused in astonishment.

And now, who does not know your name in the realm where the god
of music, Apollo, dwells?
Springs of delight flow into everybody's heart where your
compositions skillfully resound.
You know how to work magic in the secret realm of sounds; the
listener's mind carries him to paradise;
Forgetting everything, his grief and painful suffering, he is
surrounded by charming, blossoming May.

Though you were not recognized immediately at home, and though
foreign countries were the first to celebrate you:
You did not deny that your Czech homeland was dear to you, that
both your home and your family are in the Czech lands.
And unashamed of your Czech name, of your dear, sweet Czech
motherland,
No matter how much your name is glorified, you want to place
everything on the holy altar of your motherland.

O, ardent thanks to you; may the good Lord protect you for us, bless
you, work further with you;
So that your music would make the forests and meadows rejoice, so
that you may present the Czechs and all mankind with many more
compositions.
Thanks also for your having honored our town with your presence,
For granting us a moment of bliss—the town will preserve your rare
favor in its memory.

O, prince of music, your alluring, brilliant star is calling you over the
far sea;
May a new aurora of fame rise there for you; your motherland is
happy that the whole world knows you.
Your imagination is as vast as the sea you will soon be sailing across
into the distance;
May the Slavic melodies resound even there; even there the Czechs
will enjoy fame in music.

O, do not forget your dear motherland as your fame will be rising to
the sky;
Always remember: "Each to his own," that in the Czech lands this is
heard the strongest!
O, may the Lord's angel accompany you everywhere, protect you on
your artistic pilgrimage,
As the wreaths will adorn your features—say: "In the Czech
motherland is my cradle."

May you not be dazzled by the glory of the world so that you may
always have your dear motherland in your mind,
So that your star may bring you back in good health, so that you may
keep on singing for your motherland, for the dear Czechs.
"O, God be with you, God be with you"—thus we call to you in
parting; may the almighty Lord of the worlds accompany you;
Good luck on your way; may you arrive in the lucky city where soon
you are to set up your tent.

But when one day your heart fills again with longing and your feet
stir in the direction of return,
And following the inner voice of the heart by which everyone is
bound in his heart to his own country:
O, know then that all the Czech hearts will go to meet you, will even
come flying to meet you;
That the arms of all, be they from cities or villages, will lovingly
open—to embrace you.

Boh. Hakl

Karel Knittl (1853–1907) was a composer, educator, and conductor. He was
a professor at the Prague Conservatory and, after Dvořák's death, became
the director. The following review appeared in the periodical *Dalibor* in 1896.
It deals with the symphonic poems, based on the ballads of Erben, that Dvořák
had recently completed. [Ed.]

Dr. Dvořák's New Orchestral Works

KAREL KNITTL

Just before the end of the current concert season we were quite surprised by an event of extraordinary significance. Maestro Dvořák
joined the rank of composers of symphonic poems. There is no doubt

that for a long time each newly published work of the Czech symphonic composer has been eagerly anticipated. The tension this time became almost feverish. One could almost read in the features of many listeners gathered on the 6th of June, by special invitation, in the big auditorium of the Rudolfinum, the question: how will the composer treat this genre of music whose realm he is entering for the first time today? Let us answer it promptly: he treated it with originality, in every respect. That Dvořák would maintain the singular character of his work in musical matters had never been doubted. Not one among our living composers can address the heart in the specifically touching Czech manner the way that Dvořák can. That becomes immediately apparent in the opening bars of all the three symphonic poems based on subjects from Erben's *A Bouquet of Flowers*: "The Water Goblin," "The Noon Witch," "The Golden Spinning Wheel." Look, the water sprite making himself a pair of shoes up in the poplar tree over the lake is Czech; Czech is the little boy standing at the bench, playing with his toys and—screaming; Czech is the king on a black horse. As soon as the first tones of each poem are heard, you feel at home, familiar sounds caress your ears, you are enveloped by the sweet charm of your native country. Happily you bathe in the delightful atmosphere, grateful at heart that the composer dwells on certain scenes longer than you might expect the text of the poem to require. The mysterious sounds of "The Noon Witch" cast an indescribable spell over you; it is her voice indeed: a howling windstorm. You listen to the words of the enamored king and to the girl's responses in the poem "The Golden Spinning Wheel" interpreted for you by the English horn and the violin, feel the cheerless sadness of the water realm painted for you by unusually chilly harmonic combinations for the wind instruments.

The charms of Dvořák's new compositions highlighted here will come as no surprise to his admirers; they were expecting them as they expect a sunny summer day, certain in the knowledge it will come without fail. But a surprise of a different kind has been prepared by the composer: it is the way he approaches the subject matter, or, rather, the way he garners melodic material for the intricate fabric of each composition. It is original and yet at the same time so simple, uncomplicated. We might say: the orchestra recites Erben's poems. This writer listened to the above-mentioned new works while following the text of Erben's *A Bouquet of Flowers*. The melodic line in the most remarkable spots of each composition under discussion stems from the cadence of the lines, the precise enunciation of words providing it with its rhythmic structure. When the witch roars her "Give me the child"; when the water sprite's wife sings her lullaby; when the golden spinning wheel hums its strange song, and so forth, you can always supply the melodic phrase of the spot with the text—and you will actually get a nicely rounded song.

Thus what we have here is in fact a singular manner of musical interpretation: in some places the orchestra does not play; it actually sings.

Needless to say, the success of the new works justly corresponded to their value: they were received with enthusiastic cheering. The conservatory students followed with pleasure and with apparent interest the high-spirited conducting by Mr. Bennewitz. The art of production and the art of reproduction walked hand in hand in harmony not frequently encountered on the concert stage. It was an occasion for sincere joy.

·

The following document is a translation and reproduction of the entire program of a concert that was held in 1892, shortly before Dvořák's departure to the United States. We have included virtually all the written material that appeared, including the dedicatory poem, the program, descriptions of the artists, and notes dealing with the music. [Ed.]

Volume 9   Number 3

The Lyre

The official publication of the music club "Dalibor," in Hořice
"MUSIC IS OUR ELEMENT!"
Hořice, 15 March 1892

"The Lyre" is published on the fifteenth of every month, and members of "Dalibor" receive it gratis.—Every citizen of good repute may become an active or contributing member of "Dalibor."—Monthly dues are 25 crowns.— Publisher: Music club "Dalibor."—Editor: Prof. Alois Rublic.

To Dr. Antonín Dvořák

Your great name with the voice of its fame
Vibrates through the wide spaces of the land,
Before it, enthusiastically competing in their worship,
Are the gratitude of the motherland, the admiration of foreign
    countries.
Today both of them are inviting you into their midst
To salute you and to add green branches to your laurels:
Your genius is thus blessed by the gods
That everybody understands the depth of its language.

Everyone adorns his forehead with the musical jewels
Which the Muse always lets drop from your soul like tears,
Through them he is lifted into heavenly spaces
And even finds delight in making their metal ring.
And the specialist, on the other hand, scrutinizes
The intricate fabric of the construction, examines the pinions of the
  ideas
Till, deeply moved, he claps his hands so stingy with praise
And himself opens up the ranks of your epigons.

Indeed, your compositions are heard with amazement everywhere,
The whole world greets them with jubilation . . .
Yet only a Czech can truly understand the feeling at the bottom of
  their fiery bosom
Where everything pulsates with life.
He recognizes the Czech kernel, the bond of his own blood
In each and every one of the shining garnets;
He knows that it was a Czech soul that polished all the facets
When weaving the motifs into the brocade of the work.

And though the whole world is offering you its gifts and its praise
Even beyond the expanse of the sea,
Look—our nation is partaking in one great festivity,
It will devote all its love to you.
And when tempting invitations from abroad come to you,
All of us, though weeping, are bravely calling out:
"Onward for the glory of the motherland!
But leave us your Czech heart here at home."

Jos. Pazourek

Under the auspices of the honorable Municipal Council
THE SOCIETIES OF HOŘICE:
VESNA, DALIBOR, THE NONPROFESSIONAL ACTORS' CLUB,
THE BURGHERS' SOCIETY, THE BUSINESS CLUB,
RATIBOR, SOKOL, SVORNOST, AND THE TRADESMEN'S SOCIETY
present a

DVOŘÁK CONCERT
on Thursday, 24 March 1892,
in the auditorium of the theater

Assisting the famous Maestro Dr. A. Dvořák are
the Czech virtuosos Profs. F. Lachner and H. Wihan

PROGRAM

exclusively of Dr. Ant. Dvořák's compositions:

1. Slavonic Dances, Op. 46, no. 1, for large orchestra: Dalibor
2. Trio in F minor, Op. 65, for piano, violin, and cello: Dr. A. Dvořák, Prof. F. Lachner, and Prof. H. Wihan
3. Rondo capriccioso, for violin and piano: Prof. F. Lachner and Dr. A. Dvořák
4. "The Evening Forest Set the Bells Ringing" and "A White Birch Tree Has Run Out," from Op. 63
   Mixed choirs: Vesna and Ratibor
5. a) Peace ("Silent Woods"), from the cycle *From the Sumava*
   b) Rondo, Op. 94, for cello and piano: Prof. H. Wihan and Dr. Ant. Dvořák
6. *Dumky*, Op. 90, for piano, violin, and cello: Dr. A. Dvořák, Prof. F. Lachner, and Prof. H. Wihan
7. Festive March, Op. 54, for large orchestra: Dalibor

The piano was kindly lent by Mr. Robert Rabas, the master brewer.

Beginning at 8:00 P.M.

FORMAL ATTIRE

Longer intermissions following no. 2 and no. 5
Latecomers may enter only after completion of a work
Evening box office from 7:00 P.M. at the staircase

Following the concert, a free gathering in honor
of the guests in the downstairs rooms

Dr. Antonín Dvořák

The birthplace of Antonín Dvořák is Nelahozeves, near Kralupy, where his father was an innkeeper and butcher; a memorable and very significant day for the history of Czech music is 8 September 1841, the day of Antonín's birth. Little Antonín showed a surprising affinity for music as early as his elementary school years (in Nelahozeves and in Zlonice), which reached its highest point attainable at that stage of his life when he started to take organ lessons in Zlonice; it was then that he was first introduced to orchestral parts, which he was to copy for his teacher, and already then they awoke a desire in him "to write something similar." Later on Antonín was sent for a year to Germany, and after his return (from Česká Kamenice) he was supposed to apprentice in his father's trade—however, that did not happen; after pleading with his father, he was allowed to enter the Organ School in Prague and graduated from this institute in 1859. Thereafter he played the viola in

Komzák's civil band and later, when an independent Czech theater was established, became a member of its orchestra; in 1874, however, he resigned his post to become an organist at St. Vojtěch's Church in Prague. In 1875 he received a state scholarship, which put his hitherto rather difficult situation on a more solid basis, even enabling him to give up his post as organist in order to devote more time to musical composition.

From the moment the famous musicians and writers Herbeck, Hanslick, Brahms, Ehlert, and others brought him to general attention, even foreign countries started to take note of him, and our own musical circles began to consider Dvořák's compositions as factors of indisputable value; in this respect it was Dvořák's Slavonic Dances and Moravian Duets that brought him into the arena of musical art.

Dvořák's significance increased with every composition he presented to the public and reached a point where even foreign countries began to look up to him with respect and admiration as well deserved as it was genuine, placing him in the first rank of contemporary composers; in this respect it was especially the English who recognized Dvořák's genius to a degree unknown in our country until then.

Antonín Dvořák must be justly counted among those men of our national revival who, through their tireless activities, put a stamp of fire on the period. Dvořák was victorious because he embraced the national folk songs with the ardent enthusiasm of a Czech musician, because he made use of every modern musical development in refining our Czech music, and as if by magic created a great number of musical gems that kept surging from his poetic bosom.

Needless to say, Dvořák's agile and versatile spirit tested its mettle in every aspect of musical composition; that the result was always phenomenal goes without saying. From songs to oratorios and operas, from small pieces for the piano to large orchestral compositions—what an impressive gallery of works, all of which have the touch of Dvořák's genius!

As is well known, Antonín Dvořák is an honorary Doctor of Philosophy in Prague, a Doctor of Music in Cambridge, a knight of the Order of the Iron Crown, and an honorary member of many musical and choral societies; until the present time he has been Professor of Composition at Prague's Conservatory and has now been named director of the National Conservatory of Music in New York in America.—

Ferdinand Lachner,

Professor of Violin at the Conservatory of Music in Prague, was born in Prague on 23 March 1856; he attended elementary school at St. Mary of the Snows and then high school in Panská Street. From his earliest days he showed an extraordinary liking for music; his first violin teacher was Erazim Laub, father of the world-famous Czech violinist Ferdinand Laub. He entered the Conservatory in 1870 and soon became, next to František Ondříček, one of the best pupils of Professor Bennewitz; in 1876 he left the Conservatory to become a pupil at the Organ School and at the same time continued his education in musical theory with Zdeněk Fibich. In 1879 he accepted a post as concertmaster in Vratislav, where he stayed for two years; thereafter he became concertmaster of Director Laube's orchestra in Hamburg. From there he accepted a wonderful offer to join the Czar's Theater in Warsaw. Toward the end of 1882 he returned to Prague and in 1883 was named concertmaster of the National Theater, and in 1888 Professor of Violin at the Conservatory, where he is still successfully active beside his former teacher, Director Bennewitz.

Lachner has the highest reputation as a violinist: a soft, unusually pleasing tone combined with a carefully conceived interpretation of music are the main reasons for Lachner's extraordinary popularity. He is especially valued as an interpreter of chamber music.

Lachner belongs to the most beloved members of Prague's Czech artistic community, not only because of his rare art but also for his straightforward, kind disposition.—

Hanuš Wihan,

currently Professor of Cello at Prague Conservatory, was born on 5 June 1855 in Police, near Broumov, where his father was a librarian; he attended high school in Vysoké Mýto and in Prague, but from his childhood he was attracted by music and wished to become a musician. His father opposed his decision, but his desire won and his parents permitted him to enter the Conservatory instead of high school—and thus young Wihan became a budding cellist. His beginnings at the Conservatory were not great; however, his iron diligence and tireless work resulted in Wihan's becoming upon his graduation one of the best students. In 1873 he became violoncellist and violoncello professor at the Mozarteum in Salzburg from where, in 1874, he joined Devries's famous band consisting mostly of Czech players with whom he spent a whole year in Italy and South France. In 1875 he joined the orchestra of Prague's German Theater and in 1876 became a member of Bilse's orchestra in Berlin. From 1878 until July 1880 he was concertmaster in Sondershausen and in the same year accepted the post of first solo cellist of the court orchestra in Munich; throughout the entire eight years he spent his holidays concertizing in Germany and Austria. In the summer of 1888 he was asked to become Professor of Cello at Prague's Conservatory, and to this day he fulfills the prestigious job, educating able musicians and outstanding cellists who, in the future, will bring much respect not only to their teacher but also to the Czech arts.

Hanuš Wihan is not a mere virtuoso, not a mere interpreter of compositions he plays; Wihan performs with genuine enthusiasm and through his masterly playing he transfers his enthusiasm to the audiences who are as if transfixed by his magical sounds. Wihan's playing is marked not only by technique but also by the power of his tone, above all, however, by his noble expression, by his ideal understanding of the composition; Wihan is not only a prime example of a virtuoso cellist, he is also a prime example of a teacher, and his students all but worship him. He is loved by all who come in contact with him for his noble, kind, and honest character and for his enthusiastic efforts.

A Note on Dvořák's Compositions

All of Dvořák's compositions are marked by a special characteristic: they are ours, they are Czech, Slavic. However, the Slavic character of Dvořák's music stands out in an unforced manner, without any affectation; the natural simplicity of his music is the magic spell that necessarily captivates the listener. Over the course of time, Dvořák is not the first composer to imprint the Slavic character on his music, but he does so in an original manner of his own; his compositions breathe with a thoroughly charming melodic inventiveness, and their overall mood is electrifying. Dvořák must be considered the musical herald of his Czech motherland who brought our arts to the attention of the widest circles, having lifted himself up to the first place among contemporary composers by the rich splendor of his compositions.—

The SLAVONIC DANCES, cheerful pieces that first ensured Dvořák a firm place among composers who are not only popular but also justly respected, are charming compositions, and their splendid, brilliant orchestration fully justifies the enthusiasm they meet with everywhere; however, even in their original piano version they are extremely popular. Not only book 1 but also book 2 have virtually circled the globe.— Dvořák's spirited chamber music pieces such as the Trios in F minor, B♭ major, and G minor, his splendid string quartets, his charming—and popular even in our country—Trio for two violins and a viola, the lovely Bagatelles, and so on, are genuine pearls of modern music through and through, notable for their deeply detailed composition and beautiful ideas; from among the most recent chamber music pieces we must single out RONDO CAPRICCIOSO, a composition wherein Dvořák's art is prominent, and the DUMKY TRIO, which by its modern yet genuinely Czech character, by its buoyancy and its partly cheerful, partly pensive melodies, ranks among the most beautiful and enthralling compositions of its genre.—Dvořák's numerous compositions for the piano prove that their creator is an artist of genius, independent and original. Among his recent works it is mainly the cycle FROM THE SUMAVA MOUNTAINS and other compositions that present a number of the most exquisite pearls full of sweetness and beauty.—But it is in the orchestral compositions where Dvořák comes forward as the real master. Thus a commissioned work, the FESTIVE MARCH, composed for the occasion of Their Majesties' silver wedding anniversary, proves beyond doubt that Dvořák's ingenious talent produces only works wherein fervor is joined by grace, reflecting the brilliant shine of the Maestro's great spirit. The singularly conceived and grandiose *Hussite* Overture shows an independent thinker, and the fire of imagination as well as of color glows from the Slavic Rhapsodies as much as from the two famous Serenades; the characteristic Legends, the rapturous Symphonies and others are immortal monuments Dvořák has built himself in the hearts of the Czech people, in the minds of lovers of genuine art; all Dvořák's orchestral works place their creator, preeminently and emphatically, on a lonely high plateau among contemporary composers, crowning Dvořák a victor who has easily overcome all obstacles placed in the path of Czech art in foreign countries.—Yet what a powerful spell, an alluring spell, an indescribable spell shines forth from Dvořák's numerous oratorios and operas. His *Stabat Mater* alone, notable for its profound religious majesty, contains music that touches the listener with its calm, its seriousness of conception, and its perfection of the whole as well as of the parts. His melodramatic music for *Tyl* is beautiful and spellbinding; this work is all the more noteworthy as the means employed by Dvořák to display his art in its full beauty are simple. The majestic *Hymnus*, the powerful Psalm 149, the splendid *Specter's Bride* and *St. Ludmila*, the pious *Missa solemnis* and the monumental *Requiem*—all these works, all this enormous mental activity within a short number of years! Yet even Dvořák's operas *Vanda, The King and the Charcoal-Burner, The Cunning Peasant, The Stubborn Lovers, Dimitrij*, and *The Jacobin* are superior in their unusually rare characteristic both of the whole and of details; Dvořák's operatic music is also original, Dvořák composed his operas as dictated by his ideal; the charm of the music lies predominantly in its national coloration, in its magnificent conception, in the wealth of melodies, and in its deeply emotional execution. So far, Dvořák's operas are of course not known in the music world beyond the Czech borders; but once they become known, the world will wonder at the gems it has been leaving lying idle. Perhaps the time is near when foreign countries begin to rank Dvořák as first even among opera composers; in our parts, every opera by Dvořák has been given enthusiastic recognition as a christening present already at its birth, a present full of jubilant joy and admiration.—Calm, freshness, and charm emanate from Dvořák's melodic compositions; whether they are the already famous Moravian Duets or various songs for solo voice, choral works for men's or mixed choirs among which the cycle *In Nature's Realm* is the most prominent,—they all are mostly lovely flowers, simple yet beautiful. All the perfume, all the rapture and all the desire that is concealed in these mostly short compositions!—

An article attempting to list all of Dvořák's compositions and to give them their due would be endless. Dr. Antonín Dvořák is still young, full of vigorous energy, and may God let the number of his works grow on; that all the greetings Dvořák sends the Czech people from his new home will be rare pearls is guaranteed by his phenomenal talent, enormous diligence, uncommon mental fitness, and by the inspired ideas of the creator of Slavic orchestral music that Dvořák represents, fully and uncompromisingly! May Dvořák's genius powerfully glow and shine even in faraway countries beyond the sea!—

Rc.

Dvořák's *Rusalka* is the best-known operatic work by the composer. This article appeared in the periodical *Meziaktí* (Between the Acts), a publication devoted to the theater. It featured photographs, stories, and in this case a section entitled "Aphorisms and Motives." Here one might find the thoughts of writers, musicians, and poets written in their own words. We have included photos from this periodical for several reasons. First, there were nine photographs accompanying the original article, which offer a sense of the first production. But there is another reason. We usually think of Dvořák's context as purely musical, but this magazine presents him in the wider context of contemporary intellectual life. We have also included the first page of the periodical, not only as a fascinating document in its own right but also because the Jugendstil aspect of the design suggests yet another context in which it is instructive to view Dvořák. [Ed.]

Antonín Dvořák's *Rusalka*

KAREL HOFFMEISTER

To tell the Maestro's familiar curriculum vita: it is a very simple course of life, without any special events. Only his works are its magnificent markers. Born on 8 September 1841 in Nelahozeves, he attended the

First page of *Meziaktí*, no. 220 (1901)

Wood nymphs from the opera *Rusalka*

Organ School in Prague. And then for many years he struggled to make a living. He played the viola in Komzak's band, which was later taken over by the Theater. There he remained until 1873. Then for three years he was one of the organists at St. Vojtech's Church. And during breaks between theater rehearsals and masses and private lessons he composed his works, which in those days the public hardly even learned about. It was only his *Hymnus* composed on the text of Hálek's *Heirs of the White Mountain*, performed in 1873 by Bendl and the Hlahol Choir, that placed him in a position of significance among the Czech composers. Naturally, his importance increased considerably after Simrock's publishing house, on Brahms's prompting, introduced his works on the world market. Germany became intoxicated with the fiery, undiluted wine it was being offered in classically shaped goblets by the Czech master of chamber music, by the full-blooded musician and composer of symphonies, whose like have been few since Beethoven; in the same way, cold England enthusiastically embraced the creator of oratorios and cantatas who, following in the footsteps of Handel, could fill the old and seemingly dying form with new contents of his own. The author of the *Stabat Mater*, the Psalm, *The Specter's Bride*, *St. Ludmila* has thus become one of the world's foremost composers.— For a while America borrowed the glow of his brilliant name. Now

Růžena Maturová in the title role of *Rusalka*

Prague's Conservatory, its composition department, is blossoming—
may God let it blossom for a long time—in the sunshine of his world
renown.—

One aspect of Dvořák's output has remained predominantly of local
interest. It is his operatic oeuvre. He has written a number of works for
the Czech theater. The curve marking his ascent from *The King and the
Charcoal-Burner* of 1871 to *Rusalka* shows a nice number of bench-
marks: *The Stubborn Lovers*, produced in 1874; a year later, *Vanda*; then
The Cunning Peasant, two years later, in 1882; *Dimitrij*, which was later
revised; then *The Jacobin*; and last year the Czech fairy tale *The Devil and
Kate*. It is a curve marking the evolution of a musician initially preoc-
cupied exclusively with absolute music into a dramatic composer. The
transition from formal composition to program composition, so characteristic of works from Dvořák's latest years, is probably related to his
dramatic works and to his attempt to succeed and make a mark even in
this genre, and thus expand his activity. In his symphonic poems he
made use of Czech legends; in the opera he employs a Czech fairy tale.
In this area he began with the humorous *Devil and Kate* and now continues with the tragic story of Rusalka's sad fate.—It is short and
simple.—Rusalka, charmed by human beauty, is seized by the desire
for a man and his love. Ježibaba's magic makes her human, lends her a
human body and a human soul. The price, however, is enormous:
"Should you lose the love you so desire, the curse of the powers of water
will pull you back down into the deep; and you shall suffer even while
attaining your goal, for you shall remain mute to all human ears!" And
further on: "Should you return with the curse upon you into the water
sprite's realm, you will thus also bring death to your lover!" But Rusalka
will not be frightened. Gladly she follows the Prince, who chances upon
her in the forest during a hunt, to his castle. She believes in the power of
her sacrifice.

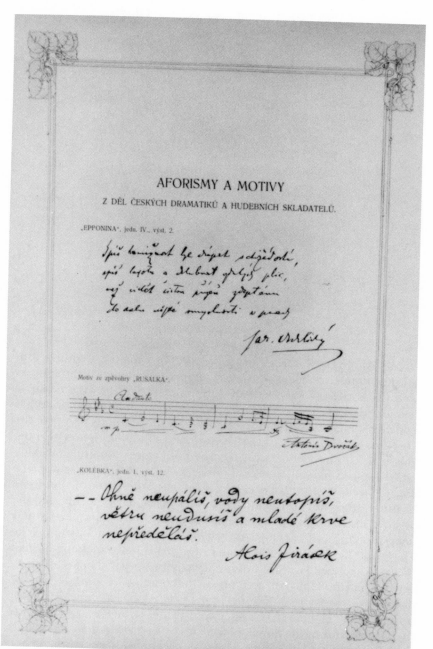

"Aphorisms and Motives" sketch, in *Meziaktí*, no. 220 (1901)

Růžena Maturová in the title role of *Rusalka*

The whole castle is busy with preparations for the wedding. But strange things are being whispered among the servants—the forester and the kitchen boy let us know a thing or two of the local gossip—namely, that the Prince's love for his pallid, golden-haired bride has cooled off, that he is now more attracted by the sensuous beauty of the foreign princess who is a guest at the castle. And soon we see that the tale is true. The Prince, provoked by the Princess and her mocking words, speaks harshly to his sad, mute sweetheart. Desperate over the loss of her love, Rusalka seeks consolation in the water of the pond.

But she does not find death in the water. Nymphs cannot die; and she is, after all, a nymph—albeit a cursed one, who cannot take part in their merrymaking and dancing. And again there is but one way to revoke the curse: her lover's blood alone can wipe off her remaining human features. Yet her love will not let her pay this price! Thus she has to suffer, half-human, half-nymph, in her mournful solitude. In the meantime, the Prince's passion for the Princess has passed. He cannot forget his pallid, bloodless, mute beauty. He searches for her and finds her on the bank of the familiar lake. He is not afraid of her love though he knows that her ice-cold embrace will kill him. He dies, happy, in her arms.

Right from the beginning we know which two elements the composer had to portray in his music. On the one hand, he had to create a

Růžena Maturová in the role of the witch in the opera *Rusalka*

number of scenes of fairy tale–like, supernatural character, to convey the mysterious atmosphere wherein a human being is but a foreign visitor, to capture the unearthly climate of the first act and, for the most part, also the last one. That Dvořák has the palette needed for such portrayals we know precisely from his symphonic poems. It is not necessary, I suppose, to call advance attention to the nymphs' playful songs in the first act and especially to the melodic beauty of their childishly simple tune glittering with the charm of diamondlike dew drops, or to Ježibaba's bizarre hocus-pocus, to the music so fittingly depicting her magic tricks. And right after the first few bars of music accompanying the water sprite's arias and stage entrances we realize that he, too, is of the other world, not of ours.

And further, we note that the action spills out into lyrical love scenes, is contained in displays of love that is full of desire, happy and fulfilled, betrayed, destroyed, desperate, and then again reconciled in death; how the composer, besides the modest intermezzo with the Princess, had to invent a considerably long gamut for capturing the nuances of erotic expression of the two protagonists, Rusalka and the Prince. We can see that the fairy tale–like atmosphere of the opera required an excellent, delicate colorist and a great master in command of first-rate tools capable of setting up the mood, on the one hand; and a master of

The witch (Marie Klánová), the kitchen boy (Vilemína Hájková), and the gamekeeper (Adolf Krössing)

superb lyrical, that is, melodic inventiveness, on the other, as has been stressed earlier.

And that is what the composer of *The Specter's Bride* and the *Stabat Mater* continues to be in this work. I am not sure which of Rusalka's arias to designate as the most beautiful. Perhaps the sorrowful, balladlike "Song to the Moon"? Or the majestic aria in classical three-part form of the second act? Or the broken, sad song "My Youth Is Gone" with its monotonous ostinato accompaniment in the last act? Or the ardent and tender scenes with the Prince? Of these I would have to mention every single one up to the closing duet, their crowning jewel. I would necessarily have to add the fiery duet of the Prince and the Princess.

One element was naturally greatly favorable to the composer's formally rounded creation; it actually inspired him to create these beautifully proportioned and yet not mechanically calculated musical constructions: it was Kvapil's libretto. In direct contrast to the short dialogue phrases of *The Devil and Kate* it is written practically without any dialogues, in broader units that in the richness of their lyrical contents and temperament are most suitable for being put to music. Thus we hear again, from the stage and in all its beauty, a melody that in the Maestro's last opera was mostly transferred from the singers to the orchestra.

Is Dvořák's new opera dramatic? The Maestro's music captures the simple story in all its particulars, always finding the one appropriate tone for the climaxes of its tragedy, sometimes highlighting them. And

Václav Kliment in the role of the water sprite in the opera *Rusalka*

it manages excellent characterization even in details. Moreover, in order to achieve firmer unity and conciseness, the composer works extensively with distinct motifs. Rusalka's motif reaches our ears in all kinds of variations, modified according to the situation. And especially the water sprite remains faithful to his stereotyped phrases that become the basis of the orchestral accompaniment of his scenes; and his playful phrase eventually recalls the lightfooted nymphs' world and their frolics. Perhaps mention should be made of the chromatic sequence of sad-sounding chords variously accompanying allusions to Rusalka's ruin; mention should be made of the repetition of Rusalka's characteristic melody, including its introductory harp cadence in the first and

Rusalka, act 2

last act as a rounding-off feature—all that is detailed work, well thought out, and, needless to say, under superb technical command.— That which is the greatest in this new work of the Maestro, that which is not arrived at by knowledge, erudition, or routine, is the power of his inspiration, of his imagination so strong, rich, and creative in every respect. Here is a source of genuine, beautiful, original music surging forth with a force found in but a few of the new operatic works.

Rusalka, act 3: Rusalka (Růžena Maturová) and the prince (Bohumil Pták)

RUSALKA: "Neither dead nor alive, neither woman nor fairy,
Accursed I wander through the shadows!"
PRINCE: "Without you it is impossible for me to live anywhere—
Can you, O, can you forgive me?"

·

Knittl's discussion of *Rusalka* appeared in *Osvěta* 31, no. 5 (1901). Of particular interest in this essay is Knittl's meditation on the contrast between fairy-tale operas and what he refers to as mythological music dramas. We may also note his close critical reading of Kvapil's text. [Ed.]

Opera

KAREL KNITTL

Rusalka, a lyrical fairy tale by Jaroslav Kvapil, with music by Antonín Dvořák. First performed at the National Theater on 31 March 1901

"Again a fairy tale" probably sighed a number of our theatergoers. "Are we then living in a fairy-tale era?" Our age—despite all realism and verism—is beginning to get a taste for this genre. The operatic field, depleted and exhausted by cultivation of myth, sees the fairy tale as a means of refreshment, even of rebirth. The current state of the opera is not unlike that of a hundred years ago. Let those so inclined set up a hundred-year musical calendar! After the death of the great operatic reformer of the eighteenth century, Gluck (d. 1787), who, through his works, revived Greek myths, the year 1791 welcomed *The Magic Flute*, one of the most beautiful musical fairy tales. One hundred years later, following the death of the great reformer of the nineteenth century, R. Wagner (d. 1883), who revived the German myths, in 1893, Humperdinck, with his fairy tale *Hansel and Gretel*, won on the operatic battlefield over every Kunihilde, Urvas, Malavike, and whatever the other forgeries of Wagner's muse are called. And since then we have been coming across new attempts in the same vein more and more frequently: we will mention just as an example the fairy tale *Barenhauter* (Bearskins) by Wagner's son, and *The Sunken Bell* by Zöllner. Let us, however, continue our scrutiny of the aforementioned hundred-year calendar: in 1817, Rossini's *Cenerentola* saw the light of the world; then, in 1821, Weber's *Der Freischütz*, and in 1826 his *Oberon*; in 1828, Marschner's *Vampire*, and in 1833 his *Hans Heiling*, practically all of them belonging to the most excellent musical fairy tales of the time; the chain was finally and almost completely broken by Meyerbeer's *The Huguenots* of 1836. We are by no means trying to prove with this list that, next to musical fairy tales, there was no room left for other operatic genres such as the romantic opera, opera buffa, or the historic opera. We are simply pointing out the fact that after an almost exclusive reign of mythology on the level of high tragedy, a simple fairy tale took over. It is thus natural to find that a mild fairy tale reaction is taking over today following a period of mythological absolutism. To us, every finely made operatic fairy tale feels like a refreshing musical bath after a stifling, upsetting, nerve-racking journey in quest of musical drama.

We rank Kvapil's *Rusalka* among the finely made, though there may be moments in it to make us pause slightly. We have no interest in trying to search in the fairy-tale literature of the past or of the present for sources that may have been used by the author of *Rusalka*, nor do we wish to criticize him for having taken over some of their themes, characters, or actions. For the purpose of opera, the water sprite remains always a water sprite even though he may be called simply Waterman here and Nickelmann or Kuhlebcrn somewhere else; and the witch remains a witch, though some may call her Ježibaba and others Wittich. Finally, it is difficult to distinguish, in the operatic versions of various fairy tales, between the personal qualities of the various "Princes." In the opera, every element representing reason or serving as a symbol is but seldom effective, and that only in specially strong cases. Otherwise it tends to disappear in the great flow of music like a little stone. Wagner's Nibelungs supply more supporting evidence in this matter than is necessary. Regarding the story of *Rusalka*, it is true that Rusalka's becoming mute is explained in the text ("before gaining love you shall suffer, to every human ear shall you remain mute"); yet it comes as a surprise when in the second act Rusalka, after her mute scene with the Prince, suddenly regains speech as soon as the water sprite emerges. Neither can one fully approve of the distribution of scenes in this act: the Prince and his retinue make two identical appearances. Finally, the third act is somewhat protracted: scenes from the first act are repeated, for example, the wood nymphs frolicking with the water sprite. However, weak points of this sort can be easily remedied with a blue pencil. Otherwise,the text of *Rusalka* contains a great deal of tender fairy tale– like poetry and language that, on the whole, is naturally noble. Moreover, its style is closely bound up with the beautiful example of Erben's ballads, as was intended by the author, and in many instances carried out with complete success. In this respect, all the scenes involving fabulous characters are absolutely splendid. Less appealing are the conversations of the "people": that of the Prince with the Princess, or the kitchen boy with the forester, though here the want of style is made up for by a genuinely comic touch.

What should be said about Dvořák's music? It is a custom in our country to compare a composer's new work with the preceding one, and the result of such examination is usually a statement of considerable progress in the development of the author's art. This kind of comparison can in no way be suitably applied to the current work, mainly because Dvořák's two latest operatic works surge from the highest level of his musical activity. Those who might find the musical inventiveness in the opera *The Devil and Kate* less rich than that in *Rusalka* should be reminded that the story itself does not allow either the time or the place necessary for its full development. The merry, fresh vein of the composer's inventiveness was practically checkmated by the barren text; the composer was forced to suppress the powerful flow of ideas. *Rusalka*, on the other hand, offers Dvořák the widest range for his compositional preferences. It is full of lyrical passages in which the Maestro's fragrant melodic invention finds a natural home. Everything in *Rusalka* is practically drowning in the sweetly sorrowful melos so specific to Dvořák, and even in places where the swiftly changing mood of the dialogue instantly requires the use of characteristic musical phrases and offers a chance to work with themes and motifs, the musical yarn is fluently spun together to form an easily perceivable whole.

This is done without any self-conscious linking so that the listener gets through the process effortlessly, happy in the knowledge that he has not become lost in a minor labyrinth.

To be sure, these motifs are of such texture and color as always to break distinctly through above the surface. In this respect Dvořák has had excellent training. For certain incidents and situations in his symphonic poems composed on the texts of Erben's ballads he was obliged to search for the most appropriate sharply focused musical figures. Coming up with a comprehensible characteristic in instrumental music is a much tougher nut to crack than doing the same thing in vocal music or even in opera. The depiction or the action contained in the latter meet the composer halfway, thus the relatively lesser impact of dramatic music in the concert hall. Dvořák's ability to capture a sense of self-evident truthfulness in the chosen poems, whether in imitating the sounds of the animal kingdom or in musically depicting the sometimes charming, at other times horrifying supernatural phenomena, is by now known throughout the world of music and recognized everywhere without reserve. We follow this aspect of Dvořák's compositional activity with admiration because it is attained through the simplest of means, does not strive for virtuosity, and is always accompanied by that enviable quality, a simple naiveté free of any clever calculation, of which, in the sky of the musical art, only stars of the first magnitude can boast.

By describing the principal characteristics of Dvořák's recent music we have at the same time stated the reason why the listener remains captivated by *Rusalka* from beginning to end. Right after the overture has transported him into a fairy-tale atmosphere, the listener is enthralled by the charm of the wood nymphs' song echoing through the silent moonlit night, amused by their playful scene with the water sprite, whose motif—scary but with a comic touch—swiftly becomes engraved in his memory; with sympathy he listens to Rusalka's words of yearning, follows Ježibaba's magic tricks (and especially the effective *valse infernale*) while his mind is vividly recalling horrifying pictures of witches conjured up long ago by his childhood imagination; he is touched by the hunter's song sounding from afar, thrilled by the Prince's love protestations. In the second act he enjoys the comic scene between the kitchen boy and the forester, which is built on a lively polka rhythm, and he allows himself to be entirely carried away by the merriment of the wedding celebration, especially by the charming ballet music whose muffled sounds merge with the tender song of the wedding guests. The third act, as mentioned before, offers little new, either in the scenic development or in the atmosphere of the libretto; thus it is

natural that the musical material, with the exception of the forester–
kitchen boy–Ježibaba trio, is predominantly derived from the preceding acts, needless to say, with appropriate colorations as called for by
the sorrowful lamentations of the betrayed Rusalka on the one hand
and, on the other, by the Prince's stormy declarations of love, seething
with amorous fire even at the point of death.

There is not one single opus among Dvořák's recent works from
which one could not select an important and convincing illustration of
every kind of musical beauty. At present, it is primarily the area of
instrumentation in which Dvořák achieves new and utterly astonishing
effects drawn from the characters of the various instruments. We intentionally disregard the mixing of certain colors for the purposes of
depiction and focus our attention on the use of one color, that is, of one
instrument. In *Rusalka* we are impressed by the unusual yet extremely
characteristic use of the piccolo to play exquisite phrases that, in terms
of depiction, sometimes sound like a gentle breeze and other times like
ghastly rustling. This is undoubtedly a new effect. The timbre of the
instrument is employed in ways already prefigured by Haydn (in his
Seasons, where it accompanies the farmer's voice), which later—as far as
we know—fell into complete oblivion. (The screaming of the two pic-
colos accompanying Caspar's song in Weber's *Der Freischütz* is something entirely different.)

In spite of these rare qualities of the new opera there are critical
voices, albeit in the minority, that would deny him his genuine and
indisputable success and apply the yardstick of music drama to *Rusalka*.
There is no better way of doing violence to an artist than trying to judge
his performance from a vantage point that is completely foreign to
him. It is just like chastising someone who has nicely cleared a hurdle
for not leaping over it. Let us always pass our judgment in accordance
with the artist's intentions. He who writes music dramas or dips his pen
in that style should be measured by the Bayreuth yardstick. But to
apply the same criterion in order to judge a work totally free of similar
ambitions is incomprehensible. As far as we are concerned, we admit
without hesitation that the use of declamatory style alone, coupled with
the use of leitmotifs, without appropriate characteristics and compelling expression, and lacking a grand conception, will never reconcile us
to that part of dramatic-musical literature that has appropriated
merely the body of music drama, searching in vain for its soul, heart,
and feeling.

There was a time when it was deemed fashionable to look condescendingly askance at everything lacking the imitation-gold glitter of a
pseudo–music drama. Today, even in the country where musical

drama was born, one is beginning to hear voices of authority speaking against this kind of overrated judgment. It has been recently pointed out how much Germany wronged Verdi by expecting from him a drama of the kind produced by Wagner's reform, without recognizing the wealth of artistic truth, power, and greatness Verdi put into his full-blooded renditions of various dramatic situations. Verdi's artistic creed never deserved the kind of condemnation it was accorded especially in Germany, and also in our country. Let us read what the Maestro has to say in his letter to Countess Maffei:

> To imitate the truth slavishly may be a good occupation, but to find the truth through one's imagination is better, much better. The words "to discover the truth through one's imagination" are only seemingly a contradiction in terms; just try to look for the truth in the pope's words—I mean to say in Shakespeare's. Falstaff may have possibly crossed his path; but he has hardly ever met an archvillain of Iago's sort and certainly never the angelic characters of Cordelia, Imogena, Desdemona—and how full of true feeling are these personalities! To imitate the truth faithfully may be a beautiful occupation. But it is then mere photography, not painting.

We mention these matters because we feel that Dvořák's operatic output is not being properly estimated in our country. There may come a time when we reexamine our views. If all the omens are right, we are on the threshold of a great flowering of fairy tale and comic opera. This will certainly and justly give Dvořák his due. For Dvořák, too, seeks and finds the truth through his imagination!

NOTES

1. *Zlatá Praha* 18, no. 45 (1901). [Ed.]

2. He is referring here to the success of Dvořák's *St. Ludmila* in England. [Ed.]

3. The word *našinec* literally means "one of ours," or an "ours-nik"—in other words, one of our own countrymen. [Ed.]

A Discussion of Two Tone Poems

Based on Texts by Karel Jaromir Erben:

The Wood Dove and

The Golden Spinning Wheel

LEOŠ JANÁČEK

TRANSLATED BY TATIANA FIRKUŠNÝ

It is well known that Leoš Janáček was one of Dvořák's great champions. He performed many of the older composer's works in Brno and even gave several premieres. Between 1897 and 1898 Janáček published discussions of Dvořák's four symphonic poems based on the poetry of Erben. We include two of these: *The Wood Dove* (*Holoubek*) and *The Golden Spinning Wheel* (*Zlatý kolovrat*). They are particularly interesting for a number of reasons. First, they are further documentation of Janáček's peculiar and powerful literary gifts; he manages to combine a reading of the poem with a sophisticated yet idiosyncratic analysis of the compositions. Second, the approach taken reveals the way in which one creative mind sees itself through the works of another. Janáček is particularly concerned with the works' dramatic potential and the way in which these compositions break down the boundary between speech, music, narrative, and static fairy tale. These were central concerns in Janáček's own compositions. Finally, Janáček makes us aware of the exciting and quite innovative strategies Dvořák employs in his symphonic poems. Janáček's analysis and discussion make it even clearer that his own efforts in the same realm, involving works such as the *Ballad of Blaník*, *The Fiddler's Child*, *Amarus*, and even *Taras Bulba* owe an enormous debt to Dvořák's example.

Writing about the music of Schubert in the *Century Illustrated Monthly Magazine* in 1894, Dvořák says: "We should return to the symphonic dimensions approved by Haydn and Mozart. In this respect Schumann is a model, especially in his B♭-major and D-minor Symphonies; also in his chamber music. Modern taste calls for music that is concise, condensed, and pithy." Certainly the symphonic poems are a conscious realization of this ideal, and Janáček's discussion of the works emphasizes this view. [Ed.]

The Wood Dove (on the Text of K. J. Erben's Poem):
A Symphonic Poem Composed for Large Orchestra,
by Dr. Antonín Dvořák

> By the cemetary a narrow road;
> There she walked, weeping, a young, pretty widow.

The widow, a "lovely rose," is accompanying her husband on his last journey.—Violoncellos and double basses mark the solemn strides of the funeral procession by a characteristic rhythm:

Arching above this rhythm, cast in two voices, is the plaintive melody in violins and flutes whose beginning, variously altered, appears many times throughout the composition, either representing a genuine expression of grief or, in diminution, conveying the sinful longings of the beautiful widow; then it returns adapted for a lively dance, and again different wedding music is playing "prettily" above it. Let us listen:

However, the mood is broken up by the very same motif, appropriately altered in the flutes:

Now we are already near a new variant of the same motif in the form of a lovely Czech dance

in the introduction as well as in the development:

In the trio, above the same motif, we hear "pretty" wedding music:

Thus, from one kernel, a whole composition has sprouted whose unity and coherence do not require support from a text; this is a well-known virtue of Dvořák's symphonic poems.

Yet do not believe the sobs of the beautiful widow. The shrill discord of dissonant seconds

and the touching melody

cut so sharply into us that we sense all the falsehood and hypocrisy of the wailing and crying!

Soon we learn the truth.

Cheerful sounds of trumpets (from a distance, behind the orchestra) suddenly invade the gloomy funeral music—and

> A handsome youth is riding by,
> A feather on his hat.

With the tiny notes of the previously introduced flute motif the frivolous mind of the widow shakes off and easily discards her mourning.

> One day she was crying,
> The next day passed quietly,
> On the third her grief
> Slowly died away—

and the whole orchestra breaks into the sound of a merry wedding feast.

We can easily understand that the widow followed the youth's "words of wisdom":

> Since your husband is dead,
> Take me for your husband—

for the motif of the cheerful trumpets and the dance motif intertwine in the introduction:

The dance is presented full-length, and its lively spirit is enthralling.

After an easily comprehensible period, always subdivided into two groups of 3/4 time, with a piercing augmented fourth

the subsidiary coda is expanded by a mischievous distribution of melody over two bars instead of one

The composer continues to compress and concentrate his ideas into increasingly shorter units until, having once more slipped from the new key into the original one (from C into B, into C), he lets them unfurl again in all their breadth—and calms the listeners' minds after so much tension.—

> Keep laughing, dear bride!
> You look very pretty;
> The dead one in the ground
> Has but deaf ears!
> . . . .
> The one you offered your potion to
> Will not come back to life.—

This quiet melody now played in the upper register, then spoken in the middle one by the cellos, then again falling deep down in order to move, with even greater force, high up and finally, full of its original icy calm, to flow

> Into time that passes, changing everything in its wake:
> What has not been, will come, what used to be, is gone—

This quiet melody could be sung as follows:

Three years have passed since the dead man was buried;
fresh grass is growing on his grave.
On his grave fresh grass, near his head an oak tree,
a white dove likes to perch on it.[1]

How closely the melodies of the instruments match the words!
In the same way one could join the text to the bass clarinet's
recitative:

Stop cooing, stop calling, stop howling into my ear:
Your cruel song is piercing my soul!

This is the truly dramatic part of the composition. We can almost see
the widow throwing herself in despair into the chilly waves that rush to
catch up with one another and the brief flashes of her white dress
within them.

The unlucky woman
Tried to find herself a grave.

The mournful funeral sounds are heard again, combined with the
dove's cruel calling:

The hollow sounds of the flutes are filled in by the dark clarinet and,
above the oboe's $G\flat^2$, the trembling tone ($G\flat^3$) of the harp. Under the
heavy chords pressing against one another

we can almost feel the heavy stone weighing down on the unlucky
woman's body.

Yet no stone can ever
Be as heavy
As the curse
Attached to her name!

Compared to Dvořák's other symphonic poems composed on Erben's texts the dramatic part of *The Wood Dove* is rather brief. However, melodies evolve into more complex and larger forms (in the funeral music as well as in the wedding music). That the composer was trying to make his point mostly by purely musical elements is also shown by the quiet tones of a march appearing once more at the end of the composition, although the text of the poem reads:

> They pulled her up onto the bank,
> Buried her in secret.

Using recollection as a ribbon, the composer tied the work tightly together, thus augmenting its musical integrity.

As a postscript I include here an excerpt from a letter by the composer.

Prague, 7 March 1898

. . . I looked at my manuscript, but even there I found the same mistake you wrote about. It should therefore be as follows:

Viola:

and the flute should have:

also the second time around, all half-tones.

This dissonant progression in half-steps should probably indicate the widow's crying, or rather "sobbing."

I am also enclosing a program, namely the program I wrote according to the music as it progresses in regard to the various scenes and characters indicated in the poem.

Cordially, . . .

The program is here reprinted:

THE WOOD DOVE

Symphonic Poem for Large Orchestra,
Based on K. J. Erben's Ballad

Andante, marcia funebre. (Crying and wailing, a young widow follows the coffin.)

Allegro—lento. (A handsome youth meets her and tells her to forget her grief and take him for her husband.)

Molto vivace. (Soon the young widow gives up her mourning and celebrates her marriage to the youth at a noisy, merry feast.)

Andante. (In the meantime, grass has overgrown the grave of her first husband, whom she poisoned; a young oak is growing at its head; a wild dove is sitting on it, and its mournful cooing resonates throughout the countryside. Its lamentation reaches all the way to the heart of the treacherous woman who, overcome by remorse, loses her mind and seeks death in the waves.)

Lento, tempo di marcia. (Epilogue.)

[Source: *Hlídka* 3, no. 15 (1898): 277–82]

Whereas Janáček's analysis of *The Wood Dove* comes complete with large chunks of the poem and Dvořák's own short description, his discussion of *The Golden Spinning Wheel* is more diffuse. For that reason I include the following brief synopsis:

A king, riding in the woods, falls in love with a beautiful girl, Dora (Dornička). He orders the girl's stepmother to bring her to the castle; he would like to marry her. On the journey, however, the stepmother and her own daughter kill Dora, bring her eyes, hands, and feet to the castle, and substitute the daughter for Dora. The king is deceived by the ruse and celebrates a festive wedding. The king commands his new queen to spin and goes off to war. A mysterious old man, having found Dora's mutilated body, sends his boy to the castle three times to exchange golden parts of a spinning wheel for various parts of Dora's body. He then brings her back to life. When the king returns he is shown the golden spinning wheel, which, when spun, divulges the story of the murder. The king goes back to the forest and reclaims his real love, Dora. [Ed.]

Dr. Ant. Dvořák's *The Golden Spinning Wheel*

"Richter, the court orchestra conductor in Vienna, wins—see also my ⊕ (p. 50) to ⊕ (p. 53), by which I shortened the score of *The Golden Spinning Wheel*."—At a concert in Brno on 8 May 1897 the composer himself conducted this very piece without cuts. And thus three times in a row a similar tableau is presented, containing every single detail, truthfully following the story: the queen, the first time around, exchanges "our Dora's legs" for the golden spinning wheel, then the arms for the golden spindle, and the eyes that will "rekindle the dead fire" for the golden distaff.

Only Old Testament trombones together with agitated timpani could capture the supernatural apparition in music:

> And suddenly from somewhere among the forest rocks
> There appeared the strangest old man:
> A gray beard down to his knees

who with a distinct motif

commands the boy:

> Do not, however, exchange it for anything
> But legs.

The difficult, hard road

exquisitely matches the character of the seventh-chord progression.

(I do not include the remote bassoon note E, though it is bound into

the whole pattern of chordal combinations based on the soft key of E minor.)
The instruments, especially the flute, when

> The boy is sitting at the gate
> Holding the golden spinning wheel

match the text to such a degree that one can sing along in syllables

If only I could have that thing made of the purest gold!

Go, mother; he should name his prize for that spinning wheel
made of gold—

and it also corresponds to the melody of speech:

Buy it, my lady! It's really cheap—

A slight echo of the motif

smudges the sharp features of the dialogue, and the picture consolidates. It is not necessary to tell at length that the same motif, in an appropriate variation, superbly illustrates the trotting of the black horse at the very beginning of the piece and that the same motif resounds with a lovely melodic wave by which

> A girl like a blossom
> The world has never seen such beauty

appears to the nobleman who

Stands there, forgetting what he wanted.

In the part of the composition hitherto described, the dramatic characterization is stretched to the point of melodic precision of speech and dialogue; as has been stressed before, this degree of dramatic precision has never before been used in symphonic poems by any other composer. However, Dvořák's singular dramatic style will stand out even more clearly when we begin to consider his treatment of time. That will bring us to the boundary line of Czech musical currents.

And one more tableau, similar in its epic length, from *The Golden Spinning Wheel*:

The king is cheerfully returning from war.

The rallying cries of horns and trumpets cut into the hum of the festivities. With a cordial song the king greets his supposed wife, for whom the golden spinning wheel will soon spin inescapable downfall.

Come, my lady, sit down
And, since you love me, spin a golden yarn.

This is followed by a delightful musical depiction of the spinning wheel's ill-fated performance for the lady. Wobbling, the spinning wheel begins to spin, but

Woe, what a song!

In the mercilessly harsh voice of a whirring trill the horns and trombones bring forth their accusation by means of the motif that, with the color of blood, fired up the merriment at the first wedding—deceitfully arranged—and that sounded mournfully in the "sales conversation":

> Whirrr—you're spinning an evil yarn!
> You've come to deceive the king:
> You've killed your stepsister,
> Removed her limbs and eyes—
> Whirrr—it's an evil yarn!

Rocks crashing down upon one's soul—such is the effect of the dominant chord (C♯–E♯–G♯–B), played tersely, with dragged bows, by the whole orchestra over the lingering tones

at the words:

> What kind of a spinning wheel you have
> And what strange things you play on it!

The spinning wheel whirs on a trill

in the violins; the viola and the harp force their strings into chords:

And somewhere among all the high notes, through the plaintive melody of the piccolo and the clarinet, suddenly the inexorably rapid blend of an E♯–F♯ whistles:

And thus, for the third time, the same, yet never tiresome, musical picture is repeated, always richer in color and confirming the inevitable fate by the combination of its basic keys (first time in E minor, second time in F♯ minor, and third time in A♭ minor).

> Of the mother the shrew,
> Of the daughter the snake.

The souls of those who listen with their whole hearts to *The Golden Spinning Wheel* are profoundly stirred three more times. The first time we are moved by the king's yearning melody; the second time, the cheerful strings of the harp vibrating above the whole orchestra during the wedding feast pull us into the tumultuous dance; and the third time we rejoice over the skillful mixing—immediately, in the first few bars of the composition—of the metallic sound of the horseshoes, played by the contrabassoon, into the rhythm of the black, spirited horse's canter. Here are short examples thereof:

Triplets are tearing up the cellos; a harsh ringing sound comes out of the rumbling echo of the large drum, and the cymbals spark off the contrabassoon on the contrabass note F_1, always on the first quarter-beat of the bar; and thus

> A nobleman is riding from the forest
> On a black, spirited horse;
> The horseshoes are cheerfully clicking.

The words of toasts heard through the commotion and murmur of the wedding reception are dying away; from the castle courtyard piercing sounds of the harp float into the splendid halls

terse, yet in harmony with the hushed murmur of the low-pitched instruments:

But

> There was a wedding—a full-fledged sin;

thus even the main motif of the delightful scherzo scene bounces in a frightening manner

on the low F♯$_1$ of the drums and the double basses, and right after, the infernal sound of horns playing in unison crashes through:

I conclude my analysis of Dvořák's latest compositions with the heavenly motif played by the violins on the waves of rounded tones of clarinets and flutes supported by solemn trombones and double basses.

> If your hand hasn't been promised,
> You must be my wife!

> . . . I want your daughter to be my wife,
> Your stepdaughter.

> Where are you, my dear Dora? Where? Where?

Thus into the series of *The Golden Spinning Wheel*'s delightful melodies the most touching one is woven three times; the warm rays emanating from it warm up even those who thought their hearts frigid.

This part is always metrically animated by the four sixteenths of the bassoons, to which correspond the other four of the flutes in every bar; in addition, soft clarinet sounds highlight every chord with two fully arpeggiated sixteenth-note sextuplets. Tender music!

[Source: *Hlídka* 2, no. 14 (1897): 594–600]

NOTE

1. In the original, Janáček placed the Czech text directly below the music.

Index of

Names and Compositions

List of Contributors

Michael Beckerman is Associate Professor of Music at Washington University in St. Louis. He has written articles on Janáček, Dvořák, and Martinů and is currently President of the Czech and Slovak Music Society. He is the author of *Janáček the Theorist* and *Janáček and Czech Music*, both forthcoming from Pendragon Press.

David Beveridge is Associate Professor of Music at the University of New Orleans. He is the author of *The Sonata Forms of Dvořák* (Stuyvesant, N.Y., forthcoming) and of articles on Brahms, Dvořák, Rubin Goldmark, Janáček, Mozart, Schumann, and Voříšek. He served as Director of the Dvořák Sesquicentennial Festival and Conference in America, held in New Orleans in 1991.

Leon Botstein is President of Bard College, where he is also Professor of History and Music History. He is the author of *Judentum und Modernität* (Vienna, 1991) and *Music and Its Public: Habits of Listening and the Crisis of Modernism in Vienna, 1870–1914* (Chicago, forthcoming) as well as Music Director of the American Symphony Orchestra and Editor of *Musical Quarterly*.

Tatiana Firkušný has collaborated with Robert Jones on many translation projects, including Těsnohlídek's *The Cunning Little Vixen*, with illustrations by Maurice Sendak (New York, 1985), and Karel Čapek's *From the Life of the Insects* (Highland Park, N.J., 1990). She received the Virginia Faulkner Award for Excellence in Writing in 1992.

Susan Gillespie is Vice President for Public Affairs and Development at Bard College, where she has also taught German poetry. Her published translations of German works include several that appeared in *Brahms and His World*, edited by Walter Frisch (Princeton, 1990), *Mendelssohn and His World*, edited by R. Larry Todd (Princeton, 1991), and *Richard Strauss and His World*, edited by Bryan Gilliam (Princeton, 1992).

Joseph Horowitz is the author of *Conversations with Arrau* (New York, 1984), *Understanding Toscanini: How He Became an American Culture-God and Helped Create a New Audience for Old Music* (New York, 1987), and *The Ivory Trade: Piano Competitions and the Business of Music* (New York, 1990). He serves as

Artistic Adviser to the Brooklyn Philharmonic Orchestra and to the annual Schubertiade of New York's 92nd Street Y.

Jan Smaczny is Lecturer in Music at the University of Birmingham. He has published articles on many aspects of Czech music and is currently completing a new critical biography of Dvořák for J. M. Dent's Master Musicians series. He is also a regular contributor to the *Independent*, *Opera Magazine*, and BBC Radio Three.